The Disappearance
of Amy Cave

Pat Flagg

D THE
isappearance
OF Amy Cave

A TRUE ACCOUNT OF MURDER
AND JUSTICE IN MAINE

 DOWN EAST BOOKS / ROCKPORT, MAINE

1   3   5   4   2

Down East Books
P.O. Box 679
Camden, ME 04843
BOOK ORDERS: 1-800-685-7962

LIBRARY OF CONGRESS CATALOGING-IN-PUBLICATION DATA

Flagg, Pat, 1927–
    The Disappearance of Amy Cave / by Pat Flagg
        p.   cm.
    ISBN 0-89272-477-3 (cloth)
    ISBN 0-89272-499-4 (paper)
    1. Murder—Maine—Hancock County. 2. Murder
—Investigation—Maine—Hancock County. I. Title.
HV6533. H36 F58 2000
364.15'23'0974145—dc21
                                        99-54658

Preface

WHEN EVIL INVADES YOUR HOME through the television screen, you can turn off the set or distance yourself emotionally. In 1984, when there was a murder on the shores of Taunton Bay, I had no such choice. I lived across the bay and knew the murdered woman. Even if I had not been a reporter assigned to cover the crime, I could not have distanced myself from this story.

My consuming need to know why and how my friend was killed was only partly satisfied as I reported the story for the local newspaper. But then, when I decided to write a book and Hancock County Sheriff Bill Clark generously gave me access to investigation reports and to his staff, I learned more than I ever expected.

Sheriff Clark and his staff shared with me not only behind-the-scenes facts, but their feelings as well. The case, bizarre even in their experience, touched everyone's emotions.

Long after the events described in these pages ceased to make news headlines, the tragedy and irony of the story still haunted me. Talking with townspeople and with friends and family of Amy Cave revealed to me the deeper and sadder human story behind the accounts presented by both local and national media.

Most of the people I contacted during my research were amazingly forthcoming, but one important figure—Amy's killer—declined to be interviewed. All quoted material from this source is taken from taped interviews, courtroom transcripts, and recollections of other participants.

I found that I could not write this account only in the third person. As a woman, I had strong reactions to the gender issues involved in the case. Also, when I was a reporter I had never been allowed to editorialize, and now I wanted to make personal observations about the law and the courts and the participants in this drama. Then, too, sometimes I myself was a participant. Therefore, beginning in Part 2 of the book, I increasingly tell the story through my own eyes, in the first person.

For events when I wasn't present, such as during the initial investigation, I have reconstructed scenes and paraphrased dialogue based on specific recollections of the people who were there. Sometimes even police officers recalled details differently when describing the same event. (Cops are human, too, one of them reminded me.) In those instances I used the version recalled by the most people.

I am very grateful to Bill Clark and everyone in his department—Chief Deputy Richard Dickson, Lieutenant Nate Anderson, Jail Administrator Richard Bishop, and the deputies, dispatchers, and corrections officers—for their help. And I am grateful to Susan and Richard Cave, who graciously took time to talk to me when all they wanted was to forget the murder that took their aunt's life just as she was embarking on a new adventure. They wanted to focus on the good things.

I did, too, and after my initial research, I set my writing aside. Eventually, two friends with whom I met weekly to write helped me get back on track; Donna Fricke and Pati Burton encouraged, listened, and critiqued, always with patience and good humor.

Copy editor Barbara Feller-Roth was very helpful, especially by reining in my tendency to "throw in the kitchen sink." I appreciate, too, the eagle eyes of associate editor Alice Devine and senior editor Karin Womer, who had the final say.

Many people have played a part in telling this story of the murder on Taunton Bay. I thank all of them.

Part One

Chapter One

THE HOUSE ON EVERGREEN POINT STOOD VIGIL over Taunton Bay one lazy fall day after the other, waiting for a neighbor, a delivery person—anyone—to notice what had happened.

Canada geese flocked into the bay, honking among themselves as they settled in coves to rest before the long trip south. An occasional great blue heron flew over Burying Island in lingering farewell to the nest where it had raised its young.

Linda, a neighbor who lived in a trailer on the main road through North Sullivan, sauntered along the half-mile driveway to the house on Evergreen Point, three tomatoes from a late garden cradled in the crook of her left arm. Gifts for Amy. A thank-you for lunch the week before when they'd chatted about men, or the lack of men, in their lives, and about the elderly woman in the red house on the shore whose antique jewelry, Amy suspected, was being carried off by workers who visited daily.

Linda knocked on the kitchen door, then shifted her gaze through the pines and spruce to the bay below. She followed the flight of a gull in the distance as it swooped and cut through drifting puffs of mist. She waited, then knocked again on the door. Still no answer. Drawing in a breath of tangy salt air, she raised her hand for a third knock. She hesitated, then, sighing, let her hand fall to her side. No sense in trying again. Amy's car was there, but maybe she was napping or was out for a stroll on one of the trails along the bluff.

Linda placed the tomatoes on the deck railing where Amy would be sure to spot them from the kitchen window above the sink. Then she set off down the gravel drive toward home.

1

Heavy mist settled over the house behind her, turning the wood siding an even darker brown. Inside, the phone rang and rang and went unanswered.

In late afternoon, the mist lifted and the sun appeared low across the water, casting a purple tinge on the bank of Amy's west-facing living room windows. Later, light from the full moon fingered its way through slits in the drawn drapes and crept across the thick carpet. A jangling phone broke the quiet, echoed through the large rooms, and finally went silent, unanswered again.

Early the next evening, another neighbor drove his pickup truck down the long driveway and stopped next to Amy's car. He'd never seen her car parked outside before, and at such an odd angle, as though the driver had jumped out in a hurry. Frowning, he reached into his glove compartment for a flashlight. It worried him not to see even a single light inside the house.

"Amy!" he called, rapping sharply on the kitchen door. He waited briefly for the porch light to be flicked on. When it wasn't, he pounded on the door and raised his voice. "Amy, are you there? It's me, Crawf." Still calling out, he circled the house, tapping on the windows and flashing the light over the dark panes.

Back at the driveway again, crunching across the gravel to Amy's car, he stopped short, his heart pounding suddenly at a loud snapping sound beyond the big pine. He held his breath and listened as something heavy moved away slowly, stealthily. Exhaling cautiously, he told himself that the unseen creature was probably just a deer. Maybe even a moose. He played the flashlight beam over the car's front seat and rear seat, then tilted the red plastic lens cap against the car window to search the floor. Nothing. He turned the handle on the driver's side door and the door opened. It wasn't like Amy to leave her car outside, unlocked. He'd better go home and call Iva. She had tried for days to reach Amy by phone before asking him to check the house, and she was waiting to hear from him now.

Crawford drove his truck back out the long driveway, veered onto the tarred surface, and a minute later turned into the driveway of a white house set back from the road on a knoll. It was his mother's family homestead, where he lived alone except for an old friend, the black woolly dog now rubbing against his leg, its thumping tail demanding his attention. He pulled the phone across the kitchen counter and perched on a stool. "Not now, Satan," he told the dog.

"Iva? Crawford. . . . I couldn't raise Amy. The house is dark, and, a funny thing, her car's outside. She never leaves it out, even in the daytime. Drives it right into the garage with that opener thing, you know?" In an absentminded gesture, he reached down to stroke the head insistently nudging his foot.

Iva said she too thought it strange that Amy's car wasn't in the garage. When she heard how it was parked, at such an odd angle, she said they should call the sheriff. She would do that in the morning.

Crawford suggested they were probably getting stirred up over nothing. At least he hoped it was nothing. He said he had to leave for his night shift at the front desk of the Holiday Inn in Ellsworth, but he'd check with her the minute he reached home in the morning.

Corporal Skip Bouchard, senior dispatcher at the Hancock County sheriff's office in Ellsworth, handled the call from Iva Patten in North Sullivan at 9:05 on Wednesday morning. He cut short her apology about bothering busy officers with something that would probably amount to nothing. "Ma'am, you did the right thing. We'll be glad to check it out for you. Now, what's the woman's name? . . . Amelia Cave, C-A-V-E? And where exactly does she live?"

As he listened to the caller, who spoke calmly but was obviously worried, Bouchard jotted down key words, which he would enter into a daily log and flesh out with details on an incident card, referred to in the office as the IC. "I'll send someone down as soon as I can. You'll meet the deputy at the end of Mrs. Cave's road? . . . Oh, it's *Miss* Cave? Well, thanks for calling us, Mrs. Patten."

Twenty minutes later, when Lieutenant Nate Anderson checked in on his two-way car radio, dispatcher Bouchard relayed all the information he had about the missing Cave woman.

Iva Patten was a trim woman in her seventies with a deep voice and no-nonsense manner. A widow for sixteen years, she'd retired from a career in nursing ten years ago and moved to the small home built by her husband as a weekend retreat on the shore of Taunton Bay. Windows on three sides of her small living room looked out on the bay, which today was calm and sparkling in early morning sun. Now, in her favorite armchair facing the view she loved, she was too distracted to enjoy it.

Her mind was on her neighbor in the next cove to the east, around the point. And on the phone call she'd just made. She hoped she had not sounded like an old busybody, rambling on with too many details.

She had told the man at the sheriff's department about not being able to reach Amy by phone before the meeting they'd planned to attend together last Sunday. And that Amy hadn't shown up at the meeting or answered her phone since then. And that when she checked with Spike Havey at the post office, he said Amy's *Wall Street Journals* and other mail had been piling up for a week now.

She'd explained about Crawford Hollidge going over last night and finding Amy's car parked outside in that strange position. And that she'd looked in the windows of Amy's house again this morning with her neighbor Merrill Taylor, a retired policeman, and had found nothing. Except a dead partridge—a detail she'd left out, thank goodness. She recalled how her stomach felt at the sight of the beautiful, lifeless bird below Amy's window. Iva had called as many of Amy's friends as she could think of, but none had any news of her. It just wasn't like Amy to go away without telling someone.

Iva sighed, realizing she'd been building up a case to justify her call to the sheriff, when she was startled by the shrill ring of the phone still under a hand in her lap. She recognized the voice of Glenn Askeborn calling from across the bay in Hancock. Glenn and Amy had become close friends this past year, Iva knew, after discovering they'd both moved to Maine from Long Island, New York. Glenn was one of the people whom Iva had called earlier. Iva hadn't remembered Glenn's last name, but she got the number from Charlie Wheeler, Glenn's neighbor, who ran an oil burner service and doubled as chief of the Hancock volunteer police.

Glenn said that she, too, had been trying to reach Amy and was worried about her. Hearing that sheriff's deputies were on their way to Amy's house, Glenn said she'd be right over and would meet Iva at the end of Amy's drive.

Iva had barely pulled off the main road and parked her car when Glenn drove in. She seemed even more nervous than usual, smoking one cigarette after another and spilling the cup of coffee she'd brought with her. Impatient for the deputies to arrive, she insisted they drive to Iva's to call the sheriff again. Iva didn't think it necessary, but Glenn's tension made her so uncomfortable that anything seemed better than waiting in the car with her.

Glenn followed Iva into her house and announced that she'd make the call. "No," Iva said firmly. "I started this and I think I should finish it."

The dispatcher assured Iva that the officers were on their way.

"Quite a place," said Lieutenant Anderson with admiration as he and Sergeant Pete Brady pulled up behind the white-over-tan Oldsmobile parked in the yard. Amelia Cave's house was more impressive than most in North Sullivan, especially with the view it commanded from the top of an eighty-foot bluff. Anderson—in his thirties, tall, slim, and curly headed—and Brady, who was much shorter and, at forty-four, the oldest patrol sergeant on the force, had just circled the house, searching for an unlocked door or window, when Iva and Glenn drove in.

Mutt and Jeff, thought Iva, smiling for an irreverent moment before she caught a sobering glimpse of gun handles protruding from the men's leather holsters.

Lieutenant Anderson handled the introductions and began asking questions about Amy. Iva tried to answer—after all, she had been the one to alert the sheriff's department—but Glenn kept interrupting her. Iva grew increasingly irked. Getting frantic wouldn't help find anyone. She always remained calm in a crisis. As a nurse, she hadn't fallen apart even when one of her patients died, no matter how attached she'd become to the person. She approved when the young lieutenant took charge, interrupting Glenn and striding to the cruiser to radio his office for a locksmith.

The phone at TLC, the locksmith in the next town, was being handled by an answering machine, the dispatcher told him.

"Don't leave a message," Anderson said. "We need to do something now."

He walked to Amy's two-car garage and grasped the handle on the door nearest the house. He'd already tried lifting the overhead door. Now he turned the handle and heard the click of a lock just as Glenn, standing next to Amy's car, called out to tell them she could see an automatic door opener in the car.

"Damn!" Anderson said. If he hadn't turned the handle, the opener would have raised the door.

Anderson reached for his nightstick and swung it against a pane of glass above the lock, shattering it. He reached inside, turned the handle, and nodded at Brady to try the opener. The door lumbered up on its track. Brady followed him through the shadowy garage to a side door into the house. It too was locked.

"Here we go again, Nate," Brady said with a chuckle, making sure the women couldn't hear him. "More breaking and entering."

The glass in the upper half of the side door resisted blow after blow of Anderson's nightstick and even a metal bar he found on the garage floor. When it finally gave way, shards of glass crashed to the floor on the other side. Nate reached in gingerly, turned the brass knob, and stepped into a hallway. It led to another door, but this one, he was relieved to find, was unlocked. It opened into the kitchen.

"Why don't you wait here until we look around," Nate said to the women standing behind him. In a minute he returned and invited them into the kitchen while he and Brady searched the rest of the house.

Standing by the kitchen counter, Iva and Glenn glanced down the long sweep of Amy's brown-carpeted dining and living room to the raised brick fireplace in a corner of the far wall. A blue quilted comforter lay rumpled in an armchair with magazines strewn on the floor beside it.

Iva looked around at the familiar bare walls and sparsely fur-
nished room, wondering what Amy's home would reveal about her to
strangers. The deputies wouldn't know how carefully she'd chosen
everything, waiting until she could afford just what she wanted. They
wouldn't know she'd lived there a year before buying the elegant
Ethan Allen dining room set. Or lived two years with nothing on the
long wall of picture windows and sliding glass doors before she had
the drapes custom made.

Iva turned away, uncomfortable, as though she'd been spying on
someone sleeping, someone unable to protect herself by conveying
the subtle but clear signals that let others know how close to stand
and what to notice or pretend not to notice.

"She's not in the house," Anderson announced from the doorway.
They'd searched everywhere, including an apartment and laundry
room in the basement. Nothing seemed out of order, although a red
light on a panel in the master bedroom indicated that the burglar
alarm had been set off. Maybe he and Brady had activated the alarm
when they broke into the house. Or maybe it had already been set off
by someone else. Whenever it happened, Security Central in Bangor
should have responded by contacting the local sheriff's department.
But when Anderson called his dispatcher, Bouchard said he hadn't
heard from the protection agency. Nate told him to find out why.

Nate then asked Iva and Glenn to come with them and look
through some of the rooms on the ground floor—two bedrooms, a
full bathroom, and a smaller half bath—to see if anything struck them
as unusual.

Amy's leaving her house with her bed unmade and papers scattered on it seemed out of character to them both. Iva thought the
neatly folded clothes on the bathtub rim suggested that Amy had
planned to take a bath and something had interrupted her. Whatever
it was, she certainly wouldn't have left the house for long without her
blood pressure medicine, which she had to take daily. Iva asked if she
might look in the medicine cabinet. When Anderson told her to go
ahead, her eyes fell immediately on the bottle of pills she hoped she
wouldn't find.

It would be helpful, Anderson said, if they could figure out what Amy had been wearing when she left the house. So Iva and Glenn searched through the closets in the two bedrooms and the large walk-in closet in the hall. The deputies stood by, watching them. Iva, relieved to find Amy's closets in order, resolved to straighten out her own closets the minute she had time. They found Amy's gray tweed coat, the one she'd be apt to wear on a trip out of town. Her red winter parka with the hood was missing.

On the kitchen counter next to the sink were three cups, three saucers, a spoon, eggshells, and a coffee can—not in keeping with Amy's usual neatness, the women said. And neither was the refrigerator dish on the counter that, when Anderson pried it open, released the odor of spoiled food. Next to the dish, three bananas had turned dark brown and mushy. Fall flowers in a jar had withered and dropped petals onto the counter. Brady opened the refrigerator and lifted out a carton of milk to read the expiration date: October 2.

"My God!" Glenn exclaimed. "That was eight days ago."

"Yes, it was," Iva observed dryly. "And our postmaster, Spike Havey, said Amy hasn't picked up her mail for about a week, either."

Anderson turned to Iva. "How would you describe Amy's frame of mind lately?" he asked.

Iva hesitated, weighing breaking a confidence against sharing information that would help find her friend. "Well, she's been a little concerned that the local people aren't treating her right."

Glenn was less reticent. "Amy's been disturbed for some time. She thinks people are out to get her. That they're talking about her behind her back."

"Really?" Anderson said. "Iva, you mentioned 'local people' not treating her well. Isn't Amy from around here?"

"No. Amy's lived on Evergreen Point for only the last two to three years. Before that she lived on Long Island with her mother, and with other relatives after her mother's death. But she always worked," Iva added quickly, wanting them to understand that Amy was an independent woman. "She worked in a school department and saved her money for early retirement and a home of her own."

"How old a woman is she?" the lieutenant asked.

Iva and Glenn looked at each other. "What do you think, about sixty?" Iva suggested.

"In her late fifties, I'd say," Glenn answered. "Fairly old to be living on her own for the first time, in my opinion. Amy loves her new home, of course, but she expected her family to visit more often, and she's lonely. She asks everyone she meets to come see her."

"Some of us think she isn't careful enough about who she invites," Iva said.

"Oh?" said Anderson.

"I mean, she asks perfect strangers, without knowing anything about them. She expects everyone to be as good as she is. She's too trusting."

Anderson asked if they knew how to get in touch with her relatives. Neither of them did, but Iva said she'd get him the number of good friends in New York State who were Amy's neighbors in summer. They might know. Glenn said he should contact Felix and Gusti Duschek, who had been at Amy's a week ago for dinner. They lived in Hancock, but they didn't have a phone, so someone would have to go to their house, she said.

Anderson stood by his cruiser radio while Chief Deputy Richard Dickson was dispatched from the sheriff's department to the Duschek home, at the end of Stabawl Road. After only a few minutes, Anderson heard Dickson reporting back to dispatch, his words not revealing anything to the public who listened to the police band on scanners: "These people were at the party's house last Wednesday, just a week ago. Everything was fine when they left. They thought the party was somewhat depressed, though."

"I copied him," Anderson said as Bouchard started to relay Dickson's message. "Find out if Debbie Palman and her canine can come to the scene. And check with Number One. I think he ought to come down. I'll stand by."

Minutes later, Bouchard reported back that Warden Palman was at a doctor's appointment but he'd left a message for her with state police dispatch. The sheriff, referred to as "Number One" in the message, would be down shortly. Anderson returned to the house to thank Iva and Glenn for their help.

"I'm sorry we didn't find Amy inside," he said.

"Maybe it's just as well," Iva said with a knowing look.

"Well, yes," he agreed. "Now we can hope she's just away someplace having a great time."

As Iva and Glenn left, Anderson promised to keep them informed. Leaving Brady to stand guard, he set off for a quick search along the trail that Iva said Amy sometimes walked.

On the bay side of the house, Nate let his weight propel him down the bank to a shelf of level ground where a path led into the woods. He scanned the bay, orienting himself.

Across the water, few houses interrupted the sweep of tree-lined shore from Hancock on his left to the Franklin town line somewhere in front of him. Egypt Stream, the boundary between the towns, was hidden behind an evergreen-studded island—Burying Island, he thought it was called. The high Sullivan shore on which he stood jutted to a long point on his right and blocked his view of the bay's widest expanse and its head at Hog Bay in Franklin. At low tide, as Taunton Bay emptied behind him under the bridge connecting Sullivan and Hancock, most of the shore bordering the three towns became mudflats. If it were low tide now, he knew, he'd see clam and worm diggers hacking with their hoes in their favorite spots along the flats.

Nate turned and headed in a northerly direction toward Franklin. Above, on his right, a few scraggly spruces struggled for a foothold on lichen-covered cliffs. On his left, rock outcroppings and a wooded bank sloped sharply to the water. It was in this direction that Amy Cave, if she had been out for a walk and lost her balance, would have fallen. He was aware of what he might find at any moment. Nevertheless, reflected sunlight from the bay dancing over the trunks of trees and along the path before him put a spring in his step.

Being outdoors like this was the best part of his job, even when he had to hide for hours waiting to pounce on whoever showed up to tend a marijuana plot. Sometimes, when nobody showed, he'd leave his business card behind. It was a cat-and-mouse game that he thrived on. Last spring, standing in line in the feed store behind a suspected pot grower buying a huge bale of fertilizer, he'd asked pleasantly, "Shall we load it into my car now or wait until harvest?" Sooner or later, he'd calculated, he would face that guy in the courtroom.

The trail, which had been declining but was now nearly level with the bay, ended in front of a camp with boarded-over windows. Amy's summer neighbors, Nate thought, the ones Iva said he ought to call. A white card on a door at the rear of the camp caught his eye, and he climbed the back porch steps for a closer look. A message to would-be burglars informed them that there was little of value inside, and the few major appliances were marked and registered with the sheriff's department. Nate chuckled at the last sentence: "You are welcome to enjoy the sunset from our front porch." Nice try, he thought, but it probably wouldn't work. There was a rowdy bunch in town with too much time on their hands. Sullivan wasn't the only town where summer homes were broken into; it was a popular sport all over Hancock County. Snowmobiles and four-wheelers made even the most remote camps accessible these days.

Nate began retracing his steps up the trail, remembering all the burglaries he'd worked, all the tracks he'd traced in the mud and snow. When he was new on the job, he'd followed a beautiful trail of boot prints across a barren, snow-covered field. Only later did he learn that it wasn't a field at all but a saltwater bay where the treacherous ice seldom froze solid. He wondered if Taunton Bay ever froze over completely. Probably not in the channel where the current was strongest. Next summer, maybe, he'd bring his boat up through the falls and explore this bay. He looked up to see that he was back at his starting point below the house, and he decided to continue along the trail in the opposite direction.

The sight of Amy's house set him thinking about how much he'd like to find the woman who lived there. How much he'd like telling Iva and Glenn that he'd found their friend. In the tight-knit community in Aroostook County where he'd grown up, folks looked after one another—as they should, he thought. He'd always liked helping people, especially elderly ones such as the man who had called a couple weeks ago complaining about two young people who'd moved into his house and refused to leave. Nate had searched the house and found no one. The man insisted that the people were there. Shaking with fear, he showed Nate a newspaper picture of two smiling faces in an ad for laundry soap. So Nate arrested the picture and took the newspaper into custody. Then he called the Department of Human Services. The social worker promised to look in on the old man and do what she could to help.

Nate noticed that the incline, now on his left, was growing steeper, until it terminated in a sheer granite cliff—one of North Sullivan's old quarries, he realized. Unlike the town's other murky, rain-filled quarry, which his department often dragged to find a ditched stolen car or truck, this one was open faced, its history of mining, which had ended more than a half century before, naked to the eyes of a passerby. Apprehensive about the dramatic drop so near the missing woman's home, Nate scoured the underbrush at the base. He found nothing. The path continued on to the east, but Nate decided to return to the house.

The sheriff should be there by now.

Chapter Two

As Nate approached the top of the bank in front of Amy's house, he could see the sheriff standing in the driveway with Brady. "Hey, Bill," Nate called, "about time you showed up." His boss, grinning, waited for Nate to reach them.

Sheriff William Clark, in his mid-thirties, was only three years older than his lieutenant. The shock of brown hair falling over his forehead added to an already boyish look. He was dressed casually in tan slacks and sweater. No uniform today.

Clark, a local boy from Franklin, had earned the respect of fellow officers during his twelve years in law enforcement. He'd been at the top of his class in the police academy and in every training course thereafter. Four years ago when he ran for sheriff, he was a lieutenant with the Ellsworth Police Department. After winning the election, he'd chosen fellow officer Richard Dickson as his chief deputy. Together they'd made changes that had shaken up the sheriff's department. Some of the changes had been good, some not so good, he'd admit. With no training for the job of sheriff, he'd learned under fire, drawing praise from some and stirring up resentment in others. Even disgruntled employees, however, admitted that Bill was a "damn good investigator." What he still liked best was working a case in the field with his men.

"I figured you'd have this thing solved by now," Bill kidded Nate as he joined them. "By the way, Pete answered Amy's phone while you were gone."

The Bangor Window Shade Company had called, Brady explained. They'd been calling all week trying to set up a delivery to

Miss Cave. This was the first time anyone had answered her phone.

"Did they say when they talked to her last?" Nate asked.

"He thought they'd made one recent delivery—a couch they'd up-hostered—and now they have something else to deliver. The guy who called didn't know all that much. He said the manager would know more. He'll call us."

"Good," commented Nate. When Brady said he had to leave for Lamoine to investigate another matter, Nate turned to Bill. "Want to take a look in the house?"

Nate took the sheriff on a tour of all the rooms, directing his attention to the kitchen—with its three coffee cups on the counter, the spoiled food, and the expiration date on the milk carton—and to the bedroom, with the papers on Amy's bed. Bill scanned the pages facing him. "I see that J. T. Rosborough's her agent," he said. "Maybe they can shed some light on why Amelia was checking her homeowner's insurance policy now."

Not wanting to risk contaminating a potential crime scene or being discovered by Amy in her home, they decided to set up head-quarters in the garage. They carried in a radio and power pack from Bill's cruiser and placed them on top of an overturned box. The cruiser radio was more powerful than their portables and would make contact with dispatch in Ellsworth more certain.

Nate called dispatcher Bouchard and told him to round up deputies and wardens for a search of the woods around Amy's house. He also told him to call the Rosborough agency and find out if any-one there had heard from Miss Cave.

When Bouchard radioed back, he said Wendy Spearin at Rosbor-ough's had received a call from Amy just last week, on Thursday morning. Amy wanted to raise the deductible on her house, so Wendy had sent her an amended policy. Wendy gave Bouchard an address for Amy's relatives in Massapequa, Long Island, and he'd left a message on their answering machine asking someone to call the sheriff's office in Ellsworth.

"So, what have we got, Bill?" Nate asked, initiating a familiar thinking-out-loud process they engaged in. "Amy Cave places a call to her insurance agent last Thursday morning. And she's a neat woman, we hear, who would probably make her bed each day."

Bill joined in the speculation. "It looks like she didn't sleep in her bed again after making that phone call. We can assume that Thursday was the last day she was in her house."

"That was six days ago," Nate said, "and no one's heard from her since. If she took a trip somewhere, she sure left in a hurry, leaving food out and dishes unwashed. And not taking her medication with her."

"Even if she was called away suddenly, wouldn't she have contacted someone here by now?" Bill asked. "And what about those three coffee cups? I wish we knew who paid her a visit. And why her car—"

The radio crackled and Bouchard's voice interrupted them. Iva Patten had called with a New York number for Amy's summer neighbors, the McMillens, and Bouchard had called them. They said they hadn't heard from Amy recently. Then, following a suggestion from Wendy at the insurance agency, Bouchard had contacted a close friend of Amy's, Ruth Kane, at The Ellsworth Motel. She hadn't seen Amy since late summer. At that time, she said, Amy had seemed quite depressed.

"Hasn't someone else said the same thing?" Bill asked when Bouchard signed off.

"The Duscheks," Nate said. "They saw Amy last week and said she seemed depressed then."

Bouchard, on the radio again a few minutes later, told them that Ruth Kane had called back from the motel to say that another friend—Ruth Church, in Hancock—thought they ought to get in touch with a woman whom Amy had been seeing a lot lately. Her first name was Glenn and her last name was Aska-something.

"Askeborn," said Nate quickly. "She was over here this morning with Iva Patten. She doesn't know anything."

At the sound of a car, Nate and Bill looked out to see Dave Gordon, corrections officer at the jail, arriving to help search the woods around the house. Nate glanced at his watch. It was nearly two o'clock. Warden Palman still hadn't shown up with her dog, and there weren't enough people for the kind of tight grid search that the wardens would conduct. Nate sent Gordon and two part-time deputies to scout the area east of the house toward the mouth of the bay.

Gordon, happy not to be stuck inside the jail on such a perfect fall day, set off through the woods and, before long, lost sight of the men on either side of him. The trees thinned to low scrub growth. Pushing through bushes covered with thorns that plucked at the trousers of his summer uniform, he was considering turning back when he spotted two houses in the distance. Maybe he'd find someone there to ask about the missing woman. He approached them, but no one was around. He continued past the houses through a stand of poplars into a cemetery—an old one, judging from the huge oaks and lichen-covered gray tombstones. He stood for a moment listening to the raucous call of ravens and deciding whether to proceed down the grassy slope to the bay, which he could see through the trees. He glanced at the tall monument in front of him and was startled by the name chiseled there.

Gordon. His own name.

He set off down the steep slope, scanning the terraced rows of tombstones to his left, half expecting to see a body propped against the back of one of the stones. Struck with the irony of looking for a dead body in a cemetery, he laughed aloud. Reaching the bottom of the slope, he turned around and was dismayed to see that he had a long climb back. What had he been thinking of, anyway, wandering so far from the house and acting like a kid hunting for ghosts in a graveyard?

Well, he thought, he didn't need to mention his escapade to the others. Anyway, maybe one of them had already found the woman closer to home.

Nate and Bill, following the trail past the old quarry where Nate had ended his search earlier, heard a sound at the same time and stopped to listen. Tracking the steady tapping noise to a rocky point at the end of the trail, they found a modern house built in a clearing. As they rounded the front of the building, they surprised a man nailing trim on a large window still bearing the manufacturer's stickers. They introduced themselves.

The man put down his hammer and extended a hand. "John Guertler," he said amiably. "What can I do for you?"

Guertler lived in Massachusetts, he explained, and had come to Maine to work on his new house over the Columbus Day holiday. He hadn't seen Amy for several weeks. Sometimes she walked over to visit along the same trail they'd just taken, but she wouldn't have ventured off the trail, he said. She wasn't that sure of her footing.

"What's the rock wall out there?" asked Nate, gesturing to the end of the point where a pool had formed behind a barrier of boulders between the land and the bay.

"You saw the old quarry on the trail back there?" Guertler asked. "Hopewell Quarry. Those rocks are what's left of a causeway to the wharf where vessels loaded up with granite."

"I guess Sullivan used to be a thriving little port," said Bill. "How do you suppose they got the granite down here from the quarry?"

"By ox-drawn cart, I hear," Guertler said. "And by gravity. The causeway was built on just the right downgrade to the wharf"—he tucked his thumbs in the tool belt around his middle and grinned— "although they say that on at least one occasion a load of granite overshot its mark and landed in the bay."

"That so?" said the sheriff, grinning too as he and Nate turned to leave. "Well, let us know if you hear anything about Amy."

Guertler leaned down to pick up the hammer he'd laid on the deck. "Sure will. I hope you find her soon," he said. "Amy's a good person."

Bill, already walking away, turned and, with his arm extended in a half wave, half salute, called back, "Thanks. We'll find her."

The others had returned to the house by the time Nate and Bill arrived. No one, not even Warden Palman, who had joined the group with her search dog, Lobo, had found anything.

Nate left to talk to Spike Havey in the tiny North Sullivan Post Office, which, as Nate told Bill when he returned, was not much bigger than a postage stamp itself. Amy had been at the post office about nine days ago and had phoned at mid-morning a few days later, on Thursday. Havey told her she had a lot of mail. She hadn't picked it up or called again.

Area hospitals and the ambulance service had no word of Amy, the dispatcher told them. But word of the missing woman was spreading through the community. The sheriff, already well aware that not much gets by people in small towns, wasn't surprised when one person after another began dropping by Amy's house.

Merrill Taylor, who took care of Amy's place sometimes, told Bill he was positive that Amy wouldn't go away without letting him know. As Taylor left, Cecil Havey, a member of the Sullivan volunteer police, dropped by to say that he'd checked Amy's house during patrol two nights ago. He hadn't been on patrol the previous week, but that night her lights were on and her car was parked outside just as it was now.

Havey was just backing out of the driveway after sharing this information when Bill spotted a large gray sedan approaching in the distance.

"You ever hear about the Germans trying to land two spies off Hancock Point in the Second World War?" he asked Nate.

"I don't think so. Why?"

"All it took to foil their plan was one person spotting strangers trudging along the point road in long black coats and homburg hats, which no local person would wear. That person passed the word to the Hancock constable, who called the FBI."

"Yeah? They catch the spies?"

"The feds, as I remember the story, eventually tracked them to New York City and arrested them." Bill watched the sedan pull up next to the garage. "The local network seems to be operating pretty well here today."

Sandy Bryan stepped out of the sedan in front of Amy's house and introduced herself as Iva Patten's daughter. The young girl with her was her daughter, Beth, who knew Amy and her habits as well as anyone, her mother said. Sometimes, when Sandy gave Beth a note for the school bus driver, he'd let Beth off one stop early at Amy's road and Amy would meet her there. She'd stay at Amy's until her mother or grandmother came to pick her up.

Bill knelt beside the youngster. "I have a little girl not much bigger than you, Beth. How old are you?" She told him she was seven.

Beth thought the sheriff was nice, but she wasn't sure about all those men in uniform standing around outside. And why was everyone asking her questions in that extra-nice voice as though she were a little kid? Of course she knew where Amy kept her pocketbook, she told them, leading them into the house. Sometimes Amy laid it on the kitchen table and sometimes on her bed. But she really kept it in the cupboard under the counter next to the dining room table. Beth opened the cupboard door to show them. Amy's pocketbook wasn't there. She caught the look that her mother and Sheriff Clark exchanged above her head.

"Beth, can you remember the last time you were here at Amy's house?" the sheriff asked.

"It's been a while, maybe three or four weeks," Beth said. "Amy didn't say anything about going away, but I can show you where she keeps her suitcases, if you want." She led them to the closet in the hall. Both the blue suitcases were there. She pointed out the place in the front hall where Amy took off her shoes before entering the house. Amy liked other people to do that, too, and gave them special socks to wear. Amy's brown shoes were there. She must be wearing her L.L. Bean boots, Beth told them, the ones you wear without any shoes.

Did Amy seem happy the last time Beth was there? the sheriff asked.

Beth wondered what he meant. Amy was always happy, laughing and giving her bear hugs. Sometimes Amy hugged her too hard, though. And tickled her too hard. But she wouldn't tell Sheriff Clark things like that, or that Amy made her eat everything on her plate, even yucky lima beans.

So nothing seemed to be bothering Amy? the sheriff asked.

Beth thought a minute. She and Amy had looked at the album with pictures of Amy's family. And played cards. When her grandmother picked her up, they were playing bingo. No, she didn't think Amy had been upset, she told the sheriff. It was weird standing by the table where they'd played Go Fish a million times, talking about Amy and she wasn't even there.

"Well, Beth, thank you very much for your help," the sheriff said, reaching out to put a hand on her shoulder.

She didn't know she'd said anything helpful. "You're welcome," she answered, and she secretly crossed her fingers to make a wish that nothing bad had happened to Amy.

"Pretty little girl, isn't she?" Bill said as Beth and her mother drove away.

Nate agreed. "Very grown-up, too."

Inside the house, Brady, who had returned from Lamoine, was focusing his camera for a close-up of the cups and saucers on the kitchen counter when the phone in Amy's bedroom rang. Bob Cochrane, president of the company that had installed her security system, asked to speak with the sheriff.

Cochrane had spoken with Amy about three weeks ago, he told Bill. She'd seemed worried about some problems in the area that she preferred not to discuss on the phone. She said it was a matter for the police. Cochrane's records showed that they had installed the alarm system two years ago on April 25 and it had been set off only two times, once last July by one of her relatives, a young child, and again today. He assumed that was when the deputies broke into the house. He didn't know why the alarm hadn't registered in his office. He said he wanted to test the alarm at the house and would be coming down soon.

On his way down the hall to the garage, the sheriff spotted Brady in the living room. "Pete, we'll need a shot of the alarm panel on the bedroom wall," he said.

"I've already done that," Brady told him as the shutter clicked and a flash illuminated the armchair and magazines on the floor beside it.

"Good man," Clark said, continuing down the hall. As he opened the door to the garage, he heard laughter and saw Richard Dickson perched on the bottom of an overturned aluminum boat, swinging his long legs, entertaining the others with his special brand of dry humor.

"What'd I miss?" Clark asked.

"Don't ask, and consider yourself lucky, Bill," Nate said. "Hey, Richard, tell Bill what you told us about those people who were here a week ago."

"The Duscheks," said Dickson. "Felix and Augustine Duschek.

People call her Gusti, though. If you're looking for someone who had coffee with Miss Cave, it wasn't Felix and Gusti. Amy served them hot cider just before they left at seven in the evening. In mugs, not cups."

"That was last Wednesday?" Clark asked. "Then someone else was here after they left. Either later that night or the next day. The last contact Amy had with anyone we know about was Thursday morning when she talked with her insurance agent."

"Oh, yeah," Dickson cut in. "Mrs. Duschek said her husband talked a long time with Amy about her insurance. She was worried about money, and he told her to raise her deductible."

Dickson, complaining about the hardness of his perch, stepped down from the boat, stretched to his full six feet, and began pacing the cement floor. Amy had other visitors while the Duscheks were here, he said: two clam diggers. Amy and Gusti were outside when they showed up, and Gusti came back into the house while Amy talked with them. She said that Amy didn't seem particularly concerned afterward. Said the fellows had parked their truck on a nearby side road and while they were clamming on the shore someone had blocked the truck in with logs and rocks and had taken the key from the ignition. Gusti said that when she and her husband left a little later, they didn't see a truck.

Nate suggested that maybe Pete Brady would know who clammed in the area. It was his town, and sooner or later he found out pretty much everything that went on in it.

The sun had disappeared below the horizon, and someone had turned on the lights. A chill was settling into the garage, and Nate reached to the overhead door to close it against the damp air. The door had just rolled down and clunked to the floor when Nate saw the headlights of an approaching car. He lifted the door and greeted the driver, who was walking briskly toward him.

"Pete Hartford," the man said, introducing himself. "I have some information you might be interested in."

"Come on in," Nate said and pulled down the door again after him.

Hartford was a member of the Sullivan volunteer police and had just heard on his scanner that they were looking for Amelia Cave. He and his wife, Arlene, had been on patrol on October 4, last Thursday night, and according to his records had checked Miss Cave's house at 9:37 P.M. They didn't see her. In fact they'd never seen her. They always drove in, flashed their blue light to let her know it was the police, turned around, and drove out. Last Thursday, they had to back out because a car blocked the small turnaround area they always used.

"Did you notice what kind of car it was?" the sheriff asked.

"Sure. It's the same car that's there now. Parked the same way, too."

"Parked just like that? You sure?"

"Yeah, I'm sure. We didn't know it was Amy's car because we never really saw her car. It's always inside the garage with only the white roof showing. Her porch light wasn't on last Thursday. It never was, but usually we saw a light somewhere inside. We didn't see any light last Thursday."

When Hartford left, Nate drew the sheriff to a corner of the garage. "Bill," he said, "I think it's time we called in the state police."

Bill didn't immediately agree. Sure, there were increasing signs of a suspicious disappearance, but that was a far cry from homicide. It would be jumping the gun to bring in the state police, the agency designated by the attorney general to investigate most homicides.

Nate understood the turf struggles between law enforcement agencies, as well as his boss's reluctance to let go of an investigation before he had to. But Nate got along just fine with the state troopers. Besides, he was starting to have a feeling about this case. He knew that the sheriff respected his judgment, so he stood his ground.

"Okay, Nate," Bill said finally. "Go ahead. Give CID a call."

Nate instructed dispatch to contact the state police criminal investigation division at its Orono headquarters. And to send down food for their supper. And notify the wives of the men who'd be working late.

Nate turned expectantly at the sound of a car door closing outside in the driveway. But of course it was too soon for a deputy to be returning with their grub. Bob Cochrane of Security Central had arrived to check Amy's alarm.

The alarm was functioning as it should, Cochrane determined

right away, and almost certainly had been set off today by the deputies when they broke in. Maybe there had been some problem with the phone lines.

"Oh, and I don't know if this is important," Cochrane said, "but Miss Cave owes us money. She's behind eleven payments."

"Interesting," Bill said, sending Nate a quizzical look.

Minutes after Cochrane drove off, a part-time deputy arrived with a box of sandwiches, half-gallon jugs of milk, and Ethel's homemade chocolate chip cookies. While they were eating, Bouchard, who had been asked to work a longer shift tonight, called several times with pieces of information about the woman in whose garage the deputies were having their evening meal.

Ellsworth attorney Frank Walker had just heard on the radio that they were looking for Amelia Cave. He had recently handled her purchase of the lot next to her house. She had been in his office two weeks ago and seemed in good spirits. She hadn't said anything about leaving the area. Walker mentioned that Harry Plummer had surveyed the property.

Bouchard contacted Plummer, who said he'd been at Amy's a couple of days ago but hadn't seen Amy then or, in fact, for the last several weeks.

Mac Roach, manager of the Ellsworth branch of Bangor Savings Bank, where Amy had an account, had heard about her disappearance on the nightly news. She'd been in the bank last week, he told Bouchard, and had seemed especially happy about a recent visit from her New York family.

"You wait," Nate said between bites of ham and cheese. "We'll get a call soon that'll amount to something." He heard a sound at the garage door and looked up to see a black-haired man looking back at him.

Chapter Three

RALPH'S HERE," NATE ANNOUNCED TO THE OTHERS after the few seconds it took him to recognize the apparition behind the dark glass as CID detective Sergeant Ralph Pinkham.

All six men inside—five from the sheriff's department and Charlie Marshall, warden with Inland Fisheries & Wildlife—knew Pinkham, a twenty-year veteran with the state police. When Nate rolled down the garage door after Pinkham, he felt a shift in the atmosphere, as though the temperature had dropped or the high-school principal had entered a classroom. Pinkham was friendly enough—it wasn't that—but he seemed so professional and reserved as he listened and watched you with those piercing eyes, and you were never quite sure what he was thinking. The perfect homicide investigator, Nate thought. He looked the part, too: strong jaw, solid, compact build, natty three-piece suit, and black patent leather shoes.

"Hello, Bill," Pinkham said.

Nate watched Pinkham talk with the sheriff in his soft-spoken way. Attentive and polite as he listened to details of the investigation, Pinkham made it clear that he was here just to listen and learn on the remote chance that this would turn into something nasty and his agency would be obliged to take over. By the time the three toured the house and returned to the garage, it had been established without being addressed directly that the sheriff was still running the show.

Bill, at ease now, was directing plans for a massive search the next day: Wardens would conduct a tight grid search on the ground with canines, Brady would scour the area in his plane, and deputies would search the shore in boats.

How much everything had changed since morning, Nate thought. He had broken into a woman's home expecting to find her inside, hoping she was only ill or injured. Searching for her on the trails outside, he had still pictured returning to the house and finding her there, indignant at the police intrusion into her home. Or maybe, when she heard their explanation, she'd understand and even be amused, grateful that people were watching over her. That image had receded so far, Nate realized, that now he was thinking of her as a body washed up on the shore. Too bad. Just when he was starting to know and like Amy Cave.

As Pinkham left just after eight-thirty, the sheriff was arranging for one of his men to stand guard at the house during the night.

Driving through North Sullivan, Pinkham met only one car on the road. He was about to turn onto Route 1 when he saw a state police cruiser coming off the bridge. Pinkham pulled his cruiser to the side of the road and stopped. The other vehicle eased next to his, drivers' sides together, and both men lowered their windows.

"What's going on?" asked Detective Dave Giroux.

"Everyone's leaving for the night, but we'll need you first thing in the morning," said Pinkham.

If the case turned out to be a homicide, Giroux would be the primary investigator under Pinkham's supervision.

Pinkham was still filling in Giroux when Sheriff Clark and the others drove by. The drivers signaled one another with a flick of their headlights.

Within fifteen minutes, the sheriff had arrived in Ellsworth and was turning into the courthouse driveway. After parking the cruiser in his reserved space against a brick retaining wall, he walked to the flight of steps to the new courthouse addition.

At the top of the stairs, he entered a glassed-in lobby to the sheriff's department and turned left into the dispatch office. Dispatcher Bob Larson, seated behind a high counter, was busy on the phone. Clark raised a hand in greeting as he crossed the room to a row of wood-partitioned cubbyholes on the far wall. He gathered his messages from the compartment marked Number One and, leafing through them on his way back through the lobby to his office, chose the call he'd return first. A Susan Cave had phoned from New York only twenty minutes earlier.

Susan was married to Amy's nephew Richard, she explained, and they and their three children had stayed at Amy's the last two weeks of August. Susan didn't think that Amy was visiting any of their relatives, but she'd check around to make sure. It didn't seem like Amy to leave Sullivan without telling Crawford Hollidge or someone, Susan said, or to leave her car outside or do any of the other things the sheriff was telling her. Something must be wrong. If no one in the family knew where Amy was, she and Richard would come to Maine themselves. She'd call back soon.

Clark was returning a phone call from a television reporter when Nate walked in with part-time deputy Fred Ehrlenbach. Nate signaled Bill to hurry up and finish his conversation, a hard thing for the sheriff, who was friendly with reporters and liked to talk. "You can't use all of this yet," he'd say to them, "but let me tell you what's going on so you'll have some background." It was better having the media in your corner, he'd learned. He seldom got stung confiding in them. But now he cut short the call, telling the reporter to stay in touch and that they'd probably have more for him tomorrow.

Before Clark had even hung up, Nate said, "Bill, Fred knows Amy!"

"You do, Fred? You know Amelia Cave?"

"Sure. We built her house for her."

"Ray Builders built the house in North Sullivan?"

"Yes. I designed it for her."

Bill leaned forward and planted his arms on his desk. "Sit down. Tell us what you know about Amy."

Fred settled in a chair in front of Bill's desk and was about to speak when Nate, perched on the edge of the chief deputy's desk, announced, "Fred says we won't find Amy tomorrow."

"That's right, Bill. If you didn't find her within the first hour, with the dogs and all, I don't think you're going to. She doesn't wander around outside. Amy's not a back-to-nature kind of person. More of an observer of nature."

"That so, Fred? You known her long?"

Ehrlenbach, in his brown deputy's uniform, slid forward in his chair and crossed one long leg over the knee of the other. "I met Amy in the mid-seventies when a Bangor real estate agent brought her to Ray Builders. She was looking for land, planning to build a house."

"That was ten years ago," Bill said. "I thought her house was only a couple years old."

"Well, after she bought the lot on Evergreen Point, she held off building for a few years because of the economy. Then she decided that Ronald Reagan would turn things around. Right after Reagan was elected, she started coming up from Massapequa, staying a couple weeks each time with the Kanes at The Ellsworth Motel.

"I showed her plans and took her around to look at houses. She wanted a Cape with a detached garage and an apartment over it for her family when they visited or to rent out. In a couple months, though, she settled on a ranch style with the apartment in the base-ment, 'cause it'd be cheaper."

"It's kind of a fancy house for Sullivan, isn't it?" Bill asked.

"About eighty-five thousand. More like a hundred thousand now. You call that fancy?"

"Well, yeah," Bill said. "Around here."

"People tried to talk her out of it. I helped her get financing. I re-member Bob Lakin at Bangor Savings, where she got her mortgage, questioning her about moving so far from her family." Fred shrugged his shoulders. "But Amy loves Maine. And when she makes up her mind, that's it."

Nate drew up a chair next to Fred. "You ever see her car parked like we found it today?" he asked, angling one hand against the other. "Like this, next to the house?"

"Never. She always uses her electronic opener and drives right into the garage. Closes the door before she gets out of the car. She isn't scared—she gets upset if you think that. She calls it being cautious."

"We've been hearing how depressed Amy is," Bill said. "What about that, Fred? You ever see her depressed?"

"Not in the beginning. She was too excited about building her dream house. But the first winter she lived here was hard on her. She borrowed furniture for her basement apartment and lived down there—the rest of the house was empty. You know how depressing Maine winters can get and—"

Bill's phone rang. Answering, he held up a finger in a "wait a minute" gesture, then mouthed, "Richard Cave." Apparently someone was coming to Maine—Bill was talking about meeting a plane at the Bar Harbor airport. When Bill hung up, he told them that Richard and Susan Cave were coming to Maine the next day.

"Good," Fred said. "Amy's awfully close to her family. I think when she moved up here she wasn't very realistic about how often they'd be able to visit."

"You were telling us about Amy's first winter," Bill reminded him.

"Yeah, well, even though the house was finished, I'd talk to her, oh, maybe two, three times a month. She'd say something was bothering her but she didn't want to talk about it on the phone. I'd stop in to see her, too, and she'd ask me what she was doing wrong, why she was having such a hard time making friends. I said maybe she was trying too hard, that she should relax, take it easy. I explained that Mainers are kind of private people, apt to look at anyone from away as a foreigner."

Nate and Bill laughed. "Yeah," Nate said. "Even if you move to Maine when you're a month old, you'll always be an outsider. So, have you stayed in touch with Amy?"

"Not as much." Fred replied. "Two years ago I drew her a plan for an outside entry to the apartment in the basement. Had it built that summer. This last spring she called about putting a patio outside the apartment. She sounded like her old self again. But I haven't heard from her since."

Nate, checking his watch, was surprised to see that it was nearly ten o'clock. He stood to leave. Not that his wife, Marti, bugged him about his late hours. He'd just like to spend more time with his family.

"What's Amy look like?" Bill asked. Nate paused in the doorway.

Fred seemed surprised. "Nobody's given you a description?"

"Sure. A couple people. But you're a trained observer."

Fred drew himself up in a pose of exaggerated authority. "Oh, well then, as a trained observer, I'd say she's a nice-looking woman, about five-foot-five, maybe a hundred and forty pounds. Late fifties, with gray hair—she wears it short. Kind of distinguished looking. Carries herself in an aristocratic way, you know. Bright blue eyes, a little on the hazel side—wears glasses sometimes."

Fred paused, relaxing into his normal posture. It was hard to make them see Amy as he saw her. "You know what I think of when I picture Amy? Her teeth." He laughed at himself. "I mean, they're so even, and she's got such a nice smile."

"You like her, don't you, Fred?" Nate said.

"Yeah. Amy's a good person. . . . Well, see you in the morning, Nate," he said just before Nate shut the office door behind him.

"Oh, you're coming to Evergreen Point?" Bill asked Fred.

"Yep, dispatch signed me up for the search. It's okay—things are slow in the building trade. But I better check in with Larson now. I'm still on patrol duty."

When Fred left, Bill, alone for the first time all day, sat quietly at his desk. You never know, he thought, what little detail will turn out to be helpful. It's like putting a puzzle together: you need lots of little pieces to get the full picture.

Bill reached for his phone messages and pulled out one from *Bangor Daily News* reporter Mike Gordon, who he knew had an eleven o'clock deadline. Bill dialed the number. He realized that he was forming a picture of Amy, a woman he'd never met, even though—he smiled wryly—he had looked in all her closets. And even her medicine cabinet.

Gordon answered the phone. He was just finishing a story on the missing woman, he said. He could add a few lines about the search and still get his copy to Bangor in time for tomorrow's paper.

Bill hung up the phone, straightened his desk, locked his office door behind him, and stopped at dispatch on his way out. Larson told him that Brady planned to take off in his plane at eight in the morning. He had lined up three units for the boats and another eight or so for the land search.

Larson, logging the sheriff's departure for home at 10:28 P.M., noticed how long the log was. Much of it centered on the search for Amelia Cave. It hadn't been easy finding people, many of them part-timers with other jobs, to show up on such short notice. Dave Gordon had just called to say he couldn't make it tomorrow. There must have been twenty calls from the media, besides all the usual ones. Kathy Pollenz, his relief, would be in soon, and he had a pile of incident cards to type up before he could leave.

Just before the end of his shift at midnight, Larson entered Amelia Cave's name and date of birth, 10-27-24, into two statewide police files—Missing and Wanted in Maine, and Attempt to Locate.

The dispatch door opened and Larson swiveled his chair from the teletype to greet Kathy. She'd already heard about the search for Amelia Cave.

"It's all over the news," Kathy said. "Somebody's bound to call in something that'll help find her."

"Maybe so," Larson said, reaching for his brown nylon windbreaker.

Or maybe, he thought, they would find her body tomorrow in Taunton Bay.

Chapter Four

THE PONTOONS ON THEIR SMALL PLANE SKIMMED along the surface of Flanders Pond, and the shoreline flew by faster and faster until suddenly they were airborne.

The fog that had surrounded them on the pond lay below them now. Pete Brady had radioed dispatch before takeoff and learned that the weather around Taunton Bay was sunny and clear. So was the rest of Sullivan, they saw, as they headed west toward Evergreen Point.

Brady, who'd been flying since he was fifteen, was a passenger today in the red-and-white Cessna 172 that Wes Ford used in his fishing business to spot schools of herring. Ford was at the controls. Brady was checking the rooftops and the network of roads below, orienting himself, when he saw the black metal superstructure of the Sullivan bridge ahead.

"Follow the Sullivan shore up the river," Brady called to Wes above the din of the motor. A minute later the plane banked to the right around a point where the river widened into the bay. "There's the house. See?" he directed Ford. "They're waving at us." Ford dipped the wings of the plane in salute. "Head back around the point toward the bridge," said Brady. "I saw something I want to check out."

Brady held his binoculars at an angle against the window and focused on a patch of red in the mudflats next to a large rock near the shore. Nearby, clam diggers were bending over the flats with their hoes. Brady radioed deputies at the house to contact the diggers and have them check the red object. He stayed on the radio, directing Dickson to the spot, and in a few minutes saw him emerge from the trees onto the shore, waving his arms and no doubt calling out to get the clammers' attention.

One of the figures below plodded through the mud to the red object, picked it up, and carried it to Dickson on the shore. Dickson's voice crackled from the radio in Brady's hand. "It's what?" Brady called back. "I didn't copy you."

"It's an onion bag. A red onion bag."

"Copied loud and clear. Thanks." Brady signed off and turned to Ford. "We think she's wearing a red jacket," he explained.

The plane hugged the shoreline back around the point where Guertler was building his new house, past the Cave house, and toward Franklin, at the head of the bay. Brady was struck again, as he often was, at how different he felt in the air, looking down on the place where he spent his days running around like an ant, it seemed, trying to fix things. Trying to fix people. Trying to stop some guy from beating up his girlfriend or his wife. Stop a woman from smashing the windshield or slashing the tires on the car of a real or imagined rival for her man. Trying to find out who stole a crate of lobsters from the pound, who shot this man's prize bull, cut trees in that man's woodlot.

Sometimes Brady wondered if he were making any difference at all in what people did to one another. On the ground it seemed so important. If he even noticed trees, water in the inlets along the coast, or clouds in the sky, they were just part of the background. He was always surprised when he rose in a plane to see Hancock County become a wilderness of trees interrupted here and there by a rooftop connected to another rooftop by a narrow swath through the forest. Looking down changed his point of view completely.

Below him today, blue-green channels wound through a giant mosaic of mussel bars, ledges, and eelgrass in a background of gray mud. To the south, the smoky blue Bar Harbor mountains marched along the horizon like a chain of camels.

They had flown farther than Brady could imagine a body washing from Evergreen Point. But he'd been surprised before at the combined force of current, wind, and tide, which maybe in this case had been at work for as long as a week. There was a lot of bay below them, probably more than five square miles. And maybe thirty-five miles of shoreline.

Brady scanned the Franklin shore around a horseshoe curve toward Hancock and signaled Ford to head across the bay to the opposite shore. They crisscrossed the basin, now—at ebb tide—more mud than water, until they reached Burying Island. Brady had flown over the island before and seen a few cabin rooftops among the blanket of evergreens, and the large, scraggly heron nests perched precariously in the tops of dead or dying trees. The nests were empty now, Brady saw as they flew over the rookery toward the Sullivan shore and the tan roof of Amy Cave's house.

Ford banked the plane sharply around the eastern tip of the island and followed the shore while Brady searched among clumps of kelp and fallen trees exposed in the mud for something that didn't belong there. Today that something was the body of a woman in a red jacket. Last month on the mainland it had been plots of marijuana plants. Before that, a stolen blue pickup truck. Soon, he promised himself, he'd rent a plane at the airport and not look for a thing but his own enjoyment.

As the plane rounded the western tip of Burying Island, dots of color in the channel caught Brady's attention. Lobster buoys. But worth a close look, he knew. Several years ago a fisherman pulling his traps here in Taunton Bay had found the bloated body of a man hung up on his trapline. He and Fred scanned the line of buoys and doubled back to cruise along the Hancock shore to Egypt Stream. Near an old boat beached on the shore by the stream, two clam diggers waved up at them in a friendly gesture.

Ford followed the Hancock shore to the bridge where they'd begun the search ninety minutes earlier. Brady radioed the men on the ground and signed off on the search. They flew back to Flanders Pond, their mission completed—successfully or unsuccessfully, Brady thought, depending on how you looked at it.

At his desk in the patrol room, Lieutenant Nate Anderson scribbled his initials on another of the incident reports that had been piling up for several days. He picked up the last report. Bob Palmer had investigated a complaint by a man whose van had been shot at while he was driving along Route 3 near Romer's Corner. Palmer located two boys walking along the road carrying shotguns. One of them admitted firing at a partridge but claimed he had no idea that the pellet had traveled as far as the road. Palmer had disposed of the incident, Nate saw, with a lecture on firearms safety. Nate initialed the top copy, separated the triplicate carbon form, and arranged the pages in three different piles by color.

He carried the reports to the sheriff's office and tossed the white and yellow copies onto the secretary's desk. Karen was on the phone, unable to fire off her usual kidding complaint about having to file all his paperwork. Nate settled for the scowl she sent him, and, grinning, proceeded to the dispatch office.

He placed the remaining pink copies on the counter behind which Bouchard sat glaring at him. It was a game they played. "Oh, all right," Nate said, and with exaggerated gestures began shuffling the pink sheets, arranging them by date and tapping them against the counter until the punch holes lined up. He inserted the sheets onto the prongs of a clipboard, which he returned to a corner of the counter, ready for inspection by reporters who covered the crime beat.

"Don't say I never do anything for you," Nate grumbled.

"I won't if you won't," Bouchard replied, adding pointedly, "and here's the number you asked me to get for you." He stretched from his chair to pass a slip of paper across the counter. "You were right. Brookings is a dentist." Nate returned to his desk and dialed the Bangor number.

"Dr. Brookings's office," a crisp voice answered after only one ring. Nate stated his business, and the receptionist put him on hold.

Mac Roach at Bangor Savings had told him this morning about three checks just returned on Amy's account. The last one, dated October 2, was a $25 check to a John Brookings. Roach had agreed to put a freeze on Amelia Cave's account and notify him if any more checks came back.

"Hello, Lieutenant, this is Nancy Crotty. I understand you're asking about Amelia Cave."

Miss Cave had kept a 10:30 appointment on Tuesday morning, October 2, to have her teeth cleaned, the hygienist said. Amelia had seemed lonely and had invited her and two other women in the office to visit her home in Sullivan. It wasn't the usual idle invitation, said Nancy. Miss Cave had given them explicit instructions so they would not get lost. Tuesday was only the second time they'd met her.

Nate made two more phone calls, visited the district attorney's office upstairs, grabbed some lunch in the jail kitchen, and stopped at dispatch on the way to his car. He was on his way to Ashville, he told Bouchard, and would call the office when he finished his business there.

He found the Keenan brothers' house in Ashville on a loop off Route 1. He'd heard they were the clammers who had stopped at Amy's house last week after someone barricaded their truck and took the ignition key. No one was home at the Keenans'. Nate left his card with a note asking one of them to call him at the sheriff's department.

On the return trip, Nate stopped at the Sorrento General Store on Route 1 and called his office. Mac Roach was on the phone now, Bouchard told him, with something important about Amelia Cave.

"Patch him through to me," Nate said. Roach came on the line. His first words sent a surge of adrenaline through Nate. "You're kidding. Amelia Cave's check? Is the teller sure?"

This could be the break they'd been hoping for. Nate hung up and called Key Bank to hear from the teller herself what she had told Roach. Then he jumped into his cruiser to drive to Evergreen Point with the news.

It had been a chilly forty-one degrees when Crawford Hollidge finished the night shift at the front desk of the Ellsworth Holiday Inn. Now at 10:30, the thermometer on his front porch registered seventy-five degrees, and the WDEA forecast he'd just listened to predicted the day's high in the mid-eighties.

It was good to be outside in a summer shirt again. He would walk to Amy's; the turnoff to Evergreen Point was only a quarter mile down the road. If he could just get off nicotine, maybe he wouldn't be so short of breath. Of course worrying about Amy didn't help. Slowing his pace, he told himself to stop borrowing trouble and think about pleasant things. Like when he first saw Amy, walking along this very road to the post office as he was driving home from work.

For several weeks they'd waved to each other, getting acquainted at a distance. Then one morning he stopped and offered her a lift, and she accepted a ride as far as her turnoff on the point road.

She was friendly and outgoing. He could tell she was from away; she didn't drop her *r*'s and she noticed things around her that the locals took for granted.

It wasn't long before she asked him to come see her house. He would drop in for coffee sometimes when he came home from work, then he started doing little chores for her.

That first winter when he got his new truck and plow, he offered to plow her driveway. She thanked him and said she'd just walk when her car got snowed in. The next winter, though, when he talked to her about safety and a fire truck not being able to get down her driveway, she gave in. She would insist he come in for coffee and a chat when he finished plowing. He liked to listen to her talk. She'd go on about all the opportunities there were for people to pull themselves out of the poverty she saw around her—starting a mussel farm, maybe. Anything to get off welfare. It bothered her to hear about children dropping out of school. She liked helping them, helping anybody, as long as they were willing to help themselves, too.

Crawford grinned. It seemed as though Amy was walking along the road with him, chattering away. He hadn't fretted once all the way to her driveway.

Then he saw the yellow police ribbon strung across the drive and police cars and uniformed men outside Amy's house. He recognized Sheriff Clark from his picture in the paper and seeing him on TV. The sheriff motioned him around the ribbon barrier. After a bit of small talk, Clark and a tall blondish fellow with a mustache, a state policeman named Giroux, began asking him questions that set him to worrying again. Questions about Amy's being paranoid or depressed and too friendly with strangers.

Crawford thought she was too trusting at times. He had told her so, especially when she met that state ecology fellow on her road. She'd invited him in to talk, and he'd stayed a couple of hours. "Amy, you shouldn't do that kind of thing," Crawford had told her, and she had brushed aside his concern, saying there was nothing to worry about. He wouldn't say he'd ever seen Amy depressed. Bothered, maybe—about people she trusted saying things about her and ruining her reputation.

"I have no idea of the details," Crawford told them. "I've asked her dozens of times to tell me straight out so I can help. She always says she'll take care of it herself. She wants someone to tell her how, without her spelling out the problem."

"So, you don't think she'd take her own life or anything like that?" Clark asked.

"Hell, no! Why would you say a thing like that?"

Clark was immediately apologetic. "We don't know Amy at all," he explained, "and we're just considering all the possibilities."

"I'm sorry," Crawford said. "I get hot under the collar sometimes. I guess I'm worried about Amy. I know you're just doing your job."

Giroux, changing the subject, asked when he'd seen Amy last. Crawford said he hadn't talked with her since September, but he thought he had seen her car drive past his house this week, maybe on Monday.

Crawford could tell that the news surprised them. Apparently they thought she'd disappeared before that. He wasn't sure at all, he told them. It was dark and he couldn't see inside the car. It might have been another car like hers.

As he was leaving, Crawford took in the strange scene in front of Amy's house—a half dozen cars, police milling around where he was used to plowing snow or parking his truck and having Amy appear with a warm, welcoming smile. "Come back," a voice inside his head commanded. "Amy, come back, take charge, and send all these people packing." Knowing Amy, though, she'd probably invite them in for coffee.

As Crawford walked out her driveway, he saw a car approaching slowly. The driver, a man not in uniform, eyed him solemnly and nodded as he drove past.

The sheriff observed Pinkham as he parked at the end of a line of cars in the driveway. Watched him in his three-piece suit and patent leather shoes move toward them with that smooth, coiled-spring walk of his. Pinkham had a way, Bill thought, of making you feel you should get right down to business. That you ought to tell him right away that the plane and boat search hadn't turned up a thing and the wardens were still combing the woods. That a neighbor, Linda Smullen, had stopped by to say she had lunch with Amy last week and Amy had been annoyed about something to do with the town office. So Bill filled Pinkham in with all that news, quickly adding that they had already followed up on the town office issue.

He'd sent Dickson to check with Lynn Dunbar, the town clerk, and Lynn had reported that Amy was upset because the town office was closed on Friday afternoon when she went to pay her taxes. Friday was the deadline for getting a 2 percent discount. She'd even gone to Dunbar's Store to find out why the office wasn't open, not knowing it was always closed on Friday afternoon. Amy returned the following Monday and paid her tax, less the discount, which Lynn allowed her.

Linda had dropped by Amy's again three days ago, Giroux told Pinkham, with some tomatoes from her garden. She couldn't raise Amy, although her car was there, parked the way it was now. Those were Linda's tomatoes on the deck railing where she had put them on Monday.

"We thought we'd better look in the trunk of Amy's car," Bill said. "It was about the only place we hadn't looked. We had to punch out the lock."

"Oh?" Pinkham said. "You didn't find a body or you'd have mentioned it, I assume." The sheriff and Giroux laughed.

"And we didn't do it just because some guy who's threatening to hire a private investigator told us to," Giroux said, expecting to get a rise out of Pinkham, who just fixed him with a look and waited. "Felix Duschek," Giroux said. "He thinks we're taking too long finding Amy."

"Duschek?" Pinkham inquired. Giroux turned to Bill to do the explaining.

"Felix Duschek and his wife visited Amy last Wednesday, the day before she seems to have disappeared," Bill said.

Pinkham nodded. "You've taken photos of the car?"

"Brady did," Giroux told him. "We tried to get into the trunk without breaking the lock—Bishop and I struggled for half an hour to remove the backseat and finally had to give up. Found only a few things in the trunk: some string, pieces of vinyl flooring, and a couple of other items we put into evidence bags."

"Phone call, Bill," Brady called from the front door.

As Bill left, Pinkham walked to the rear of Amy's car to check the trunk lock. They had done a clean job, he told Giroux.

When Bill returned, he said he had talked with a man from Bangor Window and Shade Company. Two of his men had delivered a divan to the house on Thursday morning and had seen Amy.

"Thursday," Pinkham said. "The day that she called her insurance company?"

"Yep. That day. Curtis Ramsey, one of the deliverymen, said that Amy mentioned speaking with her insurance agent that morning. And get this—after they carried the couch to the apartment downstairs, Amy served them cookies and hot chocolate." He paused before delivering the punch line. "In china cups with saucers. Like the ones we found on the kitchen counter."

"Didn't we find three cups?" Giroux asked.

"Yeah. The third cup was Amy's. She had cocoa with them."

"Well, now we know who was here in the house with her," Giroux said. "They say anything else?"

"Ramsey said there was no car in the driveway. Miss Cave came to the door dressed but with a towel around her hair, explaining she was just out of the shower. She had them carry the sofa to the downstairs apartment from the far side of the house—the bank was less steep

there. The men stayed half to three-quarters of an hour and left around
eleven o'clock."

"Okay," Pinkham said, "so the deliverymen place Amy here a week
ago today at eleven in the morning. We don't have anybody who saw
or heard from her after that?"

Bill thought a minute. The postmaster had said Amy called him at
midmorning Thursday, and the Hollidge fellow thought he might
have seen her car the following Monday night but wasn't sure.

"No, the deliverymen are the last ones we know about to see her
for certain."

Bill mopped his brow. The sun, directly overhead now, was hot.
Pinkham had to leave, and Dave and Bill decided that the most pressing business was lunch. Bill went inside to call the office to send down
food for ten people.

He had just returned when Nate drove in. They could tell he was
hopped up about something.

"Listen to this!" Nate called, walking briskly toward them. "Someone just opened an account at Key Bank with a large check from
Amelia Cave."

"What's large?" the sheriff asked.

"How about twenty-seven hundred dollars. Is that large enough?"

Bill turned on his heel and walked to the garage. The other two
followed him. Nobody would interrupt them there. "Who opened the
account?" Bill asked.

"Samantha Glenner," Nate said, looking from one to the other for
a sign of recognition. They shook their heads and waited to hear
more. "Well, Beth Sargent, a teller at Key Bank, read in today's paper
that Amelia Cave was missing. The name was familiar to her, and
when she remembered why, she thought the information she had
might be important."

"Yeah, Nate," Clark interrupted him. "You're enjoying this too
much. Get to it. What information?"

"I'm telling you, if you just give me a chance," Nate said with a
grin. Bill was right; he was enjoying this. "Beth said that Tuesday, the
day before yesterday, a very large woman in her forties came into Key

Bank and opened an account with a twenty-seven-hundred-dollar check signed by Amelia Cave."

"Jesus," Bill said. "You don't suppose Glenner's the person Amy just bought the land from, do you?"

Nate's face fell. He didn't want what seemed like their first solid lead to disappear with a reasonable explanation. "There's one way to find out," he said. "Send someone to the town office. They'll know who sold her the land."

Bill stepped outside the garage, spotted Brady chatting with a warden by the ribbon barrier, and sent him off to the Sullivan Town Office. Returning to the garage, he asked Nate if he knew where the Glenner woman lived.

"Glenner gave the bank an Ellsworth RFD address," Nate said. "Which tells us only that she lives outside the city in one of several towns. She told Beth she's lived at that address for two years and that she doesn't have a driver's license but plans to get one soon. Beth said Glenner used two IDs that didn't particularly impress her—a Department of Defense buying card and a card from Harbor Divers on Mount Desert Island."

"I know Harbor Divers," Nate said. "I'll give them a call."

"Good idea," commented Bill. "What else did Beth tell you?"

"She said that Glenner mentioned owning a boat that had been damaged, and a silent partner who was putting up the money to fix it. She opened a personal account, saying she might change it later to a business account. Another woman came into the bank to identify Glenner, but she wasn't much help; she didn't have an account there herself. Glenner introduced the woman as her aunt and said she'd been shopping next door at Doug's.

"And listen to this," Nate said. "The Glenner woman came into the bank again this morning and used a starter check to withdraw nine hundred dollars."

"Boy, I don't know," Bill said. "It doesn't seem as though anyone who had anything to do with Amy's disappearance would be dumb enough to cash a check when it's all over the news that we're looking for her."

"But," said Giroux, "when she opened the account two days ago, none of us knew about Amy's disappearance. When the word got out, why wouldn't someone use the money? The damage was already done. What was the date on Amy's check?"

"The fourth of October. Last Thursday," Nate told him.

"Thursday again," Giroux said. "Amy wrote a check to Glenner and vanished into thin air on the same day?" With a raised eyebrow, Giroux looked from one man to the other. "Come on, Pete, hurry up."

Lunch, delivered by a part-time deputy, took their minds off Brady and everything else for a while. Nate and Bill ate sitting next to each other on the bottom of Amy's overturned aluminum boat. Giroux perched on the box they'd used for their base radio; they were using the phone in the house now that they'd secured the scene. Nate had just taken a bite of his chicken sandwich when Brady appeared in the garage doorway. Nate stopped chewing.

Brady chuckled at the three expectant faces looking up at him and told them the news he knew they wanted to hear: "The check wasn't for Amy's land."

"It wasn't," Nate said, relieved. "So maybe we do have a lead."

"Maybe," Brady agreed. "She bought the land from some guy named Baldwin in Rhode Island. Paid seventy-five hundred dollars."

"Come on," said Nate, putting aside the last of his sandwich. "Let's go look for Glenner in the phone book." Bill and Dave followed him into Amy's living room, where Nate plugged her only phone into a phone jack. The sheriff searched the directory for Samantha Glenner's name and didn't find it. He looked around and discovered Amy's personal address book in the cupboard under the dining room counter. No listing there, either. But when Nate called Key Bank, Beth Sargent gave them a number, a 422 exchange, the exchange for the towns of Hancock, Sullivan, and Sorrento.

Nate began pacing beside the dining room table. "Okay," he said, "we call Glenner. No—first . . ." He picked up the directory to look for another listing.

Elaine Eaton at Harbor Divers was angry when Nate told her that Samantha Glenner was using a card from her business. Samantha had come in two years ago claiming she was an experienced commercial diver, but it hadn't taken Eaton long to realize that she wasn't.

Eaton hadn't seen Samantha since last year when she bought a used diving suit and tank. She'd heard, though, that Samantha was having a hard time finding diving partners. Had even thrown a guy she was diving with overboard, gear and all. The word was that Samantha was hitting the bottle pretty hard.

When Nate hung up, he told them what Eaton had said. Then he picked up the phone again.

"Are we ready?" He dialed the number that Beth had given him, and a woman answered on the second ring. "Does Samantha Glenner live at this address?"

The woman hesitated. "Yes, Samantha lives in a trailer on the property. Who is this? Why do you ask?"

"This is Lieutenant Nate Anderson of the Hancock County Sheriff's Department." He was trying his best to sound both casual and official.

Nate was stunned at the woman's response: "Oh, yes. I met you yesterday at Amy Cave's house."

After only a second's pause, his voice calmer than he was feeling, Nate asked, "Who is this?"

"Glenn Askeborn."

"Oh." Nate remembered the name and recognized the voice in the same instant. The nervous woman with Iva. "Is Samantha there now?"

"No, she's not. Why do you want Samantha?"

Nate ignored the question. "When Samantha returns, please have her call me at the sheriff's office." He hung up and turned to the others. "What have we got here? Pete, that was Glenn Askeborn, who was here yesterday with Iva Patten. She didn't say anything about seeing or hearing from Amy Cave recently, did she?"

"I don't think so. Not that I heard, anyway."

"Then what in hell was someone at her phone number doing with a check from Amy dated last Thursday?"

Chapter Five

SITTING AROUND WAITING FOR SAMANTHA GLENNER to call was not appealing to any of them, particularly Nate. It wasn't his style. He and Dave would pay a visit to the Askeborn residence, if they could find out where it was.

Maybe Charlie Wheeler, the Hancock volunteer police chief, would know, Bill suggested. Charlie was out, but his wife, Joanne, who dispatched for the police, told them that the Askeborn house was just down the road from their own.

"Let's go, Dave," Nate said on his way to the door. They were in Nate's cruiser nearly at the end of the Evergreen Point road when a car with two women inside passed them.

"You know them?" Giroux asked. Nate didn't recognize either woman. If the women were on their way to the Cave house about anything important, Bill would fill them in when they got back.

Ruth Kane, seeing the yellow ribbon ahead that blocked their way, pulled in behind a parked car with an orange light on the roof. She took a deep breath and finally looked at Amy's house.

How Amy had fussed to get that rosy tinge in the brown stain— so her home would have a warm glow, she'd said. Amy herself had always seemed like a ray of sunshine. Well, not always.

Ruth's gaze wandered over the bird feeders that Amy kept filled and the wind chimes hanging from the eaves of the house. She wondered if the comfortable old furniture she had loaned Amy for that first winter was still in her basement apartment. In the old days, she would have known things like that.

Pull yourself together, Ruth chided herself. There was no sense dwelling on how things used to be between them. She'd done everything she could to find out what had gone wrong.

Ruth turned to the woman beside her. Jo Warren had her own memories of the two Amys, the laughing, fun Amy who had lived with her one summer before her house was built, and the Amy in the supermarket last spring who, when their eyes met across the produce counter, had scurried away without speaking.

"You carry the doughnuts and I'll take the cider," Ruth said, bringing Jo back to the present. The cider, still cold in the white plastic jugs, would hit the spot on this warm October afternoon. Judging from the line of cars, there were a lot of people here searching for Amy. They paused at the ribbon barrier. "Should we duck under it?" asked Ruth. "No, here comes someone. I think it's Sheriff Clark."

The sheriff seemed pleased with the refreshments for his crew. They didn't deserve all the credit, Ruth explained. They thought that the community should be involved in the search for Amy and had asked Mr. Sanchez at Dunkin' Donuts and the folks at Merrill Farms to contribute.

"Good idea," the sheriff agreed. "And good timing." He nodded toward the dozen or so people milling about in the driveway behind him. "We're just finishing up."

"No sign of Amy?" Ruth asked, and Bill shook his head. "I'm relieved in a way," she said. "At least she isn't lying hurt somewhere. Two years ago when she was trimming some branches, she fell and cut her forehead on a rock. And another time she fell off the bicycle she was teaching herself to ride."

"Really?" said the sheriff thoughtfully. "Has that kind of thing happened often?"

Ruth hesitated, and turning to Jo asked, "Doesn't it seem to you like Amy had more than her share of accidents?"

"Maybe so," Jo answered, "Sometimes she'd call herself a klutz. But I'd remind her she was doing a lot of things for the first time in her new life. Imagine learning to ride a bike when you're nearly sixty." They all laughed. "Well, we won't keep you any longer."

"Let us know if we can help in any way," Ruth added.

"We will," Clark assured them. "Keep your eyes open for Amy on the way out, won't you?"

They drove away slowly, feeling good at having done something. It was better than sitting around waiting or worrying on the phone with Amy's other friends.

Jo wondered how she could fly off to Hawaii on Saturday not knowing whether Amy was all right. Ruth was grateful for the fall tourists, the leaf peepers, who were keeping her busy at the motel.

The threat of losing Amy brought back memories of when they were like family to each other. It would be easy to forget what they'd both known for some time.

That they'd already lost Amy.

"There's Charlie Wheeler's place on the left," Nate said as the cruiser approached a large, yellow frame house with a radio antenna towering above the tan shingled roof. "Charlie said to watch for several buildings together just down the road here on our right."

Nate slowed the cruiser and turned into a driveway leading to three buildings side by side: a gambrel-roof, two-story garage directly in front of them, a mobile home next to it on the left, and on the other side a one-story ranch-style house.

A woman, stocky with blonde hair, stepped from the door of the house onto the deck and was eyeing them coolly as they approached.

Nate introduced Giroux to the woman he recognized as Glenn Askeborn and asked if Samantha had returned. "No, she hasn't," Glenn told them.

"Samantha's living here with you?" Nate asked.

"Yes," Glenn said, still sounding guarded. Then she volunteered, "Samantha is a relative of mine." She puffed on the cigarette she'd brought outside with her and began pacing the small deck.

"How long have you known Amy Cave?"

"About two years," Glenn said, walking by, intent on her cigarette.

She snapped her head toward Giroux when he interjected, "Does Samantha have any business dealings with Amy?"

"No," Glenn answered sharply. "Samantha and Amy are only casual acquaintances."

"Did you and Samantha go to Ellsworth this morning?" Nate asked.

Glenn stopped pacing and pulled another cigarette from the pack she carried with her. She lit the cigarette and took a sharp, quick draw. "Yes, I went to Gibbs' to put air in my right rear tire."

"Anywhere else?"

"Wellby Drug and Doug's Shop 'N Save," she told him.

"Did you go to Key Bank?"

"No," Glenn answered quickly. "Only to Doug's."

"Did Samantha go into Doug's with you?"

"No, she didn't."

"Couldn't Samantha have gone into the bank while you were in the store next door?" Nate persisted.

"No. I don't like to leave my dog alone in the car. Samantha knows that. Why are you asking me all these questions?"

Giroux stepped in. "Do you know where Samantha is?"

"I don't know. Maybe she went with the fellow who comes to pick her up to work on his boat."

"Who is he?" Giroux asked.

"I have no idea," Glenn snapped.

Giroux pressed for a description of the man's vehicle—the make, the color, any detail.

"I don't know," Glenn said again, sighing. "I don't keep watch on everything Samantha does."

"Does Samantha drive?" asked Nate.

"No, she doesn't. Just why are you asking all these questions?"

"I think that's all the questions we have now," Nate said. "You'll be sure to have Samantha call me when she returns?"

"What do you want with Samantha?" The men turned to leave. "All right, Lieutenant," Glenn said. "I'll have her call you."

"Something isn't right here," Giroux said as they drove away.

"It sure isn't," Nate agreed. "You notice she never looked either of us in the eye?" He thought about the day before and tried to recall what Glenn had said. Nothing about any recent contact with Amy, he was sure. But she'd known who visited Amy the week before and steered them to the Duschek couple. Glenn had been hyper yesterday, too. Was she hiding something, or was she just nervous all the time?

Nate reached for the mike on the dashboard and directed dispatch to send Fred to Route 182. He should park off the road where he could survey the house they'd just come from and should bring his binoculars to keep track of who came to the house or left it.

This case was getting interesting, Nate thought, noticing a familiar stir in the pit of his stomach. The same kind he'd felt years ago in Hartford, Connecticut, working for the drilling company across the street from the bank.

Just a kid from Maine potato country, Nate had paid no attention to the older man working with him when the bank alarm went off. "Get down!" the man had yelled, diving behind their pickup truck. Cruisers screeched in from all sides and cops surrounded the bank, blasting the air with their loudspeakers. Nate had seen this kind of stuff only on TV, and he wasn't about to miss anything.

"When I tell you to get down, you get down!" the old-timer had scolded him afterward.

It had been all over in minutes, a false alarm. But the bank grounds were a shambles. Skid marks on the pavement. Lawns chewed up. Bushes mowed down. Nate had started laughing, and the more the older man scowled at him, the harder he'd laughed.

At the junction next to Card's Tideway Market, Nate stopped the cruiser and noticed sunlight glinting off the bay across Route 1 behind the L.A. Gray building. This was the kind of sight he'd miss if he hadn't come back to Maine. He pulled onto Route 1 and turned left toward the village of Hancock as he continued reminiscing, ignoring Giroux, who seemed preoccupied with his own thoughts.

Nate had been excited by Hartford. And appalled, too. A Coke cost a buck there, and nothing was safe. You couldn't put a pack of cigarettes on the fender of your truck without someone lifting it. In Aroostook County they'd never had to lock their doors or chain their bikes.

Not that he hadn't bounced around a lot before Hartford. He'd

married his high-school sweetheart, been drafted, served in an engi-
neering battalion until the war in Vietnam wound down, then worked
all over with the drilling company. Hartford had convinced him he'd
never live in the city, but it was the salt mines in Louisiana that finally
sent him back to Maine.

The white church spire visible from the long hill down to Merchant's garage was the first sign of the town ahead. In less than a
minute, Nate and Giroux had passed the church, two small grocery
stores, and the soldier's monument on the Hancock village green and
were driving along the straight stretch out of town toward the bridge.

Nate's thoughts drifted back to the salt mines. A steam elevator
had taken the men down to the mines seven hundred feet under the
Gulf of Mexico. He and two other fellows from the drilling company
drove around underground in their pickup all day searching for leaks
to plug in the bleak gray walls of salt. Not until you chipped off a
piece to hold in your hand could you see that the salt was really white.
They carted around dynamite that the miners' union wouldn't allow
miners to carry. That had scared him. His first night aboveground,
overwhelmed by thirst, his coveralls so caked with salt that they stood
up by themselves, he had packed up and left for home.

He remembered how good Aroostook County had looked to him
then. He'd gone to work for the sheriff's department and couldn't
imagine ever leaving The County again. But when McDonald's promoted Maxine to store manager in Skowhegan—a real prize job for a
woman—they moved and he got a job with the Skowhegan Police Department. Then Maxine was promoted to supervisor and they moved
again. He applied for a job at the state prison in Thomaston. During
the tour after his interview, he realized that he couldn't spend his days
behind locked doors in the gloomy prison. Too much like being
cooped up underground in the salt mines.

"Look at that," Giroux said on the curve approaching the bridge.
The bay they'd been circling since they left the Askeborn house,
blocked from view by trees until now, was putting on a Technicolor
display in the late afternoon sun.

"Wow," Nate said. He could cut short his private trip down memory lane, he knew, and avoid the painful thing about to come up. He glanced over at Giroux. Maybe he didn't know. Sometimes at the scene of a bad crash, though, Nate would catch a guy in his own department checking him out to see how he was holding up.

Nate had taken a job with McDonald's, maintaining restaurant equipment, mostly the big freezers, and he and Maxine were on the road a lot. One night coming home from a late meeting, Maxine had fallen asleep at the wheel. Her car flipped over and she was killed, leaving him alone with their eight-year-old son, Travis. A month later, as he was driving through an intersection, a driver on a side road ran a stop sign and plowed into the side of his McDonald's van. The elderly couple in the car died in the hospital.

Nate quit McDonald's, stayed home with his son, and started his own business.

Nate and Giroux had crossed the narrow bridge and were turning left onto the North Sullivan road.

His life was good now. He'd found Marti, a wonderful mother to Travis, and they had another son, Jason. They had good friends and a nice home in Lamoine, and he loved his job with the Hancock County sheriff's office. Thank God he'd answered their ad in the paper.

"So you're calling it a day?" the sheriff said to Warden Marshall as the two stood facing the western horizon, where a setting sun bathed the sky in a blaze of scarlet.

"Yup. It'll be dark soon," Marshall said. "The dogs haven't found anything, and we've made a thorough grid search. You turning up any leads at all?"

"As a matter of fact, we may have." Clark started to tell his longtime friend and Franklin neighbor about Glenner's check when Brady called from the kitchen door that he had a phone call. "Well, I'll talk to you later, Charlie. Thanks for your help."

Stanley Wong, a vice president and financial planner at Prudential Bache in Long Island, was returning a call from the Hancock County Sheriff's Department. Wong assumed it concerned Amelia Cave.

He was right, Clark told him. No one had seen Amy for about a week and they were worried about her. Her sister-in-law Trudy Cave, who called this morning, suggested they talk with him.

As the sheriff filled in the details, Wong became concerned, too. He and Amy had become close friends. As a matter of fact, he'd been trying to get to Maine to visit her again. He'd phoned several times last week and couldn't reach her.

Clark asked Wong if he knew anything about a check for $2,700 that Amelia wrote to a Samantha Glenner.

Wong couldn't explain it. It made no sense to him, because Amy was having a cash flow problem. He had just sold some of her stocks to give her enough cash to buy a piece of land. He couldn't imagine why she'd write a check that large, especially now. Amy was a conservative person, he said, who had worked in the business office of the Hempstead, Long Island, school district and saved her money carefully. But she didn't have a lot of it.

"A twenty-seven-hundred-dollar check?" Wong repeated in disbelief. "To a Samantha Glenner? Have you found this person?"

"We're working on it now," Clark said. "Another thing—we found a strongbox in the cabinet under Amy's bathroom sink. We're wondering whether we should open it."

"The box probably contains negotiable securities. I can't see a problem with opening it, if you think it might help."

Wong offered to come to North Sullivan if that would help. In the meantime, he'd flag Amy's account and let the sheriff know about any checks written on it, although Amy seldom used the account. She used the one in her Ellsworth bank, closer to home.

After Clark hung up, he walked to Amy's picture window to watch the sun, now a fiery globe, as it slipped behind the tops of the evergreens on Burying Island.

"You're missing a nice sunset, Amy," he said aloud, wondering if she often stopped what she was doing to stand at this window to watch. She looked like a person who'd enjoy a good sunset. In the album they had searched for a photograph to use on the news, she was usually laughing and hugging someone, or clowning around, making faces at the camera. They could tell by the captions that many of the pictures had been taken before she moved to Maine. She seemed to have a large family.

I'm not so sure this was a good move for you, Amy, thought Clark just as Dave and Nate walked through the kitchen door.

"We didn't see Samantha," Nate announced. "But we had an interesting chat with Glenn Askeborn." He leaned against the counter and propped his elbows behind him. "She's one nervous woman, Bill."

Bill sat beside Giroux at the dining room table and listened to Nate's report on their talk with Glenn Askeborn. Suddenly he broke in, "Oh, so Samantha and Glenn didn't go to Key Bank. The teller's lying, then—is that it?"

"Somebody is," Nate said. The phone on the counter beside him rang and he picked it up. It was Larson. He had Samantha on the other line, asking for Lieutenant Anderson. Nate hesitated. He wanted all his ducks in a row before he talked to Samantha. "Tell her I'll call her in the morning. Ask what time would be convenient."

Ten o'clock, Larson reported back. Samantha would wait for his call at the 422 number. Nate asked Larson to run a license check on Samantha Glenner, date of birth July 25, 1943, the date that Glenner had given Key Bank. In a minute Larson told him that there was no record of a Maine license for a Samantha Glenner.

Nate hung up and walked behind Giroux to flick a switch on the wall. The crystal chandelier over the table showered them with sparkling light, dispelling the gloom that had settled around them.

"How about talking to Glenner on our turf?" Nate asked. "With a tape recorder."

"With Ralph doing the interview?" Giroux suggested.

"Right," said Nate. "Pinkham's good." He glanced at Bill, who was listening but offering no comment. Nate reached for the phone. "Agreed?" he asked. Bill nodded and Nate called Larson back. "Did Samantha call from home?"

Although Larson wasn't sure, Nate dialed the 422 number and a woman who he knew wasn't Glenn answered. Yes, she said, she was Samantha. And yes, she and her aunt could come to the sheriff's office tomorrow. They'd wait for the lieutenant to call in the morning.

Nate was grinning when he put down the phone. "Samantha," he said, mimicking the high, breathy voice, "sounds like Marilyn Monroe."

"Really?" Bill chuckled. "Sounds interesting."

A rosy afterglow filled the sky as the three men stepped outside onto the deck. Brady was lounging against the deck railing, looking up at the sky. He'd stay until a part-time deputy arrived to relieve him. Bill told him that if Susan and Richard Cave came to Amy's house, they could stay there. Maybe instead of flying, they'd be driving up from New York.

"See you in Ellsworth," Giroux said, sliding behind the wheel of his blue state police cruiser. Bill, a passenger in Nate's two-tone-brown county vehicle, set Amy's strongbox on the seat beside him. He rested a hand lightly on its metal top, drumming his fingers in time with the music on Nate's radio.

Traffic on Route 1 was light, most of it traveling down east in the opposite lane as people headed home from work or shopping in Ellsworth. The two men said little to each other.

"Baby, baby, been waiting all my life for you," the throaty female voice on the radio chanted over and over.

Waiting. A twinge of conscience pricked Bill. Cristy wasn't waiting, he told himself. She already knew it would be another late night. She had called the office to make sure he was still planning to pick up Matt from a friend's house, and then to see if he'd be home for supper. Negative on both counts, he had told the dispatcher. The last time Cristy called, the dispatcher relayed Bill's request for her to tape the six o'clock news. There was bound to be something on it about the Cave investigation.

"Baby, baby, you're making all my dreams come true." Why did Bill feel like defending himself? Cristy understood. Sure, he had his late nights, but now that he was sheriff, things were nowhere near as bad as when it came down to a choice between his job and his marriage. That was in 1973, the year they were married.

Cristy was working as a bookkeeper from eight to five. An hour before she was due home, he'd leave for the Ellsworth Police Department. When she finally forced a showdown, he wasn't sure which way he'd go; he didn't want his marriage to end, but being a cop had been in his blood ever since he could remember.

It had been a big deal as a kid to have state trooper Ron Libby, the only full-time policeman in uniform around, say hello to him in the corner store. Even a big deal as a teenager to have Libby pinch him for speeding. After high school, when he worked at Bill's Place, where all the cops hung out, he knew for sure he wanted to be one of them. Being hired by the Ellsworth Police Department was his dream come true. Although his first night had been more like a nightmare. He chuckled.

"What's funny?" Nate asked.

"I was just thinking about my first night at the Ellsworth PD. They turned me loose with a badge and a gun and no training at all. I stopped a drunk driver and had no idea what to do. Had to call the dispatcher and ask him."

"You're kidding. They sent you out by yourself with no training?"

"That's right. You new guys don't realize how lucky you are."

That was two weeks before he and Cristy were married, he remembered. They were married on March 5, a Saturday night, and the next morning he was back at work. How had she put up with that for thirteen months before giving him an ultimatum?

Sheriff Merritt Fitch had saved him from having to make a choice between his marriage and his job. The county commissioners had finally okayed hiring the sheriff's department first full-time investigator, and Merritt offered him the job. The hours were long, but he could set them himself. He'd come home for supper, spend the evening with Cristy, then go back to work.

Nate turned at the foot of State Street and headed up the steep hill. Halfway up on the left the courthouse loomed, all the windows dark except in the sheriff's department at the rear. Bill promised himself that he'd get home for supper with Cristy and the kids tomorrow night.

Nate parked the cruiser against the brick wall beneath the "Reserved—Lieutenant" sign. Parking was a problem here and every-place in downtown Ellsworth.

Sudden bright light swept into the car, spotlighting both of them. They turned toward the source and were blinded by the headlights of a vehicle that pulled alongside the old jail behind them and stopped. Dave Giroux had been right behind them. He joined them on the steps to the department and waited in the lobby while they checked the dispatch office for messages.

Bill dropped a half dozen pink message slips on his desk and placed Amelia Cave's strongbox beside them. Nate brought a small power drill from the patrol room and in short order had drilled through the lock. He lifted the lid and pulled out a neat bundle of folded parchment documents. A single sheet of lightweight paper fell to the desk. Nate scanned the typewritten lines at the top of the page.

"I'll be damned. Listen to this: 'Sullivan, Maine 04644, January 21, 1983. I promise to repay Amelia Cave within ninety (90) days the sum of $427.83 paid to Harbor Divers.'" Nate looked up. "There's no signature. Just a typewritten name: Samantha Glenner."

"To be repaid in ninety days," Bill repeated. "What was that date?"

Nate checked the heading. "January 21, 1983. Almost two years ago."

The IOU from Glenner set off a stream of speculation. Had Amy ever gotten her money back from Samantha? If so, why would she keep the note in her strongbox; wouldn't she at least have marked it paid? If not, why would she have given Glenner another $2,700 when she was scrounging around for cash herself, was worrying about a 2 percent discount on her property tax, and was behind eleven payments to the security company?

Even Stanley Wong, her financial advisor, said she'd been having a problem with cash flow, Bill reminded them.

Giroux knew that Samantha was going to have some explaining to do. He'd call Ralph Pinkham now, tell him about the IOU, and make sure he'd be down tomorrow when they brought Glenner in. Ralph conducted a good interview, they all knew, so smooth and low-

key that you didn't realize how sharp he was until you thought about
it later.

Brady walked into the office from the inside hall with a handful
of eight-by-ten pictures taken at the Cave house and placed them on
the sheriff's desk.

"I didn't know you were in the darkroom, Pete," Bill said. Brady
smiled his crooked, shy smile and looked up with the others as Fred
Ehrlenbach entered from the lobby. Brady greeted Fred and returned
to the darkroom.

Fred had just finished surveillance at the Askeborn house. The
only movement had been a short trip from the house in late afternoon by a man, presumably Mr. Askeborn. There'd been no sign of
Samantha.

"You didn't see Samantha come home?" asked Nate. "I talked to
her on the phone. You suppose she was there all along when Dave and
I were there?"

Fred wanted to hear about Nate's and Giroux's visit to the Askeborn house. Bill, having already heard the story, sorted through his
pile of messages and, as talk flowed around him, called Larson on the
interoffice line. Larson told him that there had been no word from
Susan or Richard Cave. The last flight into the Trenton airport had already landed, but there was another late flight into Bangor.

"Keep me posted," Bill said and began returning calls: to the
media, to someone from MDI Search and Rescue who wondered if
they'd be needed in Sullivan again tomorrow, to one of the county
commissioners, and to his sister Rosemary.

Forty-five minutes later, he stood up, stretching, and realized how
tired he was.

"I'm going home to watch the six o'clock news," he announced,
"if Cristy remembered to tape it."

"You'd better plan to watch it tomorrow night, too," said Nate.

"Yeah?" Bill knew there was a punch line coming.

"Yeah. Tomorrow we're going to find Amelia Cave." Everyone
laughed.

"Okay, laugh if you want to." Nate stood up and joined Bill at the door. "But you guys should realize by now that I have my own special, built-in radar."

Even Ehrlenbach, a part-time deputy, knew about Nate's intuition. But he knew he was a kidder, too. "So, Nate, tomorrow your radar is going to lead us to Amy Cave?"

"No," Nate replied on his way out the door. "Samantha's going to do that."

Chapter Six

FRIDAY WAS ANOTHER BEAUTIFUL INDIAN SUMMER DAY; it was sunny, and the temperature was already in the mid-fifties by 8 A.M. Giroux had heard that it might reach the high eighties by afternoon. He bounded up the steps to the sheriff's department with the energy he always had when an investigation was starting to take shape. At 8:30, when he entered the sheriff's office, Chief Deputy Dickson, in obvious good spirits too, waved a sheet of yellow paper under Giroux's nose.

Dickson pointed to several handwritten numbers on the paper and explained that they were two different sets of birth dates and social security numbers for Samantha Glenner. Dickson paused to enjoy the look of surprise on Giroux's face. Glenner had given one set to Key Bank and the other to the Hancock Town Office a year ago when she applied for some kind of assistance. Dickson's wife, Karen, the Hancock town clerk, had recognized Samantha's name when he mentioned it last night. This morning she'd looked through her files and found Glenner's application.

"Karen just called me," Dickson said, smiling broadly. "Seems like Samantha has something to hide, wouldn't you say?" Dickson didn't wait for an answer. "According to the application, Samantha owned a '73 blue AMC. Now we can check for an out-of-state license with the addresses she gave—New York City and Patterson, New Jersey."

"Can we get a copy of this?" Giroux asked.

Dickson shot him a Cheshire cat grin. "I already asked Karen."

Ten minutes later, Giroux and Nate walked into Bangor Savings Bank to talk with Mac Roach in person before questioning Glenner.

Roach had just called the main office in Bangor to see if the

58

$2,700 check had been returned there yet. It had. The memory of the teller at Key Bank had been accurate. It was Amelia Cave's check, dated last Thursday, signed on the back by S. Glenner. On the memo line on the front, someone had written "Loan."

"We're checking the validity of the signature now," Roach said. "You know, that check just about cleaned out Amy's account. It brought her balance down from thirty-one hundred dollars to four hundred dollars." Nate and Giroux exchanged looks.

"I think we're on a roll here," Nate said on their way across the bank parking lot to Dave's car.

Just before nine, the two entered Key Bank on the opposite side of High Street and asked Beth Sargent to repeat her account of Glenner's two visits to the bank.

Beth and cashier Merry Zimbalkin had a lot to say about Glenner's appearance, which had obviously impressed them. An Amazon, they called her. Over six feet, with football shoulders and long, wild-looking, frizzy hair. Graying blond, they thought. And very large hands, bigger than Nate's, Beth said. Bright red nail polish, Merry added. Both women were struck by the excessive amount of liquid makeup that Samantha wore and her heavily made-up eyes.

"You don't see many women like that around here," Zimbalkin said. "But you know, even with all that makeup, she looked kind of mannish. Maybe because of her size."

"Samantha doesn't sound exactly mousy looking, does she?" Nate remarked in the cruiser on their way back to the sheriff's office.

Dave grinned. "Not the type you'd overlook in a crowd, I'd say." He stopped for the light by Dunkin' Donuts, at the end of High Street. "And you said she sounds like Marilyn Monroe?"

In the office, Dave phoned Pinkham in Bangor to tell him that the $2,700 check was there in the bank's main office. Pinkham said he'd stop at the bank before leaving for Ellsworth.

At 10:15, when Detective Pinkham entered Bangor Savings, he was directed to senior vice president Alice McInnis. She made copies for him of the front and back of Amy's check and of her signature card, and Pinkham signed for them.

McInnis agreed to retain the original check in her office in case it was needed as evidence in a criminal investigation.

At his desk in the patrol room, Nate phoned Iva Patten in North Sullivan. Just double-checking a few details, he told her. He was particularly interested in her contact with Glenn Askeborn. Whose idea had it been for Glenn to be there when they broke into Amy's house?

Glenn's, Iva replied without hesitation. In fact, Glenn had been quite insistent about coming over and had seemed certain they'd find Amy inside. Iva was sure that Glenn hadn't said anything about seeing Amy recently, and they'd been talking together a lot in the last two days. Glenn had been calling every couple of hours to find out if there was any news, and she had asked Iva to let her know if any of Amy's relatives came to Maine so she could invite them to dinner.

"She asked me if I knew that Amy's drinking problem was back," Iva volunteered. "And I said, 'What drinking problem?' The only time I ever saw Amy take a drink was at Thanksgiving dinner a year or two ago at her house. Glenn and her niece Samantha brought a bottle of wine and the two of them drank most of it themselves."

Nate smiled to himself. "So you don't think it's Amy with the alcohol problem?"

"I certainly don't," Iva said, with a sharp edge to her voice, the first he'd heard. Iva Patten seemed fairly laid back, and he suspected it would take a lot to throw her into a flap. "I spoke to my daughter about it, too," she continued, intent on putting an end to the matter. "Sandra says that Amy has an occasional cocktail before dinner at home or when they go out to eat. That's all."

"Iva, has Glenn mentioned how she knew that the Duscheks visited Amy last week?"

"I don't think so. Just that she introduced them to Amy last spring, I think, and how friendly the three of them had become. She said she hasn't seen much of Amy herself since then."

"You said you've met Samantha?" Nate asked.

"Yes," Iva said, apparently willing to leave it at that.

"And how did she impress you?"

"I met Samantha only that one time," Iva explained, "and she was rather quiet, so I didn't really get to know her. She seemed like a nice person, though."

"I understand that Samantha is rather unusual looking."

"Oh, yes," Iva said, "she isn't someone you'd be likely to forget. She's a large girl, with huge hands and feet. I felt rather sorry for her."

"Why's that?"

"Well, she has such a lot on top, you know, and very narrow hips, way out of proportion. Her makeup job was beautiful, though—I remember being impressed with that."

"Thanks, Iva. I appreciate that you don't like to gossip about people, but my job forces me to get nosy sometimes."

"Oh, I know that, Nate," said Iva. "But you're right. I do try to concentrate on people's good points. We all have them, don't we? We may have to look harder in some people, but we can find them if we want to."

Nate was smiling when he hung up. It must be nice to concentrate on the good in people.

It was time to leave for Hancock to pick up Glenn Askeborn and Samantha Glenner. Nate checked out with Bill and the dispatcher, and on the way to the Askeborn house he stopped to speak with Charlie Wheeler, the Hancock police chief.

Charlie knew the Askeborns slightly. They'd come to see him once when they needed their oil burner repaired, and he'd given Glenn a ride just recently when her car ran out of gas. He'd seen Samantha only once, and when he got home he told his wife he'd just met Dagmar.

"Who?" Nate asked.

"Dagmar was a big, buxom blonde who used to appear on the Arthur Godfrey show. Before your time, Nate. You'll see for yourself in a few minutes."

At 11 A.M., Nate escorted Glenn Askeborn to the chair in front of the sheriff's desk. Pinkham, seated behind the desk, rose and extended his hand.

That's Ralph, thought Nate. Always polite. Cool, but polite. Nate

crossed the room and sat in a chair beside Giroux. He had a good side
view of Mrs. Askeborn.

What was it about this woman that put him on edge? One minute
she'd have a forceful set to her chin and her eyes would be shooting
sparks at him, then she'd turn skittery and helpless, and he'd feel
sorry for her. He couldn't keep up with her.

Pinkham reached out to press a button on the tape recorder. He'd
just turn this thing on, he told Glenn, and they'd carry on a conversation and pretend it wasn't there. He asked her if that was okay.

Nate eased forward in his chair and stretched out his legs as
Pinkham took charge with a steady barrage of warm-up questions.
"How do you spell your name?" "And your address is what?" "Do you
live alone, Glenn?" "Where does your husband work?" He even asked
for her middle initial. A for Anna, she said. One-liners, back and
forth. Question, answer. Question, answer. And in the same pleasant
tone, he asked, "And how did you come to know Amy?"

"Well." Glenn cleared her throat. "Mr. Harry Plummer—he's a sur-
veyor in Sullivan—and his wife have been friends of ours, oh, a long
time, long before 1980, and he did some surveying once for Amy. He
came back and he called me and said there was another lady living in
Sullivan who'd also come from Long Island, and seeing how we were
both living alone at the time, he gave me her name and telephone
number. So I called her. She had relatives visiting, so I told her to call
me back when it was convenient. She did, and we met, and from then
on we've been friends."

Pinkham nodded and asked how often they'd seen each other.
And when did she learn that Amy was missing. And what did Iva
Patten say to her on the phone.

"When did you say Iva called you?" he asked.

"Wednesday morning."

"Last Wednesday morning? That would be the tenth?"

"I don't even know what day it is today. This has got me so upset."

Pinkham, looking sympathetic, repeated, "And what did she say?"

"She told me not to be nervous, but she thought there was something wrong. She hadn't been able to raise Amy, and she'd gone down

and gotten Crawford and they'd knocked and banged on the windows
and doors. She said that Amy's car was parked in a strange way and
she knew that Amy wouldn't have parked it that way. She thought I
ought to come over right away."

Really, Nate said to himself. A little different from Iva's version.

Pinkham asked Glenn about the entry into Amy's house and
about her relationship with Amy. Then he caught Glenn's eye and held
it. "Samantha," he said. "She lives in the trailer near you?"

"Well, on our property." Glenn's eyes darted from his.

"I see. Is she a relative or something?"

"She's my cousin."

Cousin? Nate thought. The bank tellers had said a niece. And
hadn't Glenn herself told them that?

As smooth as anything Pinkham continued. "She's your cousin.
Okay. Did she go over with you the morning that—"

"No."

"You just went over alone?"

"No." Glenn hesitated. "Is it all right if I smoke?" Pinkham nodded and waited while she lit up and took her first puff.

Nate made a mental note: She needs a cigarette to talk about
Samantha.

Glenn blew out smoke in a deliberate, prolonged breath. "No,
there was—the problem is, I didn't know exactly what was wrong. I
was sure, though, that Amy was in the house. I was positive."

"How was Samantha's friendship with Amy? Like yours or—"

"No, no. I mean, I would see a lot more of Amy than Sam ever
did. When Amy would come over, she'd come to my place."

"Has Samantha been here the same amount of time you have?"

"No, she came up in '82, in November."

"And where did she come from?"

"Jersey."

"New Jersey? Whereabouts, do you know?"

"Umm, I . . . Well, see, Samantha and I never visited that often.
She moved around. I don't even know the last couple of addresses
she had."

"But you must have been in touch with her."

"No. We didn't see each other that often. She'd heard from an-other cousin of mine that Wes had gone back to New York to work and that I was living alone and I was kind of nervous on the property. And being at loose ends, she said, 'Well, I'll call Wes and ask him if he wants me to go up and stay with Glenn.' So that's what she did."

"Does she work? Did she come up here to go to work?"

"No, she didn't. She, umm, . . . Up until Wes came back this year, she just lived with me, and then when he came back, she went next door. I really have a small place."

"She does no work at all?"

"No. She's been trying to clam."

Pinkham paused and looked out the window. When he looked back, his casual, offhand manner had vanished. "One day last week, you and Samantha came into Ellsworth to do some grocery shopping."

Glenn was confused about dates. Pinkham let himself be side-tracked for several minutes before he finally asked where they'd gone on whatever day they'd been in Ellsworth. Glenn named the places they'd visited. Key Bank was not one of them.

"Did you take Samantha over to the bank?" Pinkham asked.

"Yeah, she went with me."

"Did you go to the bank?"

"No, I didn't go to the bank."

"You didn't go to the bank?"

"No, Sam did."

"Okay. Which bank?"

"Key."

"Do you know what for?"

"Well, she was going to cash a check."

Pinkham switched back to their first trip to Key Bank and touched off another go-round about the date. Glenn offered to call her hair-dresser—she'd know the day—or he could ask Samantha.

Again Pinkham refused to be drawn into Glenn's confusion over dates. "Can you think of any reason why Samantha would've had a check from Amy?" he asked.

"No, unless they were going in together on clamming or something."

"This was a check for a considerable amount," Pinkham said. "Samantha cashed it last week."

"Last week? No, I don't know anything about that."

"You didn't go in the bank with her?" Pinkham asked, his voice stern for the first time. "You didn't go into Key Bank?"

"No, 'cause I had Buster in the car."

"So, as far as you know, you've never been in that Key Bank?"

"Well, I have an account there."

Nate was floored. She has an account there? How come she hadn't let the teller know that? Pinkham, although still polite, was sounding irritated.

"We have information that a week ago last Thursday, Samantha went into the Key Bank on High Street in Ellsworth and opened an account."

"Yeah, I took her in."

"That's what I'm asking you. So you went in with her?"

"Umm, not into the bank, no. I stayed outside."

Back to square one, Nate said to himself. But Pinkham, undeterred, asked what Glenn knew about the check that Samantha had deposited into her new account. He kept pressing as Glenn rambled on about several small checks from a man whose boat Samantha had been working on. She insisted she didn't know anything about a large check from Amy.

Without warning, Pinkham stopped asking questions. He waited until Glenn looked up at him. "According to the people at the bank, you went into the bank with Samantha," he said accusingly.

"Sam came out of the bank and came up to the car and asked if I would come in and tell them who she was because she didn't have enough identification, and I said sure. So I went in—I don't know the lady's name, but I said yeah, I knew who Samantha was."

"So she just asked you to come in?"

"That's all. I asked, is there anything else? She said no, so I walked right back out the door and got in the car." Nate cheered to himself.

Leave it, Ralph. Leave it! She finally said she went into Key Bank. Don't give her a chance to take it back.

Pinkham asked if Samantha had a checkbook and Glenn said yes, but the bank had called that morning and said that all the checks that Samantha had written had bounced. Glenn had been there when the bank called, but all she knew was what Samantha had told her.

"Does Samantha use more than one date of birth?" Pinkham asked.

Good question, thought Nate.

"More than one date of birth? No, why should she?" Glenn sounded genuinely surprised.

"Just the one as far as you know?"

"Well, sure. I'd like to change mine a little bit, put back the years, but—"

"We'd all like to do that," Pinkham agreed. Well, Nate thought, maybe she isn't in on Samantha's little game-playing with birth dates and social security numbers.

Giroux cleared his throat and leaned forward in his chair. "Glenn, has Samantha ever, to your knowledge, asked Amy for . . . to borrow any money?"

"No." Glenn said quickly.

A few minutes later, at a pause in Pinkham's questions, Giroux interjected, "Does Samantha have any diving gear herself?"

"Oh, yeah." Glenn replied.

"Did she have that when she came to Maine?"

"Yeah, she did."

Giroux slid back in his chair and sneaked a look at Nate.

Was Amy's $400 loan for diving equipment at Harbor Divers just another thing Glenn didn't know about? Nate wondered.

Ralph asked about the cars in the Askeborn yard and whether Samantha had a driver's license. Glenn said that Sam knew how to drive but didn't drive now because she had no license. She and Wes had to take her wherever she went, unless the guy she worked for picked her up.

Pointing to a calendar on the wall, Ralph asked, "Do you remember the last time you would have seen or talked with Amy?"

"Oh, well, I don't . . . I talked to her for sure, because . . . Sure, I did . . . But I didn't see her this month, I think. No, I don't think so."

As Glenn prattled on about how busy they'd been, "working like beasties," Ralph repeated his question several times. Finally, Glenn told him she hadn't seen Amy since summer, when Amy's nephew was visiting in August.

Nate brought up the Duscheks and asked Glenn how she knew they had visited Amy last week. Because Felix told her, Glenn replied. Nate didn't mention that Felix had already told them this wasn't so.

Pinkham asked casually, as though for the first time, "How is Samantha related to you?"

"Ah, let's see. My uncle . . . Well, I say cousin, actually she's . . . I guess you wouldn't call her a blood cousin, but it was my uncle's brother. She's his daughter."

What did she just say? thought Nate. Her uncle's brother—wouldn't he be her uncle, too? Or, it occurred to him, her father? What's going on with these people? And what kind of hold does Samantha have over these two? She's a grown woman and they support her and drive her around every place she goes.

That was all the questions for now, Pinkham said. Maybe there'd be more later. Giroux ushered Glenn to the front lobby, and Pinkham stepped from behind the desk. He needed a breather before starting over with Samantha.

What he really wanted was a cup of coffee.

Richard Dickson was pacing the patrol room, feeling at loose ends after being kept from his desk in the sheriff's office for more than an hour now. He could see his desk through the large window in the patrol room and a similar window across the hall in his own office. He'd had a clear view while they were interviewing Mrs. Askeborn. Now Nate and Dave were showing her out the front door, and Ralph was coming out the other door toward him. Ralph nodded in his direction and continued down the hall toward the kitchen.

The patrol phone rang and Dickson picked it up. Dispatch was trying to locate Pete. Try the darkroom, Dickson suggested.

When Dickson looked into his office again, he saw a large woman standing by the front window looking out. She turned, in profile now, and Dickson's mouth fell open. My God. Those can't be real, he thought. They were the biggest boobs he'd ever seen, jutting out like pontoons. They had to be silicone implants.

The woman turned her head in his direction. He looked down quickly, pretending to read a report on the patrol counter.

In a minute he glanced up surreptitiously. The woman—it must be Samantha Glenner—had turned away. He stared, fascinated, at the boobs, much too large for her small ass. She was wearing tight black pants and a dark knit top with a sweater draped over her shoulders. It didn't have a chance of closing over her front. He hadn't even checked out her face, Dickson realized as Ralph entered the patrol room to use the phone. Pinkham paused, one hand on the phone, and asked Dickson to take a cup of coffee to Samantha. She wanted it black, he said.

Richard welcomed the chance for a closer look at this . . . this— he searched for the right word—creature.

In thirty seconds he entered the front office with a coffee mug filled to the brim and splashing over. It scalded his fingers, but he paid no attention.

"How ya doing?" he asked Samantha, who was still standing by the window.

Samantha answered in a soft, plaintive voice that he could barely hear, "Not too good, I don't think."

Dickson felt momentarily sorry for her. He stepped forward and held out the mug.

"Thank you so much," she said, reaching out one large hand to take the coffee, securing her sweater at the neck with the other.

Dickson, who still hadn't looked at Samantha's face, glanced from the mug to the floor at the large feet in shiny black low-heeled pumps. When he looked up, his eyes met Samantha's. Over six feet himself, he wasn't used to standing with a woman's eyes on a level with his. Uneasy and at a loss for words, he stepped back.

"See you," he said and left Samantha alone to drink her coffee.

Chapter Seven

NATE, TOO, FOUND GLENNER'S PROFILE STARTLING. He'd tell Marti, who as everyone knew was extremely well endowed, that she had nothing compared to the woman he'd met today. He was used to keeping a poker face, but it had been difficult a couple of hours ago when he got his first glimpse of this Amazon. She'd had a bit of a strut then. But now, sitting across from Pinkham, shoulders hunched, she seemed to be trying to hide under the sweater she clutched around her like a shield. There was something strange about her. He couldn't put his finger on it, but something wasn't quite right.

Samantha seemed more cooperative than Glenn, though, more anxious to please. She was certainly less nervous. She answered Ralph's warm-up questions in a soft, near-whisper that Nate found surprising in such a large woman. He noticed she gave Pinkham the date of birth she'd used at Key Bank. She said she couldn't remember her social security number and told Pinkham she worked for herself, that she was trying to get her boat ready to go in the water, and that she helped one of the clammers, a guy named Tony, work on his boat. "Spread some paint around once or twice, that was all," she said.

Nate thought that Samantha was suspiciously vague about her previous addresses. She said she'd moved around a lot and had no relatives left where she used to live in New Jersey. Glenn was her closest relative.

When Ralph finally mentioned Amelia Cave, Samantha sighed. "Oh, yes," she said, "I've been hearing a lot about Amy's disappearance on the TV news."

"When was the last time you saw her?" Pinkham asked.

"Exactly the time? It was Thursday, but I don't remember the exact time."

"What Thursday are we talking about?" Pinkham asked.

"Oh, uh, the fourth. I remember the date because she gave me the check."

Thursday, October 4. Nate leaned forward, alert. Samantha admitted seeing Amy last Thursday.

No wonder Pinkham immediately started talking Miranda rights, thought Nate. Samantha wanted to know if she was being singled out or if her aunt was given the Miranda warning, too. Pinkham pointed out that Glenn hadn't seen Amy since August. He began reading from a small card, a procedure that Samantha said she'd seen on TV. Tilting her head, she listened attentively as Pinkham explained her right to remain silent, that anything she said could and would be used against her in a court of law, that she had the right to the advice of a lawyer, which the state would provide if she could not afford it, and that if she decided to answer questions now, she could stop at any time.

Solemn, looking steadily at Pinkham, Samantha agreed to answer his questions.

"We have done some investigation, Samantha, and we find that you deposited a check from Amy Cave's—"

"Yeah."

"What was the amount of that check?"

"It was twenty-seven hundred dollars. But Beth called this morning and said it had been returned from Bangor unpaid."

"Right," Pinkham said. "But why did you have the check? Did Amy owe you money or—"

"No," Samantha said, and with exaggerated patience, like a parent to a young child, she explained, "Amy had loaned me money before, okay?" Pinkham nodded. "And she saw that I wasn't getting my boat in the water any faster, so we talked about it, and she said she wanted to be part of the business. She told me I was doing it haphazardly, that it should be a regular company, filed, with all the papers and all that stuff. We talked about that and I told her I didn't have the money to do it, that I'd be lucky if I had enough money to get the boat ready."

Samantha said that the conversation had taken place late Thursday afternoon a week ago.

"How can you be sure that was the day?" Pinkham asked.

"Someone hands me a check for twenty-seven hundred dollars, I remember it."

Oh, a little sense of humor, Nate thought. But Pinkham didn't smile.

"Who else was there during the conversation with Amy?" he asked.

"No one," Samantha said. Glenn was in town having her hair done. Amy had driven over in her car—she'd called a week or ten days before to arrange their meeting—and had left in about an hour and a half, a little after dark. She didn't say where she was going, but she did say she'd call her attorney the next day to take care of the paperwork for the loan.

Samantha said that Glenn and Wes had known Amy was coming over to talk about the money Samantha owed her, but when she dropped by their house after Amy had left she didn't tell them about the check. It would have upset them.

Pinkham stood and walked from behind the desk. He had a few questions to ask Glenn, he said.

I bet, thought Nate. For starters, why didn't she say that Amy was at her house just last week?

When Ralph returned from questioning Glenn, he focused on Tony. Samantha said she didn't know Tony's last name or where he lived. Somewhere across the bay, maybe in Franklin, she said. Anyway, Tony hadn't been there Thursday. Just Amy.

"But you told Glenn you went to the bank with checks from the fella whose boat you were painting," Pinkham reminded Samantha.

"I know, I know."

"Why did you lie about that to Glenn?"

"Because I knew she'd be upset with me because I accepted more money from Amy. I knew she'd be climbing the walls. She and Wes and I have argued tooth and nail about the fact that I accepted money from Amy in the first place, about a year and a half ago. I know it was a dumb thing to do."

Who's lying here? Nate wondered. Glenn had said she knew nothing about a previous loan from Amy.

Pinkham brought up the $2,700 check again. He said he had a copy of the check right there on the desk.

Samantha said she could see that and had noticed it when she first sat down. She had cashed a $900 check on her new account, to get her boat ready before the scallop season started. The money that Amy had given her before, $400, was for diving gear, and she hadn't paid any of it back yet.

"But she still agreed to give you twenty-seven hundred dollars more?" Pinkham asked sharply.

"Because I explained to her what my difficulties were. She saw that unless something happened—I either got in the water or started clamming, or something—"

Ralph stood abruptly and, as he walked toward the door, nodded to Nate to take over. "What type of woman is Amy?" Nate asked Samantha.

Looking surprised, she repeated the question. Then, turning in her chair, she looked speculatively at Nate. "I think she's, well, I'll be polite and say eccentric."

"In what way?"

"Well, in phone conversations lately, Amy was crying about big bills coming up. Then she turns around and wants to invest even more money in me." Samantha paused for a reaction. Nate stared at her until she continued. "I really don't know what kind of answers you—"

"Tell us more about her," Nate said.

"Well, she feels persecuted. She seems to feel that a lot of people have done things to her, talked about her house, that kind of thing."

"She have any men in her life?"

"I have no idea. But knowing Amy, I don't think so. None whatsoever."

"What do you mean, 'knowing Amy'?"

"Well," Samantha said, "sometimes at Glenn's when there was other company, the talk would get rather risqué, and Amy would get beet red. I don't think she's been out on a date in God knows how many years. I don't think she'd know how to behave on a date."

"Do you think she'd want to go out on a date?"

"I have no idea. I would assume so. Doesn't everybody? But I don't know whether she'd go or not, I really don't."

Pinkham, who had been standing by the door listening to the last exchange, asked casually, "What was Amy wearing when she came to see you?"

"Um, red slacks, I think. I was thinking to myself how I wouldn't wear them. And a deeper red coat and a blouse."

Pinkham strode to his desk, sat down, and changed the subject abruptly. "The reason the bank didn't honor the twenty-seven-hundred-dollar check is because they feel that it's forged. I can tell you we're certainly going to have that checked by a handwriting expert."

"What can I say?" Samantha asked. She folded her arms across her body, hugging herself.

Nate asked what she had bought with the $900 check she had cashed. Samantha said she had most of the money left and now she'd have to find a way to pay back what she'd spent. At first she said she had a little more than $800 left. A minute later she changed her story. She had all *but* $800 left. She'd bought groceries and supplies for fixing her boat.

Nate, leaning forward, asked Samantha if she had ever been married.

Samantha jerked her head toward him, glaring, then looked away. Sighing, she said yes; she'd been married to a David Glenner. They were divorced two years ago in California. Or maybe it was Connecticut, probably New Haven County. At least that's what she'd read in the papers.

Nate pressed for details. Samantha stalled. Then she folded one large hand over the other in her lap. "Oh, all right, if you really want to know, it was only a common-law marriage."

"Okay. What about your mother and father?" Pinkham asked.

"What about them?"

"Are they alive?"

"Yes, but I don't know their phone number or anything."

"When was the last time you had contact with them?"

"Many years ago. A lot of years ago." Looking at Pinkham, who said nothing, Samantha asked sarcastically, "You want an exact number?" Ralph continued the silent treatment, his black eyes piercing Samantha's. "Christmas of '76. That's when it was, 1976. Christmas."

"You don't stay in contact with them anymore?"

Samantha lowered her eyes, the show of defiance gone. "I'm not exactly favorite-person status."

"Is there any particular reason why?"

Samantha shifted in her seat. "We don't really get along."

Pinkham stood abruptly and left the room to check Samantha's statements with Glenn. When he returned, he stared at Samantha. "Why are you lying to us? I think what you're doing is trying to throw us off base about your background, about where you lived and things like that."

"I told you where I lived."

"Yes, but you were very evasive about your parents' names, for instance."

"I tried to explain that to you. If you can't believe why someone would do that, I'm sorry. If that makes me a bad person—"

"I'm not saying that makes you a bad person, but you even lied about your husband, your common-law husband's name."

"That bastard."

"But why would you? It appears to me like you're trying to throw me off base. You know, you really can't do that."

"I know," Samantha said. "Police can check things so meticulously. You can probably find out."

"Why did you lie?" Pinkham asked. "Everyone has something they don't want other people to know, but Amy's disappearance is a serious matter."

"Well, when it comes to Amy . . ."

"Yes?"

"Well, she was eccentric—paranoid and stuff like that. Ask any of her friends. She thought her telephone was bugged and the FBI had a thing on her."

"But evidently she liked you," Pinkham suggested.

"She liked people in general—went out of her way to be nice. Maybe she loaned other people money, too. I don't know. It was common knowledge that Amy wasn't starving. Talking about her stock investments and that kind of thing."

Round and round they went. Back to last Thursday. To her relatives again. Then, with no change of expression, and almost as an aside, Samantha said Wes and Glenn Askeborn were her parents.

Pinkham's eyes narrowed. That's not what Glenn just told him, he said sharply. Samantha shrugged and asked what she *had* told him. Just tell the truth, Pinkham insisted. Samantha said she was telling the truth and they didn't believe her. It was hard, Pinkham responded, when Glenn's and her stories didn't match. For example, Glenn had told them there were several cars in the driveway when she arrived home last Thursday, and she didn't recognize Amy's as one of them.

Samantha sighed, exasperated. No one else was around when Amy arrived on Thursday, so she didn't know why Glenn had said there was. Sure, she'd lied about working for Tony, and she admitted that. Tony hadn't been there at all last Thursday. Just her. And Glenn when she came home and took her—just her, because Amy was down at the boat—to Tideway Market to get a bottle of wine. When Amy finally left, Samantha had to start her car for her. But Amy did leave, just after dark, and she hadn't seen her again.

"Samantha," Pinkham said, "do you have any objection to taking a lie detector test about this?"

"Yeah. Quite frankly, I do."

"Why?"

Nate watched, fascinated, as Ralph, cool and collected, bore down on Samantha. "I mean, let's face it," he said, "you're knowledgeable enough to realize that Amy has disappeared and—"

"I understand that."

"And that you were the last person with her."

"I unfortunately understand that, too."

"Why won't you take a lie detector test?" Pinkham persisted. "Just to clear the matter up."

"Because," Samantha said, "no one believes me about my parents and how I feel about them."

"Why should I believe you?" Pinkham asked, a touch of sympathy in his tone. "I'm not saying I don't believe your feelings. I can understand why people have feelings like that. But you flat lied to me about the name of your mother and father, about where they live, about your maiden name. You've lied to me all along. Why should I believe you?"

Samantha looked at Pinkham thoughtfully. "If I were in your position, I'd feel the same way." She looked down at her hands. "But I know you're going to ask me questions about my background and stuff like that."

"I don't care about your background," said Pinkham, "if you've told me the truth about never being in trouble before. That's the only thing I'd be concerned about."

"There are other things," Samantha said, working her fingers together nervously. "I'd lose friends if they came out. I'd just rather not talk about them."

"If you have a valid reason for lying to me the way you have, you should tell me," Pinkham said in a new gentle but firm tone. "There's something in your past you don't want out."

"Look," Samantha sighed, "Glenn and I have agreed that we would not talk about this. If we had to, we'd lie about it tooth and nail, right down the line."

"Lie about what?" Ralph asked.

"About certain medical things that I would really—"

"Tell me about it."

Samantha looked at Pinkham, assessing him. "Could these gentlemen please leave?"

"Sure," Ralph said.

"Because I will not discuss this in front of anyone else."

Nate and Dave looked questioningly at Ralph. He nodded and

they stood to leave. As they walked to the door, Samantha nodded at the tape recorder and said in a voice barely above a whisper, "Would you shut that thing off? Please?"

"How ya doing, Sis?" Clark greeted the woman at her desk outside the district attorney's office, where he'd just spent the last twenty minutes.

"Hi, Bill." She grimaced as her phone rang. Rosemary's phone was always ringing. She delayed answering it. "How's it going downstairs?" she asked.

"Still questioning those two people." Bill told her.

"Good luck," his sister said, picking up the phone. She could never finish a conversation, was always being pulled in ten different directions. Bill chuckled. Her stress reduction was hanging on the wall across from her desk: Every inch was plastered with pictures of her idol, Tom Selleck.

Bill signaled good-bye and walked through the outer office—he was surprised to see no detectives, attorneys, or reporters hanging out at the moment—and headed down the hall to the elevator.

As the elevator door slid open one flight down, Bill saw Mrs. Askeborn seated on a folding chair against the lobby wall. She nodded to him, then her eyes darted from his and disappeared behind the cloud of smoke she'd just exhaled. He walked past her into the dispatch office.

Larson had just come on duty for the four o'clock shift. Bill asked if they were still interviewing. Yeah, Larson said, but only Pinkham was in there with Samantha now. Through the window behind Larson, the sheriff saw a Channel 2 truck drive up and stop. Out stepped that go-get-'em reporter whose mouth always seemed full of marbles. Bill glanced through the glass door at Mrs. Askeborn and made a split-second decision. He wasn't going to leave her there to face prying reporters.

He opened the door to the lobby. "Would you like some coffee, Mrs. Askeborn?"

"I'd love some," she said.

"And would you like to wait in a room where it's more private?" She stood and eagerly followed him to the jail administrator's office cubbyhole. At least there was a comfortable chair. After making small talk about the wonderful October weather they were having, Bill excused himself to check with Dickson in the patrol room. He returned with her coffee a few minutes later. "Can I get you anything else?" he asked.

"No, no. Thank you, though." She hesitated, evidently sizing him up. "You're being awfully nice to me. Not like Mr. Pinkham at all."

"Oh, well," Bill said, "Detective Pinkham is just doing his job. It's a tough one, you know."

"I don't care," she said. "He could be a lot nicer about it. I wish he was, because I really need to talk with someone. There's something I need to tell someone—just one gentleman alone."

What should I do now? Bill wondered. He didn't want to interrupt them in the other room.

"I'd like to tell you, Sheriff Clark," Glenn said. But he had no tape recorder, and he couldn't just horn in on the interrogation like that. He walked to the door, buying time. "Please," she insisted, "won't you listen to me?" As he stood in the doorway, waffling, Glenn announced, "Samantha Glenner is my son." Bill stared at her. "Samantha's real name is Glen Robert Askeborn." He still said nothing and hoped he was wearing a sympathetic look.

"See, you don't think it's so awful," she said. "Don't you understand, though? Sam isn't a woman." She heaved a deep sigh. "You don't even seem surprised."

"I'm not, Mrs. Askeborn," Bill said gently.

"You're not? Why not?"

"It's just not a surprise, Glenn—may I call you Glenn?" She nodded. "We've suspected it. Kind of known it, really."

"Oh, my God," she gasped. "How did you find out?" When he didn't answer, she went on, her hands fluttering aimlessly. "I thought my husband and I and Amy were the only ones in the State of Maine who knew. How humiliating." She clasped her head in her hands and lowered her elbows to her knees. Bill thought she was going to cry, but in a moment she sat up straight, her mouth a determined line. "We'll just have to sell our place and move."

"Why would you do that?" Bill asked.

"You don't know, Sheriff. People can be so cruel. This is a small community, and people aren't used to things like this, like they are in the city. That's why the three of us made an agreement that none of us, under penalty of death, would ever reveal this to anyone. And now it's all out. What are we going to do?"

Again he thought she was going to cry. Instead, she heaved another sigh and looked directly at him. "Sheriff Clark, you have no idea how hard this has been."

"Do you want to tell me about it, Glenn?"

She stared at him for several seconds, looked around the small office as though searching for a way out, then looked back at him, sighing again.

She launched into her story. Samantha was forty-one years old, she said. Until three years ago she'd been their son Skip, living in Connecticut with his wife, Martha. Or so she and Wes thought. Sometime in November, Wes, who'd returned to New York to work awhile longer, contacted Skip and arranged a visit. He found Skip living apart from his wife and—Glenn looked sharply at the sheriff, as if challenging him—found Skip dressed in women's clothes.

Glenn paused, searching Bill's face for a reaction. He looked back calmly. Reassured, she continued. Skip told Wes he'd undergone a sex change operation and was on hormones. He was their child, so of course they tried hard to understand and accept him . . . her. Wes brought Samantha home and the three of them decided on the story they would stick to with everyone but Mrs. Askeborn's sister in Connecticut, who knew the truth.

Skip, they would say, had moved to Saudi Arabia to work in the oil fields, and Samantha Glenner, a distant cousin, had come to stay with her until Wes returned home.

Glenn told the sheriff some of the things they did to hide Samantha's identity—making up stories, writing pretend letters from Skip in Saudi Arabia, and keeping Samantha away from people.

"Except Amy?" Bill said.

Glenn looked suddenly wary. "Oh. Ah, Amy."

"You told Amy the truth?"

Glenn moved her head in a slight nod. "We saw each other so often, you know, and became such good friends." She reached for a cigarette. After the first puff she shot him an appraising glance and said casually, "Sam and Amy became quite friendly." She drew in another breath of smoke. "Why Amy even loaned Sam nearly five hundred dollars that first winter. I think it was February of '81."

Bill, as casual as Glenn, switched subjects and asked about last Thursday, not sure she would admit to Amy's visit.

Glenn said that she had gone to the hairdresser in Ellsworth that day, and when she came home she saw Amy's car in the driveway with Sam outside waiting for her. Sam wanted Glenn to drive her to Tideway Market to buy some wine for Amy, who was down on Sam's boat on the shore. When they returned from the store, Glenn went into the house to prepare supper.

"Glenn," Bill said, "does Sam have a criminal record?"

Glenn's hands flew to her face as though he had struck her. She stared at him, then lowered her hands. "I suppose you're going to find out anyway." She sighed. "Sam has been in prison for armed robbery."

The second he'd asked the question, he'd seen the answer in her eyes. "You know, Glenn, you're probably going to find that Sam has something to do with Amelia's disappearance."

"No, no!" Glenn cried. "I don't believe that. It's not true. Sam couldn't have anything to do with that." She herself had seen Amy leave the yard, had heard the car start up that evening, and had stood in her window and watched her drive off.

"How could you be sure it was Amy?" Bill asked.

"Because of her plum-colored coat. I recognized Amy's coat."

"Glenn," the sheriff said sternly, "wasn't it dark out? How could you see what anyone was wearing or who was in the car?"

She stuck to the story for several minutes, then under Bill's insistent prodding she gave up. "You're right, Sheriff Clark. I couldn't tell who was driving. But it wasn't Sam. I know that. Sam came into the house as the car was leaving. She stayed with us awhile and then went over to her place. You have to believe me, Sheriff."

"Glenn, do you remember the rights we read you before you started talking to us—that anything you say may be used against you in a court of law?" She nodded. "You have to realize, Glenn, that you don't know what we know. I'd rather you not say anything than lie to us."

Glenn was considering what he'd just said when Nate appeared at the door.

Bill excused himself and walked beyond earshot of Bishop's office, then told Nate about Glenn's confession.

"We know," Nate said. "Samantha just told Ralph the same thing. Ralph wants to get together with us to plan our next move."

"A search of the Askeborn property?" Bill suggested.

"Probably. It certainly seems like the best place to look for Amy, doesn't it?"

Dickson was no longer at loose ends, no longer on the outside looking in. The patrol room had come alive around him. Pinkham was on the phone to the office of the attorney general; the Amelia Cave case had clearly become a matter for them. The sheriff and Giroux were running back and forth to dispatch, lining up troopers and deputies and wardens for an immediate search of the Askeborn property. Mrs. Askeborn and Samantha had given their permission, and the investigators would ask Mr. Askeborn for his when they got to Hancock.

Dickson looked across the hall at Samantha, alone now, hunched over in the chair that for the last three hours had been a hot seat. How different she looked to him now. Or he looked. Damn, this was confusing. And to think he'd felt sorry for Samantha and felt like comforting her. And that he'd been fascinated by her boobs, even though he thought they were implants. He was a little embarrassed about that now. Not that he'd been turned on or anything; but damn it, he felt foolish.

"Richard," Bill was saying, "I was sure glad you told me about Karen's call when you did."

"You told Mrs. Askeborn?"

"No, she came clean on her own. But I think I handled it better, already knowing, although I still didn't really believe it, you know what I mean? Karen's sharp, I know that, but until Glenn told me herself, there was that little doubt there. I'm not used to stuff like this."

Well, I am, Dickson thought. He'd seen a lot of crazy things in his years with the finance company in New Jersey and traveling around the country. Still, he didn't expect to see people like Samantha in Maine. How had Karen known, just like that, and he hadn't? Samantha Glenner had been just a name to her when she found the application in her files this morning. But when she hunted around some more and uncovered Samantha's other application for a job as secretary to the planning board, she remembered actually seeing her. She had called him back this afternoon to tell him that Samantha was a man. Just like that. So matter-of-fact. She'd known when she first saw him: Samantha Glenner was a man dressed in women's clothes.

"Hearing it from you helped me play it cool when Glenn came out with it," Bill said.

Well, now that they knew, it changed a lot of things. Now they had a name and could look into Glen Robert Askeborn's past. Glenner had told Pinkham about the armed robbery and about serving time in a federal penitentiary. They would send off an inquiry to the FBI and would look into Askeborn's service record, too. Askeborn had also been in the navy, and in 1968, while married and living with his wife in San Diego, had been given an undesirable discharge because of some trouble over his wife's young son. Samantha even admitted to having filled in the face of Amy's check herself. Because Amy was so drunk, she said. But of course she hadn't forged the signature.

Yeah sure, Dickson thought. Amy was sober enough to sign her name and drive a car but was too drunk to fill out a check. It didn't add up.

Dickson looked again at the lone figure across the hall. Samantha had told Pinkham that she had a partial sex change a couple years ago and that her face used to be beautiful when she could afford hormones and had doctors she could get them from. Now her face was getting rough again. Poor thing, Dickson said under his breath, then chastised himself for being sarcastic. It wasn't a crime to change your sex. It wasn't a crime, either, to change your name. You could use any name you wanted as long as you weren't doing it to defraud anyone. Was that why Samantha had changed sexes? Was she wanted by police somewhere? They'd find out.

The main thing now was to find Amelia Cave. If Samantha had anything to do with Amy's disappearance, Dickson thought, it wouldn't matter what sex he . . . she was.

Nate's two passengers, Mrs. Askeborn on the seat next to him and Samantha in the rear, were quiet now. No wonder, after the hours of interviewing and waiting around. Maybe, like him, they were hungry. He'd like to be going home for supper with Marti right now, changing his clothes, settling in for the evening. Glenn lit up another cigarette; in a minute when it didn't seem obvious, Nate would crack open his window. The Askeborns weren't going to kick off their shoes and get comfortable tonight, either.

After Nate pulled into their driveway and parked in the yard, Samantha jumped out and disappeared into her trailer, and Glenn hurried to the house, where a man waited at the door.

Nate radioed dispatch from his cruiser. "Call Charlie Wheeler," he told Larson, "and ask him to come to the house that he and I were talking about today." Nate still didn't know how many people they'd been able to line up on such short notice. They'd need a lot of manpower to comb all these woods. When Giroux drove in with Pinkham and parked behind him, Nate joined them for a quick conference before they all entered the house to meet Wesley Askeborn.

Wes, as he told them to call him, gave his permission right away for a search of the property. When the four of them settled in the living room, Pinkham turned to Mr. Askeborn on the couch beside him. "How long have you lived here, Wes?"

Nate, across the room by the window, was sizing up the man who was Samantha's father. Nice-looking gent, he thought. In his sixties, probably. Strong, healthy, distinguished looking, too, with that high forehead, and blue eyes that looked right at you. He was soft-spoken and direct when answering Pinkham's questions. Almost deadpan. No hint of the turmoil he must have gone through meeting his son in Connecticut dressed like a woman—finding that his son had turned into a daughter.

The door opened and Samantha walked in carrying two bottles of beer. Nate noticed that she had changed her black pumps for a pair of combat boots. She disappeared into the kitchen, where, judging from the sounds and smells, Glenn Askeborn was preparing the evening meal.

Pinkham was talking about Amy now. "Wes, we'd like to ask you about the last day anyone seems to have seen Amelia. Let's see," and he turned to Giroux, "that would have been last Thursday, Dave?"

Giroux nodded. "That's right, Ralph. Thursday, October 4."

"You and your wife must have talked about this, Wes, in view of the fact that no one has seen her since. Can you tell us what you remember about that day?"

"Of course," Wesley Askeborn said, and with no hemming around he told them that he'd arrived home from work at four-thirty and seen Amy's car by Samantha's trailer. He asked his wife if she'd seen Amy and she said no, but she'd seen Samantha, and Samantha had said that Amy was down on the boat. Around eight or eight-thirty, he'd gone to the front of the house to get a cup of coffee and noticed that Amy's car was gone. He went back to the bedroom to watch TV. He hadn't seen Amy or Samantha at all that day.

Pinkham's eyes flicked casually to Giroux. That's not what Glenn had told them. "You didn't see Samantha at all? She didn't come over to your house?"

"No. Well at least if she did, I didn't see her."

"Ah, Wes, do you know anything about a check that Samantha used to open an account at Key Bank? A check from Amy in the amount of twenty-seven hundred dollars?"

"No, I don't. I only know about . . . Sam told me about two checks from a guy by the name of Tony who she worked for, painting his boat."

At a sound beside him, Wesley turned as his wife switched on a table lamp by the couch. Ralph thanked her with a nod. Nate saw the glare that Glenn was sending her husband, but Wesley never met her look. "That's what she said," he continued. "She started an account with those checks."

"We appreciate your being so straightforward with us, Wes. Now, do you remember when you first learned that Amy was missing?"

Nate sneaked a glance at his watch. It was 5:55 and the light outside was fading fast. He could see the men standing around, shifting from one foot to the other.

He stood up and walked across the room, and as Wesley was telling them about Iva Patten's call to his wife, he stepped outside and closed the door.

In the yard, the sheriff was talking with trooper Lloyd Williams about Moose, the dog sitting patiently at his feet. Moose wasn't trained as a cadaver dog, Williams said, although he had a pretty good track record finding dead bodies. He was trained to search out live people. Moose had led him back and forth across the field next door, and they hadn't found anything. Maybe Debbie had, Lloyd said, nodding toward the road where Warden Palman was approaching at a fast clip, pulled along by the dog on a leash in front of her. She and Lobo had been tracking down a bad smell on a neighbor's shore, Debbie told them. It turned out to be just the stench of low tide. Lloyd had scouted along the shore, too, he said, and Moose had shown quite a bit of interest around the stern of an old boat there. Maybe they ought to check it out.

"Old boat?" Nate said. "Where is it?" Ralph and Dave were still inside the house, and Nate was getting impatient. "We've got Wes's okay to search, Bill. Let's go take a look at that boat before it gets any darker."

The sheriff summoned his men on the radio and deployed some of them across the field in back of the house to comb the woods beyond. He told Bishop and Lenny Ober to stand guard at the house. The rest of them set out single file on a well-trodden path through the field to the woods.

At the tree line they plunged into darkness. Following the narrow beams of their flashlights on the trail ahead, they tramped in silence for about a quarter of a mile until the woods ended abruptly.

Ahead, in the fading light they could see an expanse of rose-hued bay, and looming at the edge of the water was a white boat tilted on a homemade cradle of slender tree trunks lashed together. Other poles rose from the water at helter-skelter angles around the boat. The men stepped gingerly down a dirt bank to the rocky shore and picked their way to the boat. The stern was butted against a low rock wall that ran parallel to the bank.

"Look at that," Dickson said, pointing to the ground in front of the wall. "Someone's been digging here. See if there's a shovel any-where." Nate found one on the stern of the boat and handed it to him. As Dickson stepped forward, he sank into soft, wet soil and jumped back. There was no need to ruin his new suede boots. Straddling two large rocks next to the worked-over area, Dickson thrust the spade into the earth. Adrenaline flowing, he lifted out one shovelful, then another and another until several inches down the spade met some-thing soft and spongy.

"What the hell is this?" He prodded gently with the tip of the spade. "Seaweed. Someone has put a layer of seaweed here. Why the hell would anyone do that?"

Nate dropped to his knees beside the hole and pawed into the slimy mass. "Shine the light here," he said sharply. "Shine it right here." The beam of a flashlight caught a patch of red. Amy's coat was red.

"Oh, Christ," Dickson groaned. "It's her."

Nate cleared away another piece of seaweed and pressed his fin-gers into the red patch. It gave way to his touch.

He stood up and looked down at the hole. "What a hell of a place for a grave," he said and reached for the portable on his belt to call Ralph.

Chapter Eight

PINKHAM THANKED WES FOR HIS COOPERATION. As he stood to conclude the interview, Samantha approached from the kitchen. She followed Pinkham to the door and reached out to touch his arm.

"Will you please tell your people to be very careful not to disturb the rock wall I'm building behind my boat?" Pinkham looked down pointedly at the hand on his arm and Samantha drew it away. "I've worked real hard on that wall."

"Sure," Pinkham said and walked outside.

Deputy Ober told him that the search dogs hadn't found anything so far and the crew had already left for the shore. The door to the house opened behind them, and Ober stopped talking as Samantha came down the steps toward them.

"I just want to make sure, Mr. Pinkham, that your men are careful with that wall." She smiled at him. "I wouldn't want all my hard work destroyed, you know."

Pinkham's eyes narrowed and fixed Samantha with a penetrating stare. Under his scrutiny, her smile quivered and faded. She shrugged her broad shoulders and walked off.

Samantha had just disappeared around the corner of the house when Nate's voice came over Ober's portable as sharp and clear as though he were standing next to them: "Tell Ralph we think we've found a body that seems to be recently buried."

Pinkham frowned. "Tell him to hang on a minute," he said. "I want to think about this." He walked away, then turned sharply and walked back. He gave Ober curt instructions and in a deliberate stride headed down the path to the woods.

Ober, following Pinkham's orders, radioed a warning to Nate. "Ralph says to keep the traffic down. He doesn't want the people here to know."

No one in the Askeborn household had heard Nate's message, but others had. His words had reached the ears of people tuned in on their scanners to the band used by the sheriff's department. And Larson, in the dispatch office in Ellsworth, had picked up Nate's message and entered it into the department log at 1900 hours, or 7 P.M.

Daylight had vanished, even beyond the canopy of trees. A full moon hung low over the distant shore and bathed the bay in silver. As the men huddled in groups waiting for Pinkham, something glistening on the flats about twenty feet out caught Dickson's eye. "What's that thing out there?" he said to Fred Ehrlenbach, who had just arrived at the shore after fighting his way through the woods.

"There's one way to find out," Fred suggested.

"Yeah, but we don't know how deep that muck is out there."

"I'll give it a try," Fred said, bending over to remove his shoes and socks and roll up the pants of his uniform.

The cold mud pulled at his feet and made sucking sounds with each step. He played his flashlight over the object shining in the moonlight. In his mind it kept changing shape: It was an arm. No, a pocketbook. What was it? Ah. He grappled with the object, then raised it over his head like a trophy and called to Dickson across the flats.

"What?" Dickson yelled back.

"It's a piece of kelp. It's only a piece of damn kelp!" Disgusted, Fred grabbed the rubbery seaweed by its long root tail and flung it across the mudflats. Saltwater slime dripped down the front of his shirt. And on the trek back to shore, mud oozed over the bottom of his rolled-up trousers. He had almost reached the solid outcrop of ledge when Pinkham emerged from the woods.

"Over here, Ralph," Nate called. The detective, garbed in his trademark three-piece suit, stopped to pull on the heavy cotton coverall he'd carried with him. Then he made his way cautiously among the rocks to the figures silhouetted on the beach.

Water had seeped into the hole over the patch of red. Someone had found a battered yellow margarine container and reached into the beam of the sheriff's flashlight to scoop away the muddy water. Pinkham pulled on thin surgical gloves and, kneeling beside the hole, held out a hand. "Somebody got a knife?" Nate laid a jackknife in his palm, and Pinkham ran a thumb over the blade. "It's dull," he complained.

"Shame," Dickson's voice from the dark chided Nate. "What's a scoutmaster like you doing with a dull knife?"

Pinkham slit the red fabric carefully, lifted a corner, and pressed two fingers into the spongy matter below. Gently, he brushed away the dirt. Fine blond hairs glistened in the beam of the flashlight. Pinkham sat back on his heels. There was no need to risk disturbing the evidence by digging in the dark tonight, he said. Tomorrow in the daylight, with the medical examiner here, they would exhume the body.

The other men, who had been watching in silence, began talking with one another again. The sheriff and Pinkham moved to one side and conferred in low voices. They certainly couldn't leave the body unattended. Bill suggested posting three men on guard, two at the shore and one at the house. They agreed that Bill would provide the men for the first shift, and Pinkham would round up troopers to take over at 1 A.M. They'd try to keep this whole thing quiet, although they'd have to tell the Askeborns something. They could decide what to say on their way back through the woods. Now, they needed someone to stay behind on the shore.

The sheriff and Pinkham walked back to the men, and Bill flashed his light around. Ernie Fitch warned whoever might be about to finger him, "I ain't spending the night down here in this godforsaken place." The others laughed, but the prospect of standing guard at the grave site with the suspect at large was not appealing to any of them.

The sheriff shone the light on Ehrlenbach and kept it there. Fred was scheduled to work patrol with Jim Lepper, so they'd have to find someone else to patrol, Bill said. He promised they'd send somebody down to stand guard with Fred as soon as possible.

Fred watched the last man disappear from sight. Alone on the shore, he turned to the bay. This might not be a bad spot under different circumstances. Moonlight cast a sheen on the flats, and a light wind rose. Maybe the tide had turned. Fred shuddered in his summer uniform and sought shelter at the base of a large pine. As he sat down, his back against the rough bark, the portable on his belt crackled. It was Nate. No one, no one at all, Nate repeated, would come to the shore without calling Fred on the radio first. "Good," Fred answered. "I'm counting on that."

He looked out at the boat, about a twenty-five-footer at most, he guessed. It was those damn poles sticking out of the water at crazy angles that made everything so eerie, he decided. Looked like pictures he'd seen of Vietnam and the Mekong Delta. Maneuvering like a crab, he shifted his body around the huge trunk and turned his back on the scene. As he brushed his hand against the service revolver in his holster, his radio crackled again. Pete Brady was on his way down, Nate said.

Fred had been alone only a quarter of an hour, but he'd sure be glad to have company. The woods around him were alive with scurrying in the underbrush and rustling in the branches overhead. He thought of the moose track he'd seen across the trail on his way down. He stiffened suddenly at a sharp snap close by. "That you, Pete?"

"Yup," Brady answered. They agreed to take up separate posts apart from each other and talk on their radios as little as possible. Maybe the she-beast would be arrested and they wouldn't have to worry about her during the night.

Shortly after nine o'clock, however, another call from Nate dashed that hope.

"Things will stay as they are," Nate's guarded words informed them. "We don't want to make a move too soon and blow this thing."

So much for the idea that they'd arrest Samantha tonight. But Fred and Pete had their guns, their radios, and each other. And hot coffee and sandwiches would be coming soon. Charlie Wheeler and Jim Lepper would call before starting down, Nate had said.

In another half hour when Charlie and Jim arrived, they found Fred shivering with cold in spite of the pine needles he had piled around his lower body. More appealing to Fred than the ham and cheese sandwich they handed him was the Styrofoam cup of steaming hot coffee, which warmed his shaking hands.

Charlie and Jim lingered to chew over the events of the evening. When they left, Fred and Pete resumed their separate vigils, each now armed with a thermos of coffee.

Facing another three hours alone with little hope of further distraction, Fred could no longer shut out the thought that had been gnawing at him, demanding his attention. It was Amy out there in the cold mud and gravel. He tried to banish the unwanted image and remember her alive, smile bright, blue eyes sparkling. A happy Amy, trusting everyone. She must have felt sorry for Samantha and wanted to help her—that would be like Amy. But who had helped *her*? Could I have done something? he wondered. Maybe had her over once in a while for dinner with Elizabeth and the kids? Amy liked his kids. He thought of the lamps in their bedrooms that she had given them. But he and Elizabeth were always so busy; and besides, Amy was older than most of their crowd.

Fred jerked to attention at loud squawking and flapping close behind him. Then he recognized the unmistakable hooting of an owl and, relaxing, reached for his radio. "That scare you as much as it did me, Pete?" he whispered into the mouthpiece.

"Yeah," said Brady, chuckling softly.

The night creature had swept away the image of a smiling Amy and thoughts of what might have been. Now there was only her lifeless body out there, cold—much colder than he was, with the incoming tide seeping into her grave.

Sheriff Bill Clark and his chief deputy sat in their cruiser looking in dismay at the dark house. "Geez, Bill, it looks like they've gone to bed," Dickson said. "Maybe this wasn't such a hot idea."

"No, Richard, you were right. We don't want them hearing the news from someone else. It's only eight-thirty. Come on, let's go."

"Okay. You sure you want me to do the talking?"

"I'm sure," Clark said. Dickson had already met Susan and Richard

Cave earlier in the day. The couple had driven up yesterday from Long Island. They'd called around midnight when they arrived at the Colonial Motel in Ellsworth and again this morning. Besides, Richard looked better than he did in his grubby old clothes. To sophisticated city folks from New York, he'd seem like some hick from the backwoods.

At Dickson's first rap on Amy's kitchen door, the porch light flicked on. Richard Cave opened the door, eyeing them warily. When he recognized Dickson, his face brightened. "Come on in," he said. Only five minutes earlier a reporter had come to the door, apologizing for the disturbance and asking for the sheriff. Richard thought that the reporter's visit and now this one must mean they'd found Amy. He'd be relieved even if they said she was in a hospital somewhere. Just as long as they'd found her.

Susan appeared behind her husband. "Any news?" she asked.

"Yes, that's why we're here," Dickson said and introduced the sheriff. In Amy's kitchen, faced with the young couple looking at him with such hope, Dickson shifted from one foot to the other.

"I'm very sorry to tell you this," he said, "but we've just found a body buried in a shallow grave on the shore of the Askeborn property. We're almost sure it's Amy."

Susan let out a cry that sent chills through Clark. He stood frozen as she fell sobbing against her husband. Richard held her stiffly, the smile that had been on his face seconds ago still there.

Dickson moved back next to Bill and the two of them waited, eyes trained on the floor, until Susan grew quiet. When she raised a teary face, she was calm. "I knew it," she said. "Ever since we arrived in Maine, I've been expecting something like this."

Richard, his arm still around Susan, pleaded with Dickson. "Maybe it isn't her." Met with Dickson's relentless silence, he dropped his arm and sank into a chair at the kitchen table.

Susan sat down beside him. She was grateful, she told Dickson, that he had warned them that afternoon about Samantha and the large check that she knew Amy hadn't written. "Samantha killed Amy, didn't she?" she asked.

Dickson leaned back against the sink and deferred to the sheriff, who had remained by the door.

No longer feeling out of place, Bill stepped forward to field the questions that flowed one after the other. What would happen next? When would Samantha be arrested? Would they be able to tell how long Amy had been dead?

At a lull in the questions, Bill asked one of his own. Would Richard and Susan come to the sheriff's department tomorrow to identify the body?

Richard looked at Susan and tried to speak, but he gave up and just nodded. Pushing away from the table, he stood to walk the two officers to the door. Suddenly he grabbed Dickson by the shoulders. "You can't let them get away with this," he burst out.

Dickson waited until Richard dropped his hands.

Bill was watching from the doorway. "You really ought to try the tomatoes out here on the railing," he said, hoping to break the tension, if only for a moment. "It'd be a shame to let them go to waste."

But the thought of the tomatoes that were meant for Amy was too much for Richard. As he closed the door, tears streamed down his face. Susan held him while he wept.

Aunt Amy had lived in his home since he was eight years old. She'd played with him, gone fishing, clamming, and boating, and shared every birthday and holiday with him. He and Susan had spent summer vacations with her for the last four years. And now this.

Richard began pacing the kitchen. "She could have made it, Susan. She was getting better. Don't you think she was?"

"Of course," Susan said, indicating that he should come into the living room. Richard followed her but remained standing as she nestled into one end of Amy's soft couch. "You remember, when we were here in August, I kept asking her what was wrong? She said it was nothing, that she was just too sensitive. She was determined to pull herself together and become her old self again."

Richard paused at Amy's favorite chair and placed his hand on the headrest. "She took on too much too soon—retiring and moving away from all her friends and family."

Susan nodded. "I know she was lonely, but I never once heard her say she regretted the move."

Richard looked at Susan thoughtfully. "Amy was doing what she wanted, wasn't she? If only she hadn't been so trusting of everyone." He pulled his hand away from Amy's chair. "Damn it, Susan."

"I know. When we met the Askeborns this summer, I told Amy I didn't think they were her kind of people." She sighed. "If I'd just listened to what she was trying to tell me."

"You couldn't have—"

"How do we know?" she interrupted him. "She was trying to tell me something about a woman who was really a man, and I didn't pick up on it. Maybe if I had and we'd talked—"

"Susan." Richard's tone made her look up at him. "This isn't your fault." He sat on the couch beside her. "It isn't our fault."

Susan reached for his hand. "It's just that I'll miss her so much. She was so good to us and the kids." Susan gasped. "Oh, Richard—the kids!"

Their oldest was only ten. What would they tell their three children? That someone had murdered their wonderful Aunt Amy?

The cruiser headlights caught the crisscross maze of superstructure on the bridge connecting Sullivan and Hancock. It was the Singing Bridge to those who loved the whine of cars traveling over its metal grille bed, a nightmare to others who panicked when faced suddenly with the narrow lanes and high metal rails that let them see the rushing tide below, when they dared to look. The Department of Transportation had been promising for some time to replace the relic from the 1920s with something modern, something wider and safer.

Clark, in the passenger seat, looked out his window through the railing to a moonlit Taunton Bay and thought of his deputies standing watch on the far shore. Was it only two days ago that they'd started looking for Amy Cave?

"I was kind of shocked when you told them straight out like you did, Richard. I probably would've beaten around the bush for a while. But you didn't mince any words."

"Well, I'd already told them to hope for the best but expect the worst. What do you think, Billy? Was I too rough?"

"No, no. It just surprised me. You were . . . direct, that's all. We all have different ways of handling these things. You remember the story—"

"I know what you're going to say. It's a classic. You mean that dispatcher who—"

"Yeah, the new guy. Someone called in a fatal and asked him to take care of notification, meaning the funeral home or something."

"And he misunderstood and called the guy's wife and just blurted out, 'Your husband's dead.' Over the phone! Christ, Bill. Can you believe it?"

"See? Compared to that guy, you were Mr. Compassion. Here's the turnoff to 182. Should we drop in on the guys down at the shore?" Richard drove past the turnoff. "Naw," Bill said. It had been only an impulse, an impractical one. "Ralph's waiting for me at the office, and Karen's expecting you home."

"Right. She'll want to hear what's going on. Bill, how the hell do you think Karen knew Samantha was a man? How come we didn't see it? You think we might have been blinded by those big tits?"

"Come on, Richard. Karen's a woman. She's got a sixth sense, that's all."

"But we're the cops. Aren't we supposed to be the observant ones?" The two fell silent and listened to radio traffic the rest of the way to Ellsworth.

At the sheriff's department, Dickson said he'd come inside for a minute to see what was going on.

Larson was standing deadpan behind the high dispatch counter. "I can't decide whether to send someone out on the call that just came in," he said. Dickson raised an eyebrow and exchanged glances with the sheriff. They both knew Larson was a tease. "Yeah," Larson continued, "a guy called and said he'd just seen Amy Cave up in Bangor. At Pilot's Grill."

Grinning, the sheriff scooped up the messages in his box and reached into his shirt pocket. "Run this for me, will you?" He handed

Larson the Connecticut plate number he'd copied down earlier in the Askeborn yard, then he left the office.

Dickson waited for the response from the Department of Motor Vehicles. "There've been quite a lot of Amelia Cave sightings, haven't there?" he asked Larson.

"Yeah. The best one was about a woman at Hancock Grocery. The caller said she looked just like Amy's picture in the paper. She was sitting outside the store on a stone, talking to a jar of mustard."

Dickson laughed. "Bet you rushed a couple guys out on that one." He reached for the teletype printout from motor vehicles and was scanning it when the phone rang.

Channel 2 News was checking to see if there was any new information on the missing woman. Dickson paused in the doorway to listen. Larson sent him a conspiratorial look and said casually that there was nothing new on Amelia Cave.

Dickson shook his head and left the office.

Over the next few hours until the end of his shift at midnight, or until someone with more authority than he had released an official statement, Larson would have to bend the truth repeatedly to other reporters and anonymous callers from a concerned public. Although Amy's disappearance had set off a wave of sympathy in Hancock County and even beyond, this, after all, was a homicide investigation.

There were calls for the sheriff, too, several from the attorney general's office and one from Susan Cave. She wanted relatives' phone numbers that were in the address book the sheriff had taken from Amy's house.

Just before midnight, Larson took a call from a Sullivan man who often phoned when he'd had too much to drink. Usually Larson just listened; that's all the man seemed to want. Tonight Larson cut him short, saying he was going home to bed and maybe the man could use a good night's sleep, too. He suspected that this wouldn't be the last call from the drunk, but the next one wouldn't be on his shift. Dave Brady, his relief, had just arrived.

Dispatcher Brady, Pete Brady's son, was scanning the day log when a domestic assault complaint came in from Blue Hill. Two deputies were always sent out on a domestic. Alcohol was usually involved. Brady was still dealing with the domestic when he received a call about an abandoned car in Gouldsboro.

Then Richard Cave called. They couldn't find the cord to Amy's coffeemaker and wanted the sheriff to know in case it turned up the next day at Samantha's.

At 1 A.M., Fortier at County Ambulance called in a 10-55, a vehicle accident, on Route 180 beyond the Otis General Store. There were two serious personal injuries and a possible Code K.

Brady had to call the lieutenant on possible fatals. Nate said he was on his way and told him to call in more deputies.

Brady was rounding them up when the Sullivan man called again. Brady cut him short to respond to the radio. Brady's dad, just relieved from guard duty at the Askeborn shore, had copied traffic about the possible Code K and was on his way to the scene.

At 1:15, County Ambulance confirmed the Code K and said that two of the three injuries were criticals. Brady called for three more ambulance units and phoned the sheriff, who was always notified of a fatal.

In ten minutes Clark radioed in as he left his Ellsworth driveway.

At 1:30, shortly after the bars had closed, the Ellsworth PD brought in a man charged with driving under the influence. Brady barely looked up when officer Tommy Jordan walked the guy through dispatch to the booking room in the jail. Brady was busy calling the Ellsworth hospital, the medical examiner for permission to remove the body, and the funeral home to expect a body. He turned over a lost person complaint to Fred Ehrlenbach less than an hour after state police relieved Fred on the Taunton Bay shore. He also logged Ober off duty at the Askeborn house and a few minutes later gave him directions to the scene of the fatal.

The drunk called again, and again. Brady knew that the guy was lonely, but tonight he didn't have time to baby-sit a drunk. At least this one wasn't out on the road endangering lives.

Brady logged the transfer of one of the accident victims from the Ellsworth hospital to Eastern Maine Medical Center in Bangor. And he called the funeral home again and told them to hold off treating the body until the medical examiner arrived at 6:30 A.M. to do a blood alcohol test.

Ober came in with another OUI (operating under the influence). Brady guessed that this one, barely able to navigate, would spend the night passed out in a cell.

County Ambulance called on the way to pick up the Sullivan man and transport him to the Ellsworth hospital to dry out for a few days.

By 3 A.M. on October 13, most of the deputies had headed home to catch a few hours' sleep before returning to the Askeborn shore. Nate had stopped by the hospital to check on the accident victims. Sheriff Clark was on his way to the home of the young man killed in the crash.

For the second time that night, the sheriff was the messenger carrying news of a death in the family.

Chapter Nine

BY LATE SATURDAY MORNING IT WAS SUNNY and unseasonably warm on Taunton Bay. Sandpipers hopped along the shore, and a light breeze stirred the sea grasses at the high tide line. Dickson stood waiting for the digging to begin. It had been a morning of waiting.

Dickson had waited in Ellsworth for Pinkham to put together a warrant, then find a judge to sign it. He'd waited for the arrival of state police detectives, an assistant attorney general, medical examiners, and crime lab technicians, and had helped brief those not familiar with the case. Now he looked around at all of them milling about on the Askeborn shore; he counted sixteen. There was Hancock County assistant district attorney Ed McSweeney. That older man, his face turned up to bask in the warmth of the sun, was the father of one of the lab technicians, he'd been told.

In a light brown jumpsuit to protect his clothes, Ronald Roy, deputy chief medical examiner, lounged against a shovel. Dickson noticed that it was sturdier than the small spade he'd used last night. On the ground at Roy's feet lay a neatly folded packet of heavy blue plastic. The body bag. Roy was chatting with fellow medical examiner George Chase. Other people, standing in groups of twos and threes, were enjoying the scenery, watching an osprey dive-bomb the water and gulls riding wind currents in the cloudless sky.

How different from last night, Dickson thought. Then, this place had spooked everyone. Trooper Hugh Turner, who was at the shore when they arrived, looked exhausted from the raw, predawn vigil he'd taken over from Fred. And poor Fred. He'd gone from guard duty last night to the fatal traffic accident and this morning was covering the

Autumn Gold Race with the Ellsworth Police Department. He could not have caught more than two hours' sleep.

Dickson moved to the rear of the cradled boat, which in the daylight looked more dilapidated and less ominous, and hoisted himself onto the stern. This would be a good ringside seat.

Roy and a criminal investigation division detective—Gahagan, wasn't it?—had moved to the freshly dug hole at the base of the rock wall and were probing the mud and seaweed that Dickson had removed last night. Roy lifted a clump of soil and examined a flower nestled in a bit of fresh vegetation. A wild aster, lavender with a yellow center, like the ones growing on the bank a few yards away. Someone must have carted soil from the bank recently, for the flower was still alive. Roy handed the clump of earth with the delicate blossom to a state police detective, who bagged it carefully as Giroux logged the evidence on his tape recorder.

Roy dipped a plastic cup into the muddy water that had filled the hole overnight and scooped it dry. There at the bottom was the patch of dark red fabric slashed by Pinkham's knife. Roy pulled on blue surgical gloves, reached into the hole, and lifted the fabric. With his free hand he brushed away the mud under the fabric and exposed a patch of flesh. He motioned to Gahagan to begin digging—very carefully, he urged. There was no need to hurry.

From his perch above them, Dickson watched Gahagan and state police specialist Joe Gallant start a fresh hole next to the first one. About six inches down they stopped digging, and Roy knelt to clear away the earth with his hands. In tandem, digging and brushing, they followed the line of fabric as it angled sharply in a narrow V. An arm, bent at the elbow, Dickson thought. Or maybe a leg. Gahagan widened the trench along one side of the V and paused before starting on the other side.

The sun climbed higher in the sky and grew hot. Dickson removed his jacket, and, noticing beads of sweat on Gahagan's face, offered to spell him. Gahagan shook his head and continued digging. A screech from the nearby ledge diverted Dickson's attention, and he watched two gulls fighting over some morsel as though it were the last bit of food around. While the two squabbled, lunging and pecking at each other, a third gull swooped down and carried off the booty. Dickson chuckled. Serves you right, he thought.

He looked back at the scene below him. Something tan protruded from the mud. Tan and brown. A boot. It looked like an L.L. Bean pac boot. Roy was tugging at a piece of twine near the top of the boot. It circled the ankle and disappeared beneath it into the mud.

Gahagan dropped to his knees and helped Roy track the twine into the mud to a second boot. The twine bound the two ankles together. The body was lying on its left side, feet toward the shore. The head, which they hadn't found yet, was apparently toward the water. Roy stood, stretching, and massaged the small of his back with his thumbs. He moved to the upper part of the leg where they'd started digging a half hour earlier.

"We've got to move these rocks," Roy announced. "The rest of the body appears to be under the wall." He leaned over to heft a large stone—about twenty pounds, Dickson guessed—and passed it to a state trooper. Slowly, Roy and two troopers began dismantling a section of the eight-foot-long wall. It was low, maybe fifteen inches high and only about a foot wide. But Dickson could see that this would take some time. He hopped down from the boat and walked past Detective Downing, who was snapping pictures, to join Nate and the sheriff on a flat stretch of ledge.

"You got yourself the best seat in the house, I see," Nate greeted him.

"Yeah. You know, this whole thing is like a Stephen King movie. Last night when I needed a shovel, there one was. I could have stuck it in anywhere, but something drew me to the right spot. I dug down a little—and just when I was about to move on, there was that seaweed and then the patch of red clothing."

"Maybe they will make a movie, and you can star in it," Nate said. "Do you guys realize how lucky we are, though? In another few days an extra-high tide or a heavy rain could settle the area that's dug up and it'd look like the rest of the beach."

"Or Samantha could have widened her rock wall and covered the

whole body," said Bill. "You think we'd have found it then?" He turned
to the bay. "Look, you can see Amy's house over on the Sullivan
shore." Only yesterday he'd watched the sunset from her window with
no idea that he was looking across the bay to her grave.

Bill reached for his radio. Ernie Fitch, calling from the Askeborn
yard and sounding very annoyed, said he'd been having trouble with
reporters, and a bunch of them were headed to the shore through the
woods on a neighbor's property.

"Shit! That's just what we need," Bill said. "Okay," he told Fitch,
"we'll send someone up to intercept them. Where exactly are they?"

Once the sheriff knew their location, he sent Nate and Trooper
Hugh Turner along the shore toward the Bonthius property next door.
Entering the woods, they disappeared.

"How much do the Askeborns know about what's going on?"
Dickson asked Bill.

"All Ralph told them last night was that we were posting guards
and would be back in the morning."

"Nothing about the body?"

"No. But I can't help thinking how we might've handled it."

"What do you mean?" Dickson asked.

"Well," said Bill, "what if we'd told the family we hadn't found
anything and were coming back in the daylight to look around some
more? Made it appear that everyone had left when we really had some
guys hidden at the shore."

"Yeah," said Dickson, "and then Samantha steals down and starts
digging and moving the body and wham! Caught in the act!"

Fitch's voice on Bill's portable broke into their fantasy. "The reporters and a television crew have returned to the road 'cause the going
got too rough for them."

"Oh, too bad," Clark said, grinning at Dickson.

"Things okay down there?" asked Fitch.

"Ten-four," the sheriff answered. "Talk to you later." He clipped
the portable back onto his belt and turned to Dickson. "How do you
suppose Askeborn got Amy down to the shore?" Bill asked. "You think
they walked?"

"I don't know. Maybe he killed her in his trailer and brought her down in that wheelbarrow over there."

"I thought of that," Bill said. "We'll probably never know. I don't think he's going to tell us. And how do you think Amy's car got back to her house? If Askeborn drove it, how did he get back here? It's a long walk, about eight to ten miles around the bay, don't you think?"

"Prob'ly. We'll have to clock it. Or someone could have driven another car over and brought him back," suggested Dickson.

"Glenn?"

"Maybe. Hard to tell how far she'd go to protect her son." Dickson shrugged his shoulders, and they both started walking back to the others.

Dickson reclaimed his seat on the stern of the boat. The upper part of the body lay exposed, covered with something dark green and shiny. "What's that?" he asked Gahagan.

"A garbage bag," Gahagan told him.

"Oh, Christ. A garbage bag?" Dickson watched Roy run a hand along the bag, stop, and look up quizzically. He hadn't found the head. My God, thought Dickson, she's not decapitated, is she? Roy parted the thin plastic and exposed the collar of a red parka. He placed his hand above the collar and moved it along the neck. He could feel that it curved sharply forward under a rock. Gahagan lifted the rock away and shoveled carefully until Roy motioned him to stop. The two of them, working with their hands, laid bare the rest of the plastic bag. Roy probed the bag and felt the round, solid mass of a head. The body lay in a fetal position, head curved forward close to the knees.

All the men had gathered around the grave site and were looking down at the body lying there. Roy wanted it moved from the shadow of the boat to the ledge, about twenty feet away, where the sun was shining. Detective Downing, Brady, and the sheriff stepped forward and knelt beside Roy and Gahagan. Working their hands under the body to get a firm grip, they heaved and heaved until the mud let go. It made a loud, sucking sound.

Slowly, as though bearing a coffin in a funeral procession, they inched the body to the ledge and carefully lowered it to the ground.

Roy knelt beside the body and, glancing at Giroux to make sure he was ready with his tape recorder, pulled the garbage bag from the head.

A hood attached to the parka was drawn up over the head. Roy pulled the hood back, which revealed another plastic bag—a small white shopping bag from Doug's Shop 'N Save. He slipped it off and passed it to Pinkham. Then he reached into the mouth cavity and pulled out tightly wadded clear plastic. Another bag. He smoothed it out and read the red letters on one side: "Nature's Best Wild Bird Seed."

"We keep this absolutely quiet," Pinkham warned. "We'll be getting a warrant to look for bags like this."

Roy continued examining the body and noting his findings aloud for the tape. A ragged laceration at the side of the mouth, and in the mouth, clotted blood. The face, covered with dried mud, appeared to be that of a woman in her early to mid-sixties. Roy brushed the face gently, exposing bruises and, around the eyes, reddish purple spots— signs of hemorrhaging. Below, on the neck, a line of reddish discoloration indicating more hemorrhaging. No signs of rigor mortis.

"She looks good," Dickson said in a near whisper to the assistant medical examiner beside him. "She couldn't have been here long."

Roy noted bruises on the backs of both hands and blood on the back of the head. A ligature wrapped loosely around both ankles extended up the back of the body and was tied to a pull cord on the jacket. In one jacket pocket were two spare buttons in a small plastic bag marked "London Fog." In the other was wet tissue and yellow paper, possibly a mailing label from a magazine. Roy stood up. He'd continue his examination this afternoon on the autopsy table. He motioned to Gahagan to bring the body bag.

For the last several minutes, the sheriff and Pinkham had been conferring nearby. There were too many media people near the Askeborn house to take out the body the way they'd planned. Bill had just located Fred Ehrlenbach in his car on the Mud Creek Road. He told Fred to drive to Ellsworth, pick up Earland Linscott, load the sheriff's department aluminum boat and motor into the back of the

Ramcharger, and proceed to Hansen's Garage, a couple of miles down the road from the Askeborns. Bring the life jackets, the sheriff reminded Fred.

"You're welcome to try," Pete Hansen told Fred. "But this isn't the best place to put a boat in. It'd be easier on the next point over." Fred thanked Hansen and climbed back into the Ramcharger beside Linscott.

At Butler's Point they found two men closing their camp for the season. Sure, they said, you can get a boat in here, if you're careful. Earland backed the vehicle down the bank until he felt the wheels begin to sink in the soft earth. This wouldn't be a good time to get stuck. Besides, he'd take a ribbing from the guys. He was the mechanic, the one who kept their whole fleet in shape. He pulled on the emergency brake and got out. Together, he and Fred lifted the boat out of the vehicle and dragged it down the bank to the water.

"I don't have a clue where we are," Fred said as they set off in the small craft. "It's in that direction somewhere. Just follow the shore until we find them."

Rounding a point, they spotted Samantha's white boat across a cove and saw the men moving about. They'd put in only a half mile from the scene.

Earland slowed the motor and steered the boat into the deepest water he could find along the ledge. Fred hopped out and pulled the bow toward the men and the blue body bag, which, he was relieved to see, had already been zipped shut. He helped Bill and Ralph and two troopers lift the bag into the boat and prop it over the bow and middle seats. Then he climbed in and sat on the edge of the bow seat, holding the side of the boat with one hand and steadying the long blue bag next to him with the other.

"See you guys back in town," he called as Earland shoved the motor into reverse and maneuvered the stern through patches of eelgrass into deeper water.

As Earland shifted into forward gear and turned the boat toward Butler's Point, the blue bag shifted suddenly. Fred tensed and held his right arm rigid against the body. Sitting erect, he turned his head to look at the wake behind them and the sunlit waves slapping against the bow. The boat was bow heavy because of his weight and their cargo.

That's how Fred would think of it, as cargo. When he and Elizabeth had talked things over this morning, she'd urged him not to let his feelings about Amy drag him down. It was too late to help her now. It would not do any good, either, to wallow in hate and anger toward Samantha Glenner.

Earland cut the motor, and the boat drifted to shore. They'd have to wait for Ernie to get there with the Suburban Travel-All, or for the state police to arrive with one of their vans to transport the body.

Fred removed his hand from the blue plastic and, closing his eyes, turned his face up to the sun.

Skip Bouchard had already locked the glass door between the lobby and his dispatch office before Nate radioed in and told him to. Reporters had been calling and would soon start appearing in person, asking him questions. He usually told them what he knew about routine events. But this was a murder investigation. He couldn't risk saying anything or letting reporters stand there listening to his phone calls and radio traffic.

He did have something for them, though—the press release that Nate had left about last night's fatal accident. They might have to wait for it because he was busy, still handling calls from relatives and friends of the injured kids and arranging for deputies to interview them at the hospital. The funeral home had just dropped off a blood sample to be sent to the lab for testing. Amelia Cave's body was on its way in, and the nephew would be in, too, to make the identification. Thank goodness the jail administrator, Richard Bishop, had canceled inmate visiting; an attorney had just phoned to find out why. No problems in the jail, Bouchard assured him. They were busy, that was all.

This wasn't a good time to be short a man, but Jeff Clements, one of their full-time deputies, wasn't due back from the criminal justice academy for another two weeks. They were relying heavily on part-timers, and Bouchard had to find them and schedule them around their full-time jobs.

"Okay, I'll see that the lieutenant gets the message," Bouchard told a caller from Sullivan. He could see by the log that the man had been calling dispatch for most of the night. He sure hadn't spent much time drying out in the Ellsworth hospital; he was back home already. "Yes, I'll tell him you searched the quarry and found no sign of Amy Cave." Bouchard kept his voice polite but rolled his eyes at Dave Gordon, who entered from the jail booking room with a cup of coffee for him. Bouchard reached for the cup. "I will. Good-bye." He hung up the phone. "Ah, coffee. Just what I need."

"Oh-oh," Gordon said. "We've got company." Skip turned to the window overlooking the yard below and saw Dave Giroux getting out of his cruiser. "He's got Samantha with him, and I'm supposed to get palm and heel prints from her . . . him . . . whatever."

Gordon was embarrassed. Bishop had warned them that there was to be no kidding around about Samantha Glenner, who might be in their jail soon. They were all trying to be professional, but it was hard. Even Bishop called Samantha "she" one minute and "he" the next.

Giroux walked behind Samantha into the lobby, and they both disappeared into the sheriff's office. Pinkham followed minutes later.

Placing the tape recorder on the sheriff's desk, Pinkham motioned Samantha to a chair. Giroux sat down, too, and pulled out his notebook to jot down what Samantha had said to him on the ride in. She'd asked why he didn't put handcuffs on her, then said she felt as though she were drowning because nobody believed her. Giroux hadn't responded. There wasn't anything to say.

Pinkham, all business now, had switched on the machine and identified the time, location, and people present, then launched into another Miranda. Giroux wouldn't bet on Samantha's saying much now that they'd found the body behind her boat.

"That means that anything I say, if you feel I have to be detained or something, would be used against me?" Samantha asked.

"Right. You have the absolute right to the advice of a lawyer before any questioning, and to the presence of a lawyer here with you during questioning. Do you understand that?"

Samantha understood, all right, Giroux thought. She'd been through the system. Hadn't she done time in the federal penitentiary for armed robbery? He watched her wipe the palms of her large hands on the knees of her tight black pants.

"And you also understand that you can stop at any time in order to talk to a lawyer?"

"Yes."

"Now, having all those rights that I have just explained to you in mind, do you wish to answer any questions at this time?"

"Officer Pinkham, I really think I should have an attorney."

"Okay. That's your right."

"Because I—"

"You what?"

"I feel myself . . ." Samantha's slumped shoulders and deep sigh finished the sentence for her.

"Okay, that's it. Thank you, Samantha. Now I'll be talking with your parents. Would you like a cup of coffee?"

"Oh, would I. Thanks so much."

Samantha's interview, which ended at 2:03 P.M., had lasted just three minutes.

At 2:20, Wesley Askeborn's interview began upstairs in the court- house where, on a Saturday afternoon, no one would be around. Too many people, including reporters, were wandering around down- stairs. In the attorney's lounge across from the district attorney's office, Pinkham set the recorder between Wesley and himself on the polished mahogany conference table. Giroux leaned against the windowsill, half standing, half sitting.

Wes had gone to work in Trenton that morning and a deputy had been sent after him when the digging was finished at the shore. Glenn had been very upset. But if Wes was shaken, he wasn't showing it.

"I guess you know by now, Wesley, that we've found the body down—"

"Yes, I assumed that from what I—"

"And although I can't say for one hundred percent sure that it's Amy, I guess we're ninety-five percent sure it is . . . the clothing match and everything."

"Oh, it does match? I heard only that they found a body. That's all."

"We found her buried in a grave, buried right behind the boat. This certainly puts Sam in a compromising situation."

"That's for sure," Wesley said.

Pinkham said he wanted to go over again what Wesley recalled about Thursday, October 4, when Amy visited Samantha.

Wesley said he'd thought about that since they talked, and remembered that he and Glenn had worked that night, carting boxes from their attic to the upstairs of the garage he'd just built. They must have finished about seven-thirty. He recalled that they'd had the lights on. Amy's car was still there. Sometime around eight o'clock when he checked to make sure their doors were locked, he'd noticed a light on in Sam's trailer. Maybe it was around eight-thirty. He and Glenn were watching TV in the bedroom.

"Did you get up again?" Pinkham asked. "Or did you stay in bed?"

"No, I have a problem. When I lay down I have a tendency to fall asleep. I'm a sound sleeper."

"You told us last night that about eight-thirty, when you went down to get your cup of coffee, you thought Amy's car was gone at that time."

"I don't know if I saw it or I didn't see it when I locked the doors. I'm not positive."

"So, last night you seemed to think it was gone. Do you think now that it was gone?"

"I can't remember if it was or not."

"I'm not trying to put words in your mouth, Wes," Pinkham said. "I just want you to tell things the way you remember them. Sam didn't come to your house that night at all, is that right?"

"Not while I was awake, no. If I was asleep, I can't remember that."

"Okay. Another thing, Wes, you told me last night—and I think you've been quite straightforward with me, as I told you—you said that Sam didn't come over to your house at about seven or seven-thirty."

"That's correct."

"And you're probably aware now that Glenn told us she did."

"I am, yes."

Pinkham waited until Wesley looked up at him. "My feeling about that, Wes, candidly, is that Glenn is fibbing a little bit to cover up."

"You know, we moved up to this area, and we want everything to be nice and smooth, and everything clean," said Wes. "I mean, we don't want any problems. And figuring that, to the best of our knowledge, Sam was the last person we know of to see Amy, this is sort of a bad situation. As far as Glenn is concerned, she's going to try to protect Sam, because protecting Sam is protecting us, too."

"I understand that," Pinkham said. "But now we're talking about a murder."

Wesley sighed. "That's true," he said.

"So, Sam—the last person to see Amy—tells us that Amy got in her car and drove away that night, which we obviously know is a lie."

"Well, it would seem so, that's for sure."

"And then there's the matter of Sam cashing a check drawn on Amy's account in the amount of twenty-seven hundred dollars."

"Oh, the check," Wesley said. Giroux thought that Wes seemed relieved at the change of subject. Wes rattled on about how he and Glenn thought it was a small check from George or Tony or somebody, and he was so glad because it was hard supporting two homes and all. And that he'd been thrilled to have Sam with Glenn while he was in New York where he could make three times what he could in Maine. But when he came home, he wanted some privacy, you know. With a third person there, he and Glenn couldn't even enjoy a peaceful argument. So they cleared out the motor home they'd been using for storage, and were jockeying stuff around for Sam. So much to move, so many chores. And he was trying to work seven days a week and build their garage, too.

"Did Samantha help you build the garage?" Pinkham asked.

"Yeah, I'd have to admit to that."

"So she picked up a lot of stuff? Was quite strong?" A loaded question, Giroux thought, like asking if she was strong enough to heft twenty-pound rocks, or a dead body.

"Well, I don't know, true or false," Wesley answered. "She always claimed she didn't have any strength. Couldn't pick this up. Couldn't pick that up. Made her seem like a female. But every now and then she'd say, 'Well, come on, Dad, I want to arm wrestle you.'"

"Okay. I don't think there's anything else right now, Wes, although—"

"Please feel free to ask."

"I know, you've been very cooperative. We appreciate that. Now we're going to have to look in Sam's trailer. We'll get another search warrant for that. We're just trying to cover all the bases, you know, and do things properly."

Susan and Richard Cave were due any minute. Nate and the medical examiner had decided to unzip only the top of the body bag so Richard wouldn't have to see Amy's bound hands. Nate wished that Richard didn't have to see Amy's body in the police department garage, with the exhaust fumes, and tools, and auto parts everywhere. Earland kept a neat shop, but it was a stark place to see the body of someone you loved.

Nate turned on the faucet to the hose that Earland used to wash down the vehicles and ran water into his cupped hand. He splashed it onto Amy's face. The water dribbled down, streaking the dirt. When he washed away the dirt, her bruises showed up more clearly.

Nate gave up. There was no way to make this a pretty sight.

He saw the Caves drive up. "Here they are," he said to the medical examiner. "I'll go talk to them."

Outside, he waved Richard to a parking spot next to the wall of the inmate exercise yard. Susan rolled down the passenger-side window. Nate leaned in and asked Richard to come with him. It would just take a minute, he assured Susan.

Susan said she wanted to come with Richard. He urged her to let him go alone. There wasn't any point in both of them going through this, he said gently. Susan insisted she wanted to come.

"Tell you what," Nate intervened. "I'll take Richard in, and if he can't . . . can't make the identification, then we'll ask you to come in. Okay, Susan?"

It really wasn't okay with Susan. She thought they were treating her like a child who needed protecting. She could handle seeing Amy's body as well as Richard could. He had loved his aunt since he was a baby, and Susan wanted to be with him. But maybe they needed identification by a blood relative, for legal reasons. This didn't seem like the time to make a scene, so she nodded and, as Richard opened the car door, reached over to touch his hand.

In the garage, Nate introduced Richard to the medical examiner and steered him to the rear of the gray van. The tailgate was down, supporting the head at the top of the blue bag.

Richard had been steeling himself to look, but he wasn't prepared for the gray face lying there close enough to touch. He forced himself to lean into the vehicle and turn his head so he wasn't seeing the face upside down. He blanched. "Amy," he said. "Yes, that's Amy." He turned to Nate. "I . . . I . . . She looks so terrible. Maybe it isn't her."

Nate took his arm and led him from the garage.

One look at Richard told Susan everything. She moved into the driver's seat and Richard got in beside her. Susan started the car and backed it up. As she was about to drive forward, she saw Amy's car only a few feet away against the wall of the old brick jailhouse. Policemen had been at Amy's house early this morning to "process" the car, as they called it. Then a wrecker had hauled it away. Now, here it was, the familiar tan-and-white Olds, cordoned off behind a bright yellow ribbon.

Susan drove past the car, around the sharp turn that hugged the old jail, and out to the street. She was angry.

Amy's whole life was being taken apart. They had seized her car. Her body would soon be cut and prodded by strangers. And now she and Richard would return to Amy's home and begin dismantling that.

Chapter Ten

GIROUX, STANDING BY THE THIRD-FLOOR WINDOW in the courthouse, could see patches of sunlight on the roof of the old jail next door. The sun wouldn't be there long, he knew. It was already three o'clock when Pinkham brought Mrs. Askeborn into the attorney's conference room.

Giroux turned from the window and took a seat. From his position at the end of the long table, he saw Mrs. Askeborn's profile and was struck by how much Glenn and Samantha looked alike. He had not noticed that yesterday. Both had long, bushy hair that they parted in the center. Even the shape of their faces was the same. And their names were similar. Samantha's real name was Glen, like the mother's but without the second *n*. And now he called himself Glenner. Samantha Glenner. But the mother called him Sam, a man's name. Giroux was no psychologist, but . . .

Pinkham didn't waste any time getting down to business. The clothing on the body matched Amy's, he said. And any minute now he expected they'd have a positive identification.

Glenn seemed even more agitated than before, although at first she wasn't giving them the run-around she had yesterday. She admitted fibbing about seeing several cars in their driveway the day Amy came over. She even went along with Pinkham when he started calling it "lying." She admitted to seeing only one car in the driveway and lying about not knowing it was Amy's and about seeing Amy drive away from their house that evening. Then Pinkham asked her if she'd seen Sam after Amy's car left.

"Well," Glenn said, "I'm trying to think. Sam usually comes over every morning and evening for food for the cats, and now I can't swear if she came over that evening for food or not. I just can't swear to it."

Ralph had a lot of patience, Giroux thought, keeping the same even tone, calmly asking one question after another. "Yesterday when I talked to you, Glenn, you told me you watched Amy drive out of the dooryard in her car and Sam came over at the same time she drove out. Did you lie to me when you told me that?"

"No. I talked to my husband last night and he said the night we were waving to Amy was the time before, when she'd been over for dinner. I said no, it had to be last week, and he said no, it wasn't."

"And what do you believe now?" Pinkham asked.

"Well, if Wes said it wasn't last week, he must be right. I must've been thinking about the time Amy came over to dinner."

"But," Pinkham reminded her, "you told us yesterday you hadn't seen Amy since summer."

"I guess it was a while back," Glenn admitted.

"How could you confuse that time with just last week?"

"Because I'm so nervous I can't remember anything very well. And the only reason I lied was because I didn't want the family involved."

"But," Pinkham said, "you must understand that this isn't going to go away. Amy is dead. She's the victim of a murder. And she was last seen with Sam down behind the trailer at the boat."

"I don't know," said Glenn. "*I* couldn't see them."

Pinkham tried again. "Well, Sam told you that Amy was down on the boat on Thursday, the fourth. With her. And you went and got wine for Samantha. And you went into the house and—"

Glenn interrupted him, bringing in a third party again, as she had the day before. "Sam told me a lot of people saw Amy. She said Tony, the man Sam worked for, had come over to the boat that day, and as far as Sam knew, when she went up to meet me to go to the store, Tony was still there."

Giroux caught Pinkham's eye. Samantha hadn't claimed that anyone but Amy was at the shore. But of course Samantha wasn't saying anything to them now.

"What about the phone call?" Pinkham asked. "You said that

Samantha had talked with Amy the next morning, and that couldn't have happened."

Glenn said it did, but the call lasted only about a minute and Sam did all the talking. But when Pinkham bore down on her, Glenn admitted that maybe there hadn't been any phone call. Then a minute later she said she'd swear on her life that Sam did make that call Friday morning.

Pinkham said he sympathized with Glenn trying to protect her child because he was a parent too. But he reminded Glenn that Samantha had lied to them both.

Glenn insisted that Sam had not lied.

Giroux could tell that Pinkham was about to end the charade; he wasn't getting anywhere. "Let me ask you this, Glenn," said Pinkham. "No matter what I tell you, and what facts are brought to your attention, you won't believe that Sam lied to you, will you?"

"No, I won't say she wouldn't," replied Glenn. "She might tell me some lies. Do you tell the truth all the time, sir, every single minute of the day?"

Pinkham smiled. "I guess everyone strays from the truth a little from time to time. You seem to have made up your mind, though, that Sam told you the complete truth and that she didn't have anything to do with Amy's death."

"Yes, I certainly have."

"Is there anything I can do to convince you otherwise?"

"No, I don't think so."

"And the reason is that you're protecting her. Under any circumstances."

"I'd protect my dog, my cats, for God's sakes. I try to protect Wes. I mean, it's an instinctive thing."

"And you won't change your mind no matter what evidence you hear?"

"You can talk until the day of my death," Glenn said, "but I know Sam didn't hurt Amy." She sighed, and the wind seemed to go out of her sails. "Mr. Pinkham, you're making me so numb, I don't know what I'm saying."

"I'm certainly not trying to make you uncomfortable," said Pinkham, "although I know there's no way to do my job at this point without making you uncomfortable."

"I tell you," Glenn said, "I wouldn't want your job, because it must be difficult."

"Well, there are times when it is," Pinkham agreed.

Giroux could tell that Pinkham had given up. Glenn's hairdresser had told them that Glenn's health wasn't good and she took a lot of pills for headaches. Maybe Pinkham was thinking of that. Maybe he really did feel sorry for her. And maybe he just realized he'd come up against a brick wall.

As Pinkham turned off the tape, Giroux walked to the window. The jail roof was in complete shadow now. A movement in the yard below caught his eye. A TV news van had just pulled in and reporters and camera crews were milling about. They must know that the search for Amelia Cave was over. Someone was going to have to face them and make it official. And deal with a lot of questions to which they didn't have the answers.

"A zoo, that's what it was in Hancock this morning," Ernie Fitch complained between bites of his bologna sandwich. "Press and TV crews everywhere, and the public stopping their cars to ask what was going on."

"What'd you say to them?" the sheriff asked, wolfing down his own sandwich. It was past his normal lunchtime, and the salt air this morning had made him ravenous.

"I told them that nothing was going on," Fitch said, grinning as he chewed.

"Not eating, Bish?" the sheriff asked. They were having their lunch in Richard Bishop's office, but he was just sitting behind his desk, arms folded tightly across his chest, one cheek bulging with the plug of to-bacco that kept him from smoking. Still steaming over his trouble with the media at the Askeborn property, he glared at them both.

The door opened and Nate poked his head in.

"You get an ID?" Bill asked him.

Nate picked his way over the outstretched legs in the crowded office and leaned against the edge of Bishop's desk. "Yes. Richard Cave said it was Amy. He was pretty shook up, though. The body's on its way to Eastern Maine Medical. They'll have dental charts there to confirm what we already know."

Nate turned to Bishop. "What was going on this morning? You looked like you wanted to give that reporter a new asshole."

Bishop shifted his tobacco plug and grunted. "They're like vultures in a feeding frenzy."

"I just got a call from Carrigan at Channel Two," Clark said. "He was very apologetic. Offered to pull his crew if they were giving us any trouble."

"Too bad he didn't call when they were headed down to the shore," Fitch said. "We might have taken him up on the offer then. Our biggest problem was keeping people from parking along the main road. Reporters parked in private driveways. They weren't happy at all about being denied access to the Askeborn yard. Mike Gordon even climbed a tree across the road to take pictures."

Everyone laughed. "What the hell could you do about that?" Bishop asked.

"I got my own camera and aimed it up at him," Fitch said. "When I clicked the shutter, he hid his face. 'Course I didn't let on I didn't have any film in the camera." He chuckled. "What'd you say to Gordon when you came up from the shore, Nate?"

"Oh, I just asked him why he didn't smarten up. Told him he'd end up getting more from us if he'd cut us some slack."

"Yeah," Fitch said. "Lot of good that did. Some of them chased us down to Butler's Point road when we went down for the body. We had to post Lenny on the main road to keep 'em out."

The sheriff crumpled his paper napkin into a ball and took aim at Bishop's wastebasket in the corner. "There's a bunch of reporters outside now, aren't there, Nate?" Nate nodded. "We'll have to tell them something." Clark fired the napkin wad into the basket, a clean shot.

"Nothing to tell, is there?" Bishop asked.

"Some basics," Clark said. "That we found a body on the shore of

the Askeborn property. We'll have to say whose property—they already
know. That a relative has IDed the body. That the body's been taken to
Eastern Maine for an autopsy to determine the cause of death."

"What about an arrest?" Fitch asked. "Think they'll arrest Samantha
today? Jeez, Bish, how could you keep someone like her in the jail?"

Bishop moved his tobacco plug to the other cheek. The jail was
his domain. Warming to the subject, he forgot the media. "The first
thing we'll have to do," he explained, "is have a doctor examine Glenner to find out how far her change has gone. She might be part male
and part female."

"Jesus!" Fitch groaned.

"And what if the doc says she's really a male?" Nate asked. "You
going to put her in with the male population?"

Bishop was about to answer when the door opened again.
Nicholas Gess from the attorney general's office was looking for the
sheriff. Gess said he needed to find a judge to sign the warrant to
search Glenner's trailer.

Richard Cave had been lost in thought since leaving Ellsworth
and was surprised to see they were in Hancock already. He was usually behind the wheel, but now, from his vantage point in the passenger seat, he looked past Susan to the narrow inlet of the Carrying
Place. A full tide flowed under the bridge and swirled in white eddies
into Taunton Bay. When they'd explored the bay this summer in Amy's
new boat, Amy had told the kids about the Indians who used to ford
the inlet, carrying their canoes. And about the white settlers who dug
the inlet by hand to widen it into a canal for their lumber mill. Hancock was an island, Amy said, but you couldn't tell that from Route 1.

Once, Amy had turned off Route 1 and driven them to Hancock
Point, with its fashionable summer colony. She thought it was funny
that the local people called the huge old homes "cottages," and the
mountains that they faced across Frenchman Bay, the Bar Harbor
"hills."

Susan slowed the car as the road narrowed at the Hancock–
Sullivan bridge, which crossed the mouth of the bay. The rapids here

were so fierce that Amy had warned them not to take the boat too close. The hum of metal grates under their car reminded Richard how Amy loved hearing the sound from her house on a still day when the wind was just right. She told them it was called the Singing Bridge.

As they swung off Route 1 toward North Sullivan, Richard realized that he was seeing through Amy's eyes, saying good-bye for her. Saying good-bye to Jerry's Hardware on the left, the neat houses with manicured lawns and shrubs, the run-down places with junked cars in the yard, the post office she walked to for her mail. On the right was the road to the quarry. Amy had told them that, earlier in the century, granite blocks were cut here to pave the streets of New York City.

There was Marguerite Gordon's house. He and Amy had stopped there one December nearly ten years ago when they'd driven up from New York looking for land. They'd parked by the side of the road to look at lots on Evergreen Point and gotten stuck in the snow. Maynard Gordon—who had since died—had lent them a come-along, and a passing truck had pulled them out. When they returned the come-along, Marguerite asked them in for coffee, and Maynard showed them his mounted deer's head and the wooden items he carved in his shop. Amy bought a cutting board shaped like a lobster, Richard remembered. And two rooster napkin holders and several smaller knickknacks.

Now here they were at Crawford's big house set back from the road. What a good friend Crawford had been.

"Richard, do you remember when you helped Crawford mow his hay?" Susan asked. "And Amy and I stopped by to watch? We were very impressed."

"Crawford said I was as good as any old-timer."

Susan turned onto the Evergreen Point road. It hadn't been plowed that December, Richard remembered, and he and Amy had trudged through the snow to the point. Concentrating on the small tracks at their feet, they'd been startled by the partridge that flew up in front of them. When Amy stood on the bluff and looked out at the frozen bay cut with azure blue channels, and the snow-laden evergreens on the island in the distance, she'd turned to him with a look that told him their search was over. Amy had found her new home.

Susan spoke as though reading his mind. "Amy never wanted an old house or anything secondhand. She always wanted to build a home of her own."

"I know. I wonder how many miles she drove up and down the coast looking for the right spot. It had to be on the shore—she loved the water. When I was a kid, we used to walk for miles along the beach on Long Island, 'til my legs hurt, sometimes. And we'd go clamming together . . ." His voice trailed into silence as a more recent image intruded on the endless memories of childhood.

He had a last memory of Amy and a boat. Just two months ago, in August. They'd rowed out to the channel in the boat she had bought specially for his and Susan's visit. Armed with old onion sacks, a couple of sturdy branches for fishing poles, and sandworms for bait, they'd drifted in the warm sun and hauled in crabs until the wind picked up at the change of tide and forced them in. Then they'd dug clams on her shore and feasted at midnight, clam juice dripping down their chins, laughing so hard it drew Jennifer to her bedroom door. She had fixed them with her nine-year-old glare of disapproval and they'd all felt like naughty children, until Jen tottered sleepily across the living room and climbed into Aunt Amy's lap.

Richard felt the sting of tears behind his glasses. As the car rolled to a stop in front of Amy's house, he jumped out and hurried to the top of the cliff, looking blindly out at the bay. Damn it, why couldn't Amy still be here to laugh with them and hug his little daughter? He wiped a sleeve across his face and turned to the house.

Susan was bending over a flower box, picking dead blooms from Amy's yellow daisies. He walked to the deck and sat down on the top step next to her.

"Susan, what do we do now?"

"Phone calls to the family?" she suggested.

Richard nodded, but neither of them moved. The wind had died, as it always did at sunset. They could hear the cars crossing the Singing Bridge.

∞

Armed with a search warrant signed by Judge Jack Smith, the four men were about to leave the sheriff's department yard when a wrecker drove in and pulled up next to them. Dwayne Tobey had come from Augusta to haul Amelia Cave's vehicle back to state police headquarters. He'd need someone to sign a release and help hook up the car for the ninety-mile return trip.

No problem, Dickson said. He'd take care of it. With the release in hand, he sprinted up the steps and disappeared into the building.

Ober, Giroux, and Detective Downing chatted with the driver until Dickson returned. Then Dickson and Ober drove off in a county cruiser. Giroux and Downing followed in their state police car.

Wesley Askeborn met them outside his house. Giroux handed him a copy of the search warrant and apologized for disturbing him at the supper hour. That was all right, said Wesley, sounding apologetic himself. He said they didn't feel much like eating anyway.

Giroux nodded in sympathy and followed him to Samantha's trailer. Wesley turned his key in the lock and stood aside. "If you need me . . . ," he began in a tentative voice.

"That's all right," Giroux said. "We'll just look around—shouldn't be too long."

"Well, I'll be in the house," said Wesley, and he left them alone in his son's trailer.

The four men looked around at the clutter in the living room and, beyond a flimsy divider, the kitchen and dining area. Wire, tools, boxes, pieces of pipe, and assorted junk were piled on the floor and on every table and chair.

"This'll be fun," Ober said, grimacing. "Exactly what are we supposed to be looking for?"

Giroux scanned the warrant. "Any green garbage-type bag, white plastic bag, plastic birdseed bag. And, let's see, twine and plastic or nylon-type braided rope. And, oh yeah, the biggies—Amy's pocketbook and checkbook."

Ober and Dickson began rummaging through the contents of a white canvas bag on the living room floor. Ober pulled out a small square of folded plastic. He unfolded it and smoothed it out, then read the printing on the side. "Bingo!" he called out. "A birdseed bag."

He handed the bag to Downing, who photographed it, then placed it in an evidence bag, which he labeled.

Ober moved across the room to a green trash bag. It was full of clothes. He dumped them onto a chair and handed Downing the bag. The detective, on his knees, spread the bag on the floor. As he raised his camera, Pinkham opened the trailer door. He'd brought Samantha home and left her at her parents' house.

While Pinkham joined the search in the living room area, Ober and Dickson walked down the hall to a bathroom and two small bedrooms, which were even more cluttered than the front room. In one of the bedrooms, storage items had been shoved aside to make room for a bed. Samantha's bedroom. Ober spotted a shoebox on a shelf over the bed, and picking through the contents found a piece of braided rope. He took it to Downing in the living room and stayed a few minutes to watch their progress. As he walked back down the hall, he heard a voice he knew wasn't Dickson's. He poked his head around the door frame and saw only Dickson. Then he spotted the tape recorder.

"Who's that talking?" he asked.

"It's Samantha," Dickson said as he pawed through the contents of a cardboard box in the corner.

"Go on, it's not Samantha. It's a man."

"Yeah, it is. It's Samantha speaking in her man's voice."

"What's he talking about?" Ober asked.

"I don't know. Fantasy stuff about wheeling and dealing with big shots like the secretary of the navy, Arthur Schlesinger, and people like that." Dickson switched off the tape. "A bunch of bullshit."

"What'd you think you were going to hear, a full confession?"

Dickson grinned. "Maybe. But we couldn't use it anyway."

When they finished the search more than an hour later, they had gathered a birdseed bag, a white plastic bag, a green trash bag, and four pieces of string or rope, two of these from the top of the woodpile and the yard next to the trailer. They hadn't found Amy's checkbook or her purse.

Dickson and Ober drove out of the yard, leaving Pinkham and Giroux to deal with the family.

Pinkham knocked on the Askeborns' door. He told Wesley they were leaving and reminded a subdued-looking Samantha that they expected her at the sheriff's department the next day at 1:30 P.M. for photographs and fingerprints.

They were through following Samantha's trail of phony addresses, names, and social security numbers and would begin piecing together the real background of Glen Robert Askeborn.

On the drive back to Ellsworth, Giroux and Pinkham discussed what lay ahead. Now that the search for Amelia Cave was over, they could focus on gathering evidence to convict her killer. The next day Giroux and either Nate or Downing would begin interviewing people and collecting written statements. They would talk with Susan and Richard Cave before they left for New York. They'd talk with the Askeborns' neighbors; maybe someone had seen Amy's car leaving their property, or maybe a clammer or someone in a boat had seen something on the shore where the body had been found. They'd talk to the carrier who delivered mail to the Askeborns, and the beautician who had done Glenn's hair the day Amy visited Samantha. To Iva Patten and Crawford Hollidge again, and others in Amy's neighborhood. They might find someone who could tell them how Amy's car got back to her house Thursday night. They'd check with taxi drivers in Ellsworth to see if anyone had picked up a fare in Sullivan that night. And they'd get the autopsy results and send evidence to the lab for tests. And document everything they did.

While tracking down Amy's killer, they'd be leaving a trail for someone else. Looking over their shoulders, scrutinizing everything they did or didn't do, hoping to find mistakes, would be the constant specter of a defense attorney.

Part Two

Chapter Eleven

TAUNTON BAY HADN'T SEEMED THE SAME SINCE Friday night when Iva had called to tell me about Amy.

Now, standing on the bank looking down at my boat anchored in the cove, I wasn't at all sure I wanted to go out today. The day was mild and sunny and the water was calm, so I couldn't use weather as an excuse not to go. And I had my camera with me. But why should I set off to a place I didn't want to go? Just to take a picture for the newspaper?

My feet dragged on the path down to the beach. I looked beyond my boat to the ledge where three days ago I'd sat at low tide and watched the plane and boats searching the bay for Amy's body. Soon I'd begun searching, too, imagining that each rubbery piece of kelp or each log decaying in the mud was an arm or a leg—some part of a dead body. I'd never swim in the cove here again.

I untied the line from the old pine tree, climbed into the boat, and pushed off, then rowed out to water deep enough to start the motor. I couldn't help looking over to the Sullivan shore a half-mile away to see the tan roof of Amy's house. Amy and I had built our houses at the same time. We had been friends since she moved to Maine, although I was too busy as a newspaper reporter to see her as often as I would have liked. Somewhere at least a couple miles across the bay on the Hancock shore near the Franklin town line was her unmarked grave. I didn't know exactly where, but I was on my way to find out.

The outboard started on the first pull, and I headed the boat west along the Hancock shore. There were no houses in sight, just evergreen wilderness. At Seal Point, where on a Sunday afternoon such as this I'd usually veer across the bay to Burying Island, I kept a steady course instead and entered unfamiliar waters.

I checked my watch. It was 1:15. Nate Anderson had told me that Glen Askeborn, alias Samantha Glenner, was expected at the sheriff's department today at 1:30 to be fingerprinted and photographed. Please, please let that be where he was now. I didn't want to meet a suspected killer—a huge person, I'd heard—on the isolated shore of his property where I, a lone woman, would be a trespasser.

But where was the Askeborn property? The shoreline ahead was one long, continuous stretch of trees except for the bridge over Egypt Stream. This morning I'd driven to the bridge and clocked the mileage back to the Askeborn house. Transposing distance to the water, however, was another matter. I made an educated guess and, targeting a tall, scraggly pine, watched it draw closer and closer.

It was 1:30 when I slowed the boat and ran parallel to the shore, scanning the woods for even the hint of a trail. I'd heard only that the police had followed a trail from the Askeborns' house and found Amy's body somewhere near the shore. At a promising break in the trees, I cut the motor and drifted to shore. The beach was marshy underfoot. I tied the bow line around a boulder and climbed the bank to the woods. Oak leaves, turned yellow by crisp fall nights, glowed in the sunlight and formed a golden canopy overhead. As I walked along what seemed like an old woods trail or maybe an animal path, I searched the ground for freshly disturbed earth. With every few steps I peered into the surrounding woods and checked the trail ahead and behind. My feet on the soft floor of the forest made no sound, but someone might have heard my outboard. Anyone coming up behind me would cut off my route of escape to the boat.

I remembered what Nate had told me Friday night. A clammer, he said, was lugging a bucket of clams along a woods trail on the Askeborn property when Samantha, carrying a bow and arrows, surprised him from behind. The clam digger had obviously lived to tell about it, but Amy was dead.

I couldn't think what was so important about taking a picture of her burial site. But still I walked on. The woods were beautiful, and maybe just ahead I'd find what I was looking for. Finally I stopped. The grave was supposed to be close to the shore, and I certainly no longer was. I turned to retrace my steps and retreated at a much faster pace, no longer admiring the autumn woods.

I just wanted to get out of there.

"Pat, I think you were foolish to go off alone like that," Iva scolded me on the phone that evening. I didn't disagree. Neither did I mention that I planned to go again when I had better directions.

Iva and I, still in shock over Amy's murder, found comfort in telling each other the same things over and over. It was only last Sunday afternoon, a week ago today, that Amy had failed to show up at my house for a meeting about the environment of Taunton Bay. Amy had sent a card saying she was coming. Iva wanted to drive over with her but couldn't reach her by phone. On the day of the meeting—Iva and I now realized—Amy was already dead.

"Why on earth would you want to see that place?" Iva asked. I didn't really know. The reporter in me was always looking for a picture or a story. Beyond that, though, for some reason I needed to see where Amy's life had ended.

"I can't explain it, Iva. I know it seems crazy."

"You know what gets me the most?" Iva asked.

"I know."

"Yes, you certainly do. I'll never understand how that woman could act so concerned, call me so often to see if I'd heard anything, and never say a word about Amy's being at her house a few days before. And rush over here when I told her the sheriff's men were coming, and never say a word to them, either."

"Well, now you understand why she was so nervous."

"Nervous? I guess she was nervous. Spilled her coffee and talked a mile a minute." Iva sighed. "Pat, why would anyone hurt Amy? She was such a lovely, gentle person. She never would have hurt anyone." Iva sighed again. "Have you heard when they're going to arrest that . . . person?"

"No. Nate said he'd call me when they decide. Probably so I don't keep calling and bugging the sheriff's department."

I thanked Iva again for calling me Friday night, when Crawford phoned her with the news after Susan and Richard Cave had called him. Then I asked Iva to tell me again about meeting Samantha at Amy's Thanksgiving dinner. I'd never seen Samantha, or heard of her, either. Listening to Iva's description, though, it was hard to understand how a six-foot, strongly built man dressed in women's clothes could have fooled Iva like that. I told her so.

"I guess we see what we expect to see," Iva said, philosophical as usual. "And don't forget, we're seeing with twenty-twenty hindsight now."

Well, until it came out officially, I'd keep to myself everything that Iva had told me in confidence. We said good-bye. Tomorrow was a workday, and for a while tonight I'd try to forget what had happened on the quiet shores of Taunton Bay.

On Monday morning the *Ellsworth American* office was buzzing with talk about Amy's body being found. No one mentioned any suspect, and I kept quiet about what I knew.

Then, fellow reporter Katherine Heidinger leaned over my desk and in her Southern drawl told me everything I had so virtuously been keeping to myself.

My mouth fell open. How did she know? She said she'd just picked up a cup of coffee next door at Bub's Pub and everyone there was talking about it.

The back door of the newspaper office was only a few steps from the back door to Bub's, a small bar and restaurant. When I walked in, Bub called out from behind the counter, "Pat! Some story, isn't it?" I sat on the only empty stool and listened to Bub emceeing the discussion along the bar. Joe, beside me, had even met Samantha, Bub announced—about a year ago when she came into the pub. "Tell her, Joe."

Joe, embarrassed at first, soon got into the spirit of things. "Her boobs," he said, "that's what stood out most in my mind." Everyone laughed, including Joe.

"Stood out?" he continued. "Yeah, I said that right. Samantha was over six feet, and I'm short, so when I stood in front of her, the boobs were right in my face. I never, ever seen any that big."

As private conversations resumed along the bar, I stood up to leave with my Styrofoam cup. "Didn't you have any idea that Samantha was really a man?" I asked Joe.

Joe's eyes narrowed and he hesitated, sheepish. Then he grinned. "Naw. No idea at all. I took him as, you know, this sexy babe."

I left the pub and walked up the State Street hill to the courthouse, where I found Nate at his desk in the patrol room of the sheriff's department. I told him that the big secret about Samantha was common knowledge at Bub's Pub. He wasn't surprised. Too many people knew, he said. A man parading around as a woman in rural Maine was too unusual for people to keep to themselves. That, and a murder, too, guaranteed that word would spread like wildfire.

I'd seen Nate at the sheriff's department on Friday night after Iva called me, and I'd told him what I knew and how I'd found out. Now I told him about my unsuccessful expedition the day before. I said I wanted to try again. Not wanting to put him on the spot, I didn't ask outright where I should look. I watched him thinking over the implications of telling me. Finally he asked, "Do you know where there's an old white boat drawn up on the Hancock shore?"

"A cabin cruiser, you mean?"

"Exactly."

"Yes, I saw a white boat from a distance just this past summer."

"Well, right behind that boat is where we found the body."

"Thank you, Nate."

"Be careful," he warned. "Samantha spends a lot of time down by her boat, and it's pretty isolated there." I promised I'd be careful.

I was thinking about Nate's warning as I talked to Skip in dispatch and checked the incident cards on the counter. Maybe getting a picture wasn't that important.

Back at the office, I told Mel Stone, the paper's managing editor, what I planned to do now that I knew the location of the burial site. He didn't want me to go alone again and asked reporter Shawn O'Brien to go with me. Shawn, besides being good company, was a strapping six-footer.

When we shoved off from shore on Wednesday morning, Shawn sat in the bow, looking around appreciatively. I pointed out the eagles' nests in the two tall pines. About twenty minutes later, I pointed to the white hull of a boat on the shore ahead. Immediately our sight-seeing adventure ended and we stopped calling out to each other above the noise of the outboard.

As we drew close to shore, I cut the motor. Shawn whispered an offer to go ashore and do the picture taking. I whispered back that I'd do it, but would he please sit by the motor and be ready to start it in case we had to leave in a hurry.

Scanning the beach and the edge of the woods, I stepped onto the ledge and walked cautiously to the stern of the dilapidated cruiser. I saw Amy's grave. Muddy water filled the ugly hole, and blue surgical gloves lay discarded on the ground. I began snapping pictures, scurrying from one vantage point to another to vary the background, concentrating on only what I could see through the camera lens. From the corner of my eye, I saw something move as I crouched down behind the boat for a close-up. Shawn had stepped onto the ledge to keep me in sight. Neither of us was sure that Samantha wasn't inside the cabin of the old cruiser.

I snapped a last picture and hurried back to Shawn. We hopped into the boat and made our getaway. As the shore receded, we began breathing more easily. We were both brave now. And I was angry. I resented being afraid on Taunton Bay, my own turf. I'd be putting up my boat soon and didn't want this awful trip to be my last memory of the season.

"Shawn, is it okay with you if we make a little detour to Burying Island? Just for a quick visit?"

"Sure," he said. "Why not?"

The boat scraped bottom on the gravel beach as I looked up at the huge oak growing on the bank. Its leaves were turning brown, and the asters and beach peas had gone by. Shawn stepped from the boat, stretching and smiling, and looked up at the stone tower on the cliff to our right. My father's handiwork, I explained. So was the stone boathouse built into the bank on the shore. My family owned the island with two other families, and I had summered there since childhood.

Shawn and I climbed the steps dug into the steep bank and paused at the top to catch our breath and look around. The log cabin, its windows shuttered against approaching winter, looked forlorn to me, but Shawn enthused about what a great place it must have been to spend the summer. My spirits picked up as I led him around the cabin to the screened-in kitchen with the stone fireplace, then down the path to the spring, where cold water flowed year-round. I wished there were time to show him the rest of the island and the other camps, even though they were closed for the season, too. But our weekly newspaper would come out the next day, and I had film to develop and copy to write.

We walked back to the log cabin and looked out at the bay, the Hancock shore, and the mountains beyond on Mount Desert Island. As we chatted, facing each other, something moved above Shawn's head. He couldn't see it, but I watched, speechless, as an eagle floated down just above him. The great bird, suddenly aware of our presence, began frantically beating its enormous wings. Shawn turned to the stir, and we both watched in awe as the huge bird rose straight up, then flew out of sight above the treetops.

"Oh, Shawn, I wanted to tell you, but I couldn't talk. It was only a few feet above your head!"

I couldn't get over how big it looked, even though I knew that an eagle's wingspan was six to eight feet across.

"I saw the expression on your face," said Shawn, "and I couldn't figure out what was going on. Wouldn't you know I'd leave my camera on the beach."

There hadn't been time to take a picture anyway, but I'd never forget the image of those black talons and huge, sweeping wings. We rushed to an opening in the evergreens on a nearby cliff, but the eagle had vanished.

I glanced at the Hancock shore and felt a pang of guilt. We'd played hooky long enough. We sped full throttle across the bay and in a few minutes were standing by our cars in front of my house. Shawn offered to develop my film while I wrote my story. I rewound the film in my camera and handed it to him. He unzipped his leather case. There on top of his camera equipment lay the cold black metal of a Smith & Wesson .22 revolver.

"Shawn! What are you doing with a gun in your camera case?"

"I thought it might be a good idea. I didn't know what we'd be getting into."

"Why didn't you tell me you had it with you?"

"I guess I didn't want to scare you. I don't know how you feel about guns."

"Maybe I wouldn't have been so scared if I'd known you had that thing with you. Anyway, I'm glad you didn't have to use it."

"Me, too. We're supposed to be covering the news, not making it."

At my desk, looking over my notes, I saw that Amy's birthday was October 27. In ten days. She hadn't quite made it to her sixtieth birthday.

The medical examiner had officially identified her body and, according to Attorney General James Tierney, police were giving the investigation top priority. No one would comment on whether they had a suspect in mind.

I called an assistant attorney general, Nick Gess, for a final check, and he told me that they were still interviewing people and processing evidence at the crime lab in Augusta. But he was able to tell me one thing new: The cause of death was asphyxiation due to strangulation. Someone had strangled Amy to death.

I hung up the phone and sat quietly for a minute before beginning to write.

Shawn appeared with a handful of photos and spread them across my desk. They were all gruesome.

I chose one and wrote a sterile cutline: "The water-filled pool directly behind this boat beached on the Hancock shore of Taunton Bay is the grave site where police found Amelia Cave's body Friday evening. The next morning they dug up the grave and removed the body by boat."

I stared at the stark black-and-white picture of Amy's grave. It's true what is said about pictures. This one was worth more than a thousand words.

In the studio of her West Nyack home, Jo McMillen squinted through appraising eyes at the half-finished painting on her easel. Sunset on Taunton Bay. She was still thinking of the other picture she'd just seen on the front page of the *Ellsworth American*.

How could they put a picture of Amy, smiling, right next to one of that awful hole on the beach where they'd found her body? Newspapers were so sensational sometimes.

She and Ralph would go to Long Island tomorrow for Amy's service, of course. For Susan and Richard's sake. And for their own. Amy had been their friend for ten years.

How smart Amy had been, they thought, to have her lawyer check with them before she bought land next to theirs on Evergreen Point. When Amy herself had called, they told her they loved the point and looked forward to living there year-round when Ralph retired.

Now, after what had happened, they weren't sure they wanted to live in Maine at all.

Jo moved to her studio window and gazed out on the woods that always reminded her of Maine and made her feel good. Amy had told them that she pictured the Maine woods, too, when she felt overwhelmed with work at her desk in the school accounting office. Ralph and Amy had had that in common; both worked for school departments.

Ralph had given Amy the name of their builder and spent hours going over house plans with her when she visited them in New York or at Evergreen Point in summer.

How idyllic her dreams had seemed to them. Amy, who'd never

learned to cook, imagined herself baking bread and playing hostess to new friends and all the relatives she expected would visit constantly. And sewing curtains, and sleigh-riding in winter, or just watching the flakes swirling outside her window. When she moved, she'd brought with her the long gowns she'd worn to school functions. Jo had seen them hanging in the closet of her new home—elegant gowns, draped, bouffant, adorned with bows. She thought now that Amy had probably never had a chance to wear them in Maine.

"I've got to stop this," Jo scolded herself aloud. She'd had trouble painting since the weekend when Hal and Ruth Church called from Hancock to tell them that Amy's body had been found. And now, instead of picking up a brush, Jo stood in front of her easel, arms at her side, just looking. Raspberry—that was the color of the sunset. Not just any sunset, but a special one that had taken her breath away. It had tinted the water, rocks, clouds—everything. Squinting again, Jo decided that the painting needed more depth. She'd darken the shadows with lavender. Only not now. Later.

She walked across the room to her rocker, sat down, and stared mindlessly out the window.

Jo and Ralph had realized during Amy's first year at Evergreen Point that in spite of seeming so capable and independent, she had a helpless side. "She needs a lot of guidance" was the way Ralph put it. He couldn't understand how she could manage a large budget for the school system and yet wait until April 15 to start thinking about her own taxes. And she'd been ready to take her lawn mower back to Agway and tell them it didn't work when Ralph offered to check it for her. He discovered that the cutter bar wasn't making contact with the reel. Even after he adjusted the bar, they weren't sure that Amy ever tried cutting the grass herself again.

Privately, Ralph said that Amy was trying to cope in a world she'd never learned to deal with. He helped her all he could, but he drew the line at the bookcases she asked him to build. She was so fussy that she'd notice the tiniest flaw even inside a bureau drawer. Ralph told her he knew he couldn't build a bookcase that would please her.

Amy was good-natured about that. "That's just the way I am," she said. She took an hour to wash one window, was still eating long after everyone else had finished, and would insist on doing the dishes by herself even if it seemed to take forever. She was generous, too. She'd bring bags of groceries with her when she came to dinner at their house, which in the beginning was several times a week. She'd bring them crystal from Porteous department store. And she would chat with their kids and always seemed interested in what they were doing. She enjoyed their friends, too, and they liked her. Amy was fun.

That made it all the harder when she began to change.

They noticed it after her first winter alone in Maine. It wasn't like Amy to be depressed. She was never specific about what was bothering her, but they knew she was aware that her way of hugging everyone, including men, put off some of the wives. She stopped hugging everyone and tried hard to fit in.

Just last summer, Amy's nephew, Richard, had walked down from her house alone and very apologetic. "Amy doesn't trust her neighbors anymore. Not even you," Richard had said sadly.

Jo was brought back to the present when Brandy, her golden retriever, nudged open the studio door and settled on the floor beside the rocking chair. The dog seemed to know before Jo did herself when she needed comforting. Now, head resting on her paws, Brandy followed Jo with soulful eyes as she rocked back and forth, back and forth.

Amy had slowly withdrawn from their lives without ever telling them why, or saying good-bye. There'd always been the hope, though, that someday they'd be friends again.

Now, all they could do was say good-bye.

Even in his own house back on Long Island, Richard was unable to sleep. He rolled out of bed quietly so he wouldn't disturb Susan, then reached for his flannel robe on the chair.

He tiptoed down the stairs and paused in the doorway to the living room, wondering what he could do to stop his mind from racing. The whole family had gone to bed early, exhausted—even the children, who didn't know the truth about Amy's death. He and Susan had told them that Amy died in an accidental fall. Of course they'd have to tell their children sometime. When they were older.

Richard sat on the end of the couch next to his favorite reading lamp, his eyes too tired to read. He lay his head back against the cushion and was just starting to relax when Amy's picture appeared. The one in her blue housecoat—the picture they'd put on top of the casket. And then another image of Amy: her gray face in the van in the sheriff's department garage.

So many people had come to the funeral home yesterday for the wake, and for the service today. Amy's friends from childhood and from the school where she had worked. And all the relatives. Even Richie had come up from Florida. The McMillens had driven down from Nyack; he remembered seeing them, but had they spoken? He didn't think so.

People had been sitting quietly with their heads bowed, unlike funerals he'd been to in which they smiled and talked about the good times, celebrating a life even when someone had died after a long illness. But murder was different.

Richard stood quickly and walked to the kitchen. He yanked open a cupboard door and reached for a glass. The police in Maine had come to Amy's house several times to talk with them. They said Glenn's hairdresser had told them that Glenn had almost canceled her appointment last Thursday because a woman friend begged her to. The police believed that woman must have been Amy. Samantha had admitted that Amy was coming to talk about the overdue loan. Richard was sure that Amy hadn't wanted to be alone with Samantha when she asked for her money back.

He poured himself a glass of milk. It chilled his hands as he walked back to the couch.

On one visit, police had told them that Amy had been strangled and that the autopsy showed no alcohol in her blood. Of course not. Amy didn't drink, except for an occasional glass of wine with dinner.

Sipping his milk, Richard heard the creak of a floorboard behind him. Susan walked around the couch and sat beside him. He took her hand.

"I was just thinking," he said. "You know, Amy was only two years old when her dad moved out and her parents got divorced. That must have been hard on her." Susan squeezed his hand. "And taking care of the big house and her invalid mother all those years. She even broke off her engagement to do that. An invalid mother-in-law didn't appeal to her fiancé. Then when she moved upstairs into our house, she helped look after all us kids, too."

He remembered when he was little, watching his father and Aunt Amy doing the finish work upstairs in their Cape Cod, Amy putting up plasterboard right along with his dad. He wanted to help, too, but Amy said he should be out playing with his friends.

When Richard moved out of the house when he turned twenty-one, Amy stayed with his family for another six years, with all the other relatives around. Then she moved to Maine to live alone for the first time in her life.

Maybe she was like a hothouse flower exposed too suddenly to the elements. Any good gardener knows you harden off a plant gradually before it can live outside a protected environment.

Richard looked down at Susan's face next to him. Even in the dim light from the hall, he could see that she was tired. Not just from the funeral after being home from Maine only two days. The whole week before, they'd cleaned out Amy's house, going through all her things, making hard decisions.

They'd loaded Amy's belongings into a van, taking everything that wasn't built in. Why should they leave the chandelier that Amy loved? They weren't sure that anyone would buy a house owned by someone who'd been murdered.

Amy's murder had changed the way even they felt about her house and about Maine. They might never feel like setting foot in the state again.

Yet so many people in Maine had been good to them. He and Susan had put a poster in the North Sullivan Post Office thanking everyone for their kindness.

And when they had finished loading the van and boarding up the windows, they'd said good-bye to Amy's dream house, then driven down the road to say good-bye to Crawford. He would watch over Amy's property, just as he'd watched over her.

They had returned the furniture that Amy had borrowed from Ruth Kane at The Ellsworth Motel, reminisced with her about Amy, and set out on the ten-hour drive home to Long Island. Richard knew that every day on his way to work he would drive past Farmington's huge St. Charles Cemetery and look over to Amy's grave.

They still had the trial hanging over them, if there was to be a trial. They'd have to go back to Maine for that.

Susan's head was resting on his shoulder. Her slow, even breathing told him she had fallen asleep. She was lucky.

Chapter Twelve

A T HIS DESK IN THE HANCOCK COUNTY JAIL ADMINISTRATOR'S small office, Richard Bishop was going over a mental checklist in preparation for Samantha Glenner's arrest within the next hour.

Before entering the jail, she'd be taken to the doctor's office. If Dr. Adrian Hogben determined that Samantha had undergone a complete sex change operation, a matron would have to do the routine strip search in the jail. Ethel was standing by for that. If their new prisoner still had a penis, the male corrections officer on duty would conduct the search. If Glenner had a penis and breasts, Bishop's guys would be there to search below the waist and the matron above the waist.

Although Bishop had prepared his staff as best he could, heading into such profoundly unfamiliar territory made him uneasy.

He checked his watch. Time to leave. He'd already talked to his corrections officers, dispatch, the sheriff, and the doctor. Now, without speaking to anyone, he walked through the jail division and out to the lobby.

Giroux, Pinkham, and Nate were just leaving for Hancock to pick up Samantha, and Bishop followed them down the outside steps to their cars. They would meet him later at the hospital. Although Bishop had time to spare, he'd just as soon get away from the jail, where everyone was a little jittery. They'd been waiting for three weeks, not knowing from day to day when the state police and the attorney general's office would decide they had enough evidence to arrest Samantha. And today, November 5, when the special grand jury convened in the morning, they had waited from minute to minute to hear if the jury would return an indictment.

Bishop folded his six-foot-two frame into his vehicle and followed Giroux's cruiser out the driveway and down State Street to the traffic light. Giroux made it through the light, but Bishop didn't. He waited, drumming his fingers on the steering wheel. It was mid-afternoon before they'd heard that the jury had indicted Samantha Glenner. Mr. Askeborn and one of the Askeborns' neighbors had testified, Bishop knew. Just two witnesses. The indictment was being kept secret, pending an arrest.

Bishop arrived at Ellsworth's Maine Coast Memorial Hospital, where Dr. Hogben had an office. After parking in the small lot near the front door, Bishop settled back in the seat to wait for the others to pick up Samantha. His attitude toward her had changed since a month ago when he first set eyes on her. Then, he had thought she was a very strange woman. When he learned she was a man, he didn't know what to think. In the last few weeks, though, as they'd been digging into her past, gender had taken a backseat to Glen Robert Askeborn's criminal record.

In 1971, Askeborn and another man had robbed a trust company bank on Long Island, New York. Askeborn was armed with a .38 pistol. The two men had escaped.

Four days later they robbed a finance company in another Long Island town and tied up a customer and two employees. Askeborn had dropped his wallet at the scene and was promptly arrested. He and the other man pleaded guilty, and Askeborn was sentenced to six years in federal prison in Pennsylvania. He was paroled after three years and went to live in Connecticut, where he became involved in other small crimes—Bishop didn't know the details. With Connecticut warrants still outstanding against him, he stole away to Maine as Samantha.

The thing that bothered Bishop the most was what he'd heard about Askeborn when he was married and in the navy in California. His wife then, the first of three, had a three-year-old son. Bishop had learned that Askeborn once plunged the child's head into a tub of scalding water.

Bishop shifted uncomfortably in his seat. What had Askeborn

gotten for that atrocity? A three-year suspended sentence. Some court-appointed counselor had decided that he didn't need counseling. He was discharged from the navy as an undesirable, and that was it.

He checked his watch again. Giroux, Pinkham, and Nate should be showing up with Samantha shortly, unless she'd skipped town.

Bishop began anxiously watching every car that turned into the hospital driveway.

Across town, reporters who had gathered at the entrance to the building that housed the sheriff's department were bantering, specu-lating, and sharing bits of information. They were friendly with one another yet cautious about giving away some detail that the competi-tion might not know. No one was sure how the other reporters had been tipped off to Samantha's imminent arrest. Reporters from Ells-worth's two radio stations were less cautious what they divulged. They'd be on the air within minutes of the arrest.

"Here they come!" someone called out. Everyone rushed to a van-tage point along the stairs with Nikons and TV cameras aimed at the cruiser that was parking in one of the reserved spots along the brick wall. Shutters clicked and TV cameras rolled as uniformed officers es-corted a tall figure in black pumps, tight black slacks, and a hip-length fake fur jacket up the steps, into the lobby, and into the eleva-tor to the courthouse. Inside the elevator, the figure turned her back to the picture takers.

"Wow!" exclaimed a reporter. "That's a big one. Must be over six feet. I still don't know what she . . . he . . . looks like. She went by so fast, all I could see was dark glasses and hair."

"She had lipstick on, I think," said another reporter.

"And a lot of pancake makeup," another chimed in.

"Did you hear what she said to me?" a TV cameraman asked. "She said, 'Fuck you.'"

Everyone laughed. "Did you get it on tape? It'd be a good lead for the six o'clock news."

"Where're they going?" someone asked. "How come they didn't take her into the jail?"

No one knew, and they couldn't ask the dispatcher, because his door was locked. In a minute, however, Sheriff Clark appeared just long enough to let everyone know that Samantha would be back downstairs shortly. She'd been taken upstairs to a conference room for a briefing, as a courtesy gesture.

"Thanks, Bill," reporters called to the sheriff's disappearing back.

They'd have one last chance for a close-up of Samantha Glenner when she returned in the elevator and had to walk the fifteen or so feet across the lobby to the dispatch office. That is, if the officers brought her back by the elevator. They might choose to avoid the media by using the courthouse stairs to an inside hall of the sheriff's department.

"Someone's coming down, " announced a TV cameraman standing next to the elevator shaft.

Everyone stopped talking. The elevator door opened and Dave Giroux stepped out, then walked briskly through the path that reporters cleared for him to the dispatch office, where Bouchard held open the door. Nate escorted Samantha just as quickly through the throng to the glassed-in dispatch room. Reporters watched as they disappeared through another door into the heart of the jail.

Corrections Officer Dave Gordon looked up from his seat behind the booking desk and greeted Glenner and the two officers.

"We've explained to Ms. Glenner what to expect here," Nate said. "She says she'd like to be called either Samantha or Sam."

Bishop appeared from his office. He indicated a chair beside the booking desk and nodded to Gordon as Glenner sat down.

"All right, Samantha," Gordon said cheerfully, "we'll just play twenty questions here." With pen in hand, he read from the form in front of him. "Have you had TB? Hepatitis? Are you under psychiatric care? Are you pregnant?" Gordon chuckled. "No, I guess not. . . . Are you currently taking any birth control products?" Gordon laughed again, trying to put Glenner at ease.

Gordon was aware that his efforts weren't doing much to relieve the tension in the room. Glenner wasn't new to the booking-in process, he knew. But booking someone with long hair, makeup, and high heels who used to be, or still was, a male was new to Gordon.

Bishop, standing next to Glenner, spied a movement in the window behind Gordon's desk. He swore under his breath. Two reporters were peeking in at them from the hall off the lobby. Staring back coldly, Bishop yanked a curtain across the glass to block their view.

Gordon motioned Glenner to the camera and positioned her for several quick mug shots—a front view and two profiles. He'd taken Glenner's picture before, the day Amy's body was found, but Glenner had refused to be fingerprinted then. Gordon opened the ink pad on top of a tall file cabinet and politely asked Samantha to press her fingers into the pad. As he reached for her left hand to roll her inked fingertips and thumb across the white card, he brushed against her left breast.

He jerked his arm away. "Oh! Excuse me," he said quickly.

Samantha looked into Gordon's eyes and said softly, "They feel real, don't they?"

Gordon turned red. Bishop, clearing his throat, stepped to the cabinet next to them as Gordon finished fingerprinting Samantha. "We're going to put you in a cell by yourself," he said. He explained that they would do the strip search that was given everyone not eligible for immediate bail, then Samantha would don the fatigues that all the inmates wore. From the doctor's brief description of Glenner's anatomy, Bishop had determined a matron's presence was unnecessary.

He, Gordon, and Glenner, all at least six feet tall, stood next to one another in the cell. Gordon held a plastic garbage bag and freshly laundered green twill pants and shirt. He kept his eyes down deferentially as Bishop directed Glenner to remove her clothes, the black slacks first. Neither officer blinked as Samantha drew the pants off her long legs to reveal women's white underpants and nylon knee-highs. Bishop took the slacks from Samantha and handed them to Gordon, who folded them and placed them neatly into the bag.

"Your blouse next," said Bishop, his face expressionless, the ever-present tobacco wad held stationary in one cheek. His eyes swept casually over nylon-covered foam breasts and, around them, little dark marks like hen's feet.

My God, he thought. Stitches. They're sewn on. He was sure the breasts were a lot smaller than the ones Glenner had worn previously.

Underpants next, he indicated with a nod of his head. As Glenner stepped out of the panties, Bishop nearly swallowed his tobacco. What had Hogben gotten him into? The doctor had said that Glenner was a male, but all Bishop saw when he looked at the pubic area was hair. He didn't see a penis.

"Turn around, squat, and spread your cheeks," Bishop said, more sharply than he intended. The relief he felt when Glenner did so was quickly replaced by queasiness in his stomach. Glenner's penis was held between the legs in a small ring contraption.

Glenner straightened and said she had to use the toilet. Bishop stood by, still queasy, as Glenner squatted over the urinal and peed like a woman.

Glenner put the white panties back on and then the uniform that Gordon had handed her. She asked for the makeup case that her mother had brought to the jail while she was being booked. Without thinking, Bishop said no to that request. Then he softened.

He said they'd give Samantha her makeup before she went to court.

The door to the sheriff's office opened. The sheriff and Assistant Attorney General Nicholas Gess stepped into the lobby and were immediately surrounded by reporters.

Clark and Gess eyed the circle of eager faces and waited for questions. Reporters eyed them back, waiting for a statement.

Gess broke the ice. "At about four o'clock this afternoon, we arrested Glen Robert Askeborn, A-S-K-E-B-O-R-N, age forty-one, of Hancock. Askeborn is charged with the murder of Amelia Cave."

Reporters scribbled in their notebooks and looked up, expecting more. Gess told them that Askeborn had been indicted that morning in superior court in Ellsworth and would probably be arraigned on Wednesday.

That was all very well, but reporters had seen a woman walk by them and now they were told that her name was Glen Robert. They'd been hearing rumors, of course, but they needed more than rumors to file their stories.

A reporter on a weekly gave voice to the group's unspoken quandary: "Does the suspect have any aliases?" she asked.

"Yes," answered Gess smoothly. "Askeborn is also known as Samantha Glenner."

"So what do we have here? A male or a female?" asked a local radio newscaster.

Gess let the sheriff explain. "Glenner was dressed in female clothing when she was arrested," Clark said, "but she was examined by a physician, who determined she has the necessary organs to be classified as a male." He paused, watching the pencils catch up to his words. "She will be booked as a male, with a possible notation of transvestite tendencies."

"The classification is a technical one based on informed medical advice, for booking purposes only," Gess added.

"What do you mean by 'transvestite tendencies'? Is Askeborn a transsexual?" asked a reporter.

"Yes," Gess said, "that is a possibility."

"With transvestite tendencies," Clark said again.

More questions followed.

"Has he started a sex change operation?" "Is he taking hormones?" "How long has he been a she?"

The sheriff said they couldn't comment because of confidentiality. Gess explained that certain medical records are protected by law.

Changing course, reporters asked about the investigation. What led police to the Askeborn shore, and what evidence did they have against Glenner?

Clark and Gess again declined comment, saying that these details were part of an ongoing investigation. But they could say that Askeborn would be held in the Hancock County jail in a segregated cell, not because of any particular regulation, the sheriff said, but as a matter of policy allowing him discretion in such decisions. Askeborn would remain there at least until arraignment. After that, if he wasn't released on bail, other arrangements might be made.

Television reporters asked Clark and Gess to step outside to speak on camera. Other reporters eavesdropped in the background, hoping to hear something new. They didn't.

As the press conference ended, Stu Marckoon rushed to his KISS Radio van in the sheriff's department yard and broke the news on the air of Glen Robert Askeborn's arrest.

I returned to the *Ellsworth American* office, checked my desk for messages, and made a beeline to the darkroom in the basement, anxious to see if I'd captured Samantha Glenner on film. I rewound the film in my camera and placed scissors, opener, reel, and canister on the counter in the order I'd need them. Then I locked the darkroom door and turned off the light.

My fingers, working blind, found the release button on the bottom of the camera and removed the film cartridge. Launching into the familiar routine, I closed my eyes and relaxed against the counter, breathing slowly and deeply.

How peaceful after the bedlam in the jail lobby. I'd chosen a place against the wall opposite the elevator, adjusted camera settings by guess, and focused on a spot in thin air midway between the elevator and the dispatch doors, hoping that no one in the crowded lobby would block my lens at the crucial moment. When I heard the elevator door open and saw movement through the lens, I pressed the shutter button. I'd caught only a glimpse of the blurred figure, so close that I could have reached out and touched it.

Touched *him*? My eyes flew open and my hands started to shake. Touched Askeborn? Amy's killer?

My body was trembling, too. Thirty minutes ago he'd walked past me and I'd felt nothing at all. I'd been too busy. Now in the darkroom I was no longer the reporter concentrating on lens opening, speed, and focus.

But why was I shaking? I'd covered car crashes, fires, gravel pit cave-ins, and even other murders, and never reacted this way before.

But this was Amy's killer. What was I supposed to be, a robot with no feelings? I was furious. How could that monster even think of hurting Amy? I could see her fighting, struggling for her life, scared to death. Then it hit me: I was scared, too.

Amy's murder was too close to home. We'd built new homes at the same time and only a few miles apart. We both lived alone, and like Amy, I was probably too friendly and trusting of strangers; I was a patsy for down-and-outers.

My shaking subsided as I tended to the film, and my head took over again: I didn't know for sure that Askeborn killed Amy. I was a reporter and it was my job to be fair and objective. And I would be, I knew. In the newspaper I'd stick to facts. In the privacy of the darkroom, though, I'd allow myself to feel.

Not that I'd had much choice.

I pulled the film from the rinse water and, holding it to the light, scanned the strip of negatives. One frame jumped out from the rest. The huge figure, sharp and clear, promised to be a good print. I hung the dripping film in the drying cabinet and left the darkroom.

Upstairs at my desk I read my notes from the press conference, reached for a dictionary, and looked under *T*. A transsexual is a person with such a strong psychological urge to belong to the opposite sex that it may be carried to the point of undergoing surgery to modify sex organs. A transvestite is a person, especially a male, who adopts the behavior and often the dress typical of the opposite sex, especially for the purposes of emotional or sexual gratification.

"She will be booked as a male," Bill Clark had said. What strange phrasing. I could only imagine the problems that sexual ambiguity had created in Askeborn's life. My problem was only one of semantics.

Mel Stone looked up from the papers on his desk as I approached it. "You got a minute?" I asked.

Mel, a soft-spoken, gentle man, always had time to listen, even under deadline pressure when everyone else was frantic. Whoever had his attention had it completely.

I sat in the chair beside his desk. "Mel, I don't know whether to call Glenner 'he' or 'she.' At the jail they're using both genders in the same sentence."

"What do you think we should call her?" he asked, then laughed. "Or him. . . . I see what you mean."

"I'm inclined to go with 'him,'" I said, "because, according to what they told us, he is an anatomical male."

"You don't think intention determines gender?"

"Well, if one of my kids came to me saying she felt like a man—whatever that means—and wanted to change her gender, I'd have some feelings to struggle with, of course. But I like to think I'd respect her wishes."

"I understand," Mel said. He had sons; I had daughters.

"However," I continued, "Askeborn skipped out on warrants for his arrest in Connecticut. Maybe he changed his name and dressed like a woman to hide from the law. I don't know, Mel. I'd probably be more sympathetic to Askeborn's problems with sexual identity if he weren't accused of killing Amy."

"Presumed innocent?" Mel reminded me.

"I know," I said and stood up to leave. "Maybe the solution is to invent a new pronoun, something gender neutral, just as 'Ms.' was created to avoid defining women by their marital status."

"Why don't you work on that?" Mel suggested. "We have a few more days before press time to decide Askeborn's gender."

I laughed. "Talk about the power of the press."

Smelly fumes that I'd unleashed from the big brown bottles of chemicals made my eyes smart. I squeezed wooden tongs onto the corner of the white paper and agitated it gently in the tray of developer. When confronted with a clear picture of Askeborn, would I start shaking again? I wondered.

Under the rippling surface, an image began to emerge in the glow of the red safelight. A huge cuff on a fake fur jacket hung from a thick wrist. A large hand appeared and grew rings on the pinky and fourth finger. The head sprouted hair, which fell forward to the corners of thin, parted lips and disappeared under the jacket collar. Bangs hid the forehead, dark sunglasses the eyes. A long, chiseled nose and jutting chin appeared against a frame of frizzy hair.

So, Glen Robert Askeborn, or Samantha Glenner, here you are. You're very large. I don't know what you look like as a man, but you're a strange-looking woman. So you think putting on makeup and jewelry and letting your hair grow makes you a woman?

I had a sudden urge to wipe the lipstick from my mouth. The face in the tray mocked me. What right did it have to make fun of me? It was the phony. I wasn't.

I shoved the accusing photo into the stop tray and swished it around. I submerged it in the fix, then left it to rinse clean under a stream of running water.

Two days later, Askeborn/Glenner, in sunglasses, lipstick and rouge, a black-and-white pantsuit, and heels, pleaded not guilty to murder. Philip Foster—a lawyer retained by Mr. and Mrs. Askeborn—and court-appointed attorney Sandra Collier asked the judge to set bail and free their client.

Completely inappropriate, protested Nicholas Gess. The defendant had a record of violence and was now charged with another violent crime.

But, countered Collier, there was no risk of her client fleeing. Glenner had reported faithfully to her parole officer in Connecticut for twenty months. And in Hancock, even when she was aware of being the focus of a long investigation, she hadn't left the county. Foster pointed out that the whole family had cooperated with the police, phoning when they left home or leaving notes saying where they could be reached.

Justice Donald Alexander denied bail, citing the indictment by the grand jury and the test of "proof evident and presumption great" that the defendant had committed the crime of murder.

Guards led Askeborn from the courtroom to his cell in the jail two stories below.

Defense attorney Collier had consistently referred to her client as "she." Foster had made one reference to "he." The *Ellsworth American* opted for anatomy over psychology and called the accused "he."

Steve Coffin reached into the cooler for his daily bottle of Pabst Blue Ribbon. On his way to the checkout counter, his eyes fell on the stack of *Ellsworth Americans*. Holy shit! he thought. He knew the face that jumped out at him under the bold headline: "HANCOCK MAN CHARGED IN CAVE MURDER."

That was her, all right. Not quite the vision he'd seen last summer; the loose fur jacket in the photo hid some of her charms. He read the caption under the picture: "Forty-one-year-old Glen Robert Askeborn, also known as Samantha Glenner"—yes, that was the name—"was dressed as a woman Monday when he was arrested and brought to the Hancock County jail, charged with the murder of Amelia Cave of North Sullivan."

Coffin reached for the paper with his free hand and hesitated. Myrna usually picked up the *Ellsworth American*. But this was something he wanted to read right now. He paid the clerk and walked out the door and through the parking lot of Hancock Grocery, one eye out for traffic, the other scanning the front-page article. "Arrested more than a month after the murder . . . charged in secret indictment . . . examined by a physician at the Maine Coast Memorial Hospital . . . classified as male . . . denied bail . . . record of violence . . ."

"Hey, Coffin. How ya doin'?"

Steve looked up. "Richard, you devil! You knew all about this, didn't you?" Coffin held up the paper accusingly.

Chief Deputy Dickson, Coffin's pal and neighbor, glanced at the paper and chuckled.

"You know, I've seen this babe before. Up at Merchant's Garage."

"Yeah?" said Dickson. "When was that?"

"Oh, just a couple months ago. She was some sight, I'll tell you. Got a minute?" Coffin knew that Dickson was on his way home from the sheriff's department, but he'd put in a long day, too, both in the classroom at Ellsworth High and outside with his track teams after school. Dickson checked his watch and nodded.

"Well, here I am in Merchant's Garage, waiting to pay Rick for some small job—replacing a muffler, maybe. No, an oil change, I think it was. And into this atmosphere of grease and grime floats this giant flower. This Amazon."

Dickson grinned. Steve wasn't an English teacher for nothing. Dickson could just picture him in the classroom regaling students with his stories.

"She had on a long, flouncy dress covered with flowers. Peonies, maybe. Big red or pink peonies. With puffy shoulder deals cinched tight on her upper arms. And that tremendous bustline. I thought, What a set of boobs on this gal. You know?"

Dickson raised an eyebrow. He knew, all right.

"She had long, blond hair, which I figured out later must be a wig. I tried to be polite and not stare while she was talking to Rick in this forced sexy voice. But everything about her caught your attention."

"Yeah, I know," said Dickson. "You try not to stare, but you keep sneaking those little looks."

"That's right. I kept looking from the corner of my eye, trying to figure out what the hell I was looking at. Something about this big-breasted, blonde giant with her flamboyant way just didn't seem right. The parts didn't fit together. She had these big biceps, big triceps. I lift weights, but this was something else. Her arms were goose-pimply and red, like she'd used a depilatory or something. Her face was rough, too, and very red.

"When she left, I said, 'For God's sake, Rick, I don't understand what I was looking at.' He said, 'Oh that. That's just Sam.' I said, 'Yeah, but what is it? There's a story here, I know.' Rick just laughed and said, 'Well, Sam's a guy that doesn't know if he wants to be a man or a woman or what. He calls himself Samantha Glenner and has all kinds of problems.'"

"If he didn't before, he sure does now," Dickson said. He looked at his watch again. "I really better—" he began, but Coffin, not ready to let him go yet, cut him short.

"Richard, why didn't I know I was looking at a man? Did you, when you first saw her?"

Dickson hesitated. "Well, no. No, I didn't," he admitted, then added brightly, "but Karen did. She knew right away."

"No kidding. Hey, isn't this whole thing bizarre? You have this woman—the Cave woman. Ha! Cavewoman! Anyway, she comes up to Maine for peace and quiet and, ironically, she finds it. And you have the absolutely sad case of this poor devil, a giant, calling himself Samantha, who builds a stone wall on the shore, for God's sake. Can you imagine any clammer, any local guy, walking around it, scratching his head, saying, 'What the hell? A stone wall here?' He knows the ice will get it. What would we do for entertainment without these clowns from away?"

"Yep, it's weird, all right." Dickson had lived outside the state for years, but his roots were in Maine. "I gotta go, Steve. We still going hunting this month?"

"Sure, if you can break away from all your crime fighting."

"Hey, Coffin, we're talking deer-hunting season here. I have my priorities, you know. See ya later."

The huge hands with the rings caught Thelma Beal's eye first. She'd seen those hands before, lugging buckets full of clams into her fish market. She smoothed out the front page of the paper on the top of the seafood case and studied the photo of Samantha Glenner.

She'd been alone in the shop when the bell jingled as the tall figure pushed open her front door and asked if she wanted to buy some freshly dug clams. She'd squelched an immediate sense of uneasiness and arranged her face in a businesslike mask.

"Let's see the product," she said casually.

The clams looked good. She named a price and the woman agreed. Said her name was Samantha. They went outside to weigh the clams on a wood platform scale. As Samantha bent over to scoop the clams back into the buckets, Thelma checked her out: a practical blue skirt, simple sleeveless top, enormous bustline, and smooth, perfect hair, as though she'd just come from the beauty parlor.

The woman had looked up suddenly. Thelma was embarrassed, as though she'd been caught staring at someone's raspberry birthmark.

But Samantha's eyes held hers, sending the message, That's all right; I'm used to it.

Thelma, still embarrassed, coughed and turned to hold open the door. Inside, Samantha offered to carry the buckets into the cooler for her. Thelma felt a flash of alarm. She didn't want to be alone in the small, cold room with this disconcerting person. But she didn't want to risk offending her, either.

She stepped into the cooler and pointed to a large plastic tray on the floor. Samantha leaned over, poured out the clams, and stood to her full height facing Thelma, their bodies only inches apart. Their eyes met. Unable to stop herself, Thelma stared openly at the face covered with thick pancake makeup and was shocked to see the dark stubble of a man's whiskers.

My God, what have we here? Not in Ellsworth, Maine, she thought.

The tall figure backed slowly out of the cooler. Thelma's heart was still pounding as she laid the money for the clams into the palm of his large hand. "Thank you," he said in his strange high voice. When he left, Thelma started shaking.

She didn't think she'd been afraid. Unsettled, maybe. Now as she read the article below the picture of the familiar face, she realized that it was one thing to be alone in her shop with a strange-looking person. It was quite another to be alone with someone capable of murder.

The smell of lentil soup filled the Duscheks' large kitchen and even wafted to the downstairs workshop, where Felix was repairing an antique Seth Thomas clock.

Gusti stirred the soup and, at a sound overhead, looked up. Mimi, the gray tabby, looked down at her from a favorite perch on the beam across the center of the room. Mauzerl had taught Mimi, and Little Tot, too, to jump from the refrigerator and maneuver along the beam to the best vantage point for keeping an eye on all that went on below.

Gusti smiled, aware that Mimi's yellow eyes were following her across the room to the round table by the picture window that overlooked the road and woods beyond. She arranged napkins, soup bowls, and spoons on two flowered placemats. Samantha Glenner's picture stared up at her from the folded paper that Felix had laid on the table an hour ago.

Gusti turned the picture facedown. She and Felix were still smarting from the betrayal by Wes and Glenn Askeborn, who were supposedly their friends.

Friends don't lie to you and make fools of you.

Gusti and Felix had figured out what really happened last Monday, the day Samantha was arrested, by listening to news reports. Samantha was arrested at her home in mid-afternoon, and Wes and Glenn followed the police cruiser to Ellsworth in their own car. What the news didn't say was that while Samantha was being examined at the hospital, Wes and Glenn stopped by the Duscheks' house, near the hospital.

Felix had answered the knock at the door and was surprised to see Wes standing there. Glenn stayed in the car. Wes asked Felix if he had heard anything new about Amy's murder. Before Felix could answer, Gusti, who was downstairs making Christmas wreaths with the radio on, shouted up the stairs to them. "Come down and listen," she called excitedly. "They're saying on the radio someone's been arrested for Amy's murder and they're about to tell who it is."

But Wes said no, they had things to do and couldn't stay. He left without saying anything about Samantha's arrest.

As Felix said with disgust later when they figured out the timing of the Askeborns' visit, "They just came by to find out what we knew."

With that brief visit, they realized now, their friendship with the Askeborns had come to an abrupt end.

"Felix!" Gusti called down the stairwell. "Soup's ready." Lentil soup, Felix's favorite, drew him upstairs in a hurry. As he sat down, Little Tot appeared and rubbed against his leg. He picked up his spoon. Neither Little Tot nor the newspaper at the edge of the table could distract him now.

But whether or not Felix and Gusti spoke of it, the Askeborns and Amy's murder were nearly always on their minds. After all, it had been only a few days since they'd learned that their friends' son had been charged with the murder of another friend. And they'd thought that the son was a woman.

Glenn, whom they first met when she came to their house the year before to have an antique clock repaired, had kept Samantha under wraps until just this past summer. The paper said Samantha was known in the community as the Askeborns' niece, but Glenn had told them that Samantha was a cousin.

Sometimes when the Duscheks visited the Askeborns, Glenn would refer to her cousin and point vaguely in the direction of another room, and they'd hear stirrings behind the closed door. When the Duscheks invited the Askeborns to their home, they'd tell them to bring Samantha, too. But they'd always reply that Samantha was busy or not feeling well.

Then one evening last summer when the Duscheks arrived for dinner at the Askeborns, seated on the couch was the huge figure of Samantha. Somehow, their conversation turned to the subject of Samantha's size, and Glenn made a light remark about how difficult it was for Samantha having such large breasts. *Humongous* was the word Felix was thinking. Gusti, trying to be helpful, suggested breast reduction. Felix, trying to be helpful, too, laughed and said, "Oh, why do that? I say, the more the merrier."

Even though they'd seen Samantha several more times, in their own home, too, it had never occurred to them that she wasn't a woman. A strange-looking woman, for sure. Thinking maybe there'd been a problem at birth, Felix felt sorry for her.

They met Amy at the Askeborns last summer, too, and began their own friendship with her. They liked that she didn't gossip about people and wasn't pretentious, which they both thought that Glenn was. Eventually Amy told them about the rumor that she was having an affair with her house builder. She said there were other lies, too. She was bothered, of course, but the Duscheks thought she was handling it well. They liked Amy; she was fun and a kind person.

Since the arrest, the Duscheks had been looking with new eyes at Samantha, and her parents as well. Wes had seemed so adoring of

Glenn. He waited on her as though she were a queen. Maybe he wanted to put his foot down about Samantha, but he always let Glenn rule the roost.

If only the Askeborns had told them about Samantha instead of letting them find out from the radio. What kind of people hid their own child, no matter how different he or she was? And it had been a slap in the face when the Askeborns had stopped by to see them but said nothing about Samantha's arrest.

The Duscheks would never see Amy again, and right now they wanted nothing to do with Glenn and Wesley Askeborn. There were too many secrets, too many lies, and too little trust.

"The soup's wonderful as usual, Gusti," Felix said. She reached for his bowl to fill it again.

Mimi, crouched like a sphinx on the beam overhead, squinted open one jeweled eye to track Gusti as she passed below to the stove.

When she saw the picture flash across the TV screen on the evening news, Shirley called out to her husband, "Look, look! That's Skip."

The announcer was calling him Samantha Glenner. Shirley could never think of Skip Askeborn as a woman. He was a tall, good-looking man with absolutely nothing effeminate about him. And the Skip she knew couldn't possibly have killed Amy.

She had known the Askeborns for about ten years and had met Skip when he visited his parents, alone, then with Martha, his bride-to-be. Shirley had gone to Bar Harbor and Schoodic Point with Skip and his mother. Skip had been so appreciative about the beauty of the Maine coast, even more than Glenn, she thought.

The news of Skip's arrest was shocking enough. That he was Samantha was unbelievable. Why would that nice-looking, personable man ever want to be a woman? Shirley had been walking around in a daze, trying to sort truth from the web of deceit spun by Skip and his parents.

What was it that Glenn had told her before she met Skip? That he worked for NASA in Texas? Yes, and that he was coming out of a bad first marriage and his wife wouldn't let him or any of the family see his child.

Probably the part about marriage and the child was true. But NASA? A cover-up for his years in prison, she realized now.

All that business about Skip going to Saudi Arabia to work in the oil fields had been another cover-up, of course, to explain his disappearance when he became Samantha. But Glenn had gone into such detail about the Saudi customs, their attitude toward women, the country's extreme heat. Glenn would love to visit Skip there, she'd said, but she knew she couldn't stand the heat.

Then Glenn had told her about her niece, Samantha, who was coming to live with her after going through a bad divorce. Now Shirley understood why she'd never met Samantha. Her husband had asked her if she didn't find that strange. She hadn't, at the time.

One day Shirley had dropped in on Glenn and heard a flurry in the next room. Glenn said it was Samantha and that she didn't want to meet Shirley because she'd been scuba diving and her hair was a mess. Glenn had joked about Samantha's diving and her being from such "tough Norwegian stock."

How many other times had she been taken in? It hurt her to think of all the lies. It's true what they say about lies, she thought. You tell one and you have to tell another.

Shame must have been at the bottom of all that covering up. Maybe all the things you don't face, that you push down and cover over, build up steam and have to explode. The whole family must have felt tremendous pressure, living their lies.

Glenn had been the one who called her with the news that Amy was missing. What a time that had been. None of them could imagine why anyone would kill Amy, so they thought a maniac was on the loose in their community. People began locking their doors even during the day when they were home.

Rumors were flying, too. One day right after they'd found Amy's body, she was at the meat case in Dunbar's Store when she overheard a man telling others that Wesley Askeborn was the killer. Incensed,

Shirley had told them, "Absolutely not!" She knew these people, and Wes Askeborn was no murderer.

But the family's cover-up seemed so calculating and unnecessary. Although probably if she'd seen Samantha, she would've recognized Skip—she did when she saw his picture on the news. If she'd been told the truth, though, she was sure she would have felt compassion for Wes and Glenn. She did, even now. She'd never know if she could have found the same compassion for Skip.

Considering what had happened to Amy, she was glad she hadn't been put to the test.

Chapter Thirteen

T HE HANCOCK COUNTY JAIL, sandwiched between the Ellsworth library and WDEA radio station on the bank of the Union River, was set discreetly back from the street at the rear of the courthouse.

Samantha Glenner joined the small jail community on a Monday. At first, the underlying rhythm of daily routine kept things on an even keel. The bread man delivered his standing order at 5 A.M. as usual, and the milkman arrived at 5:30. At 6:30 the guards turned on the lights and woke the inmates. A half-hour later they unlocked the pass-through to the kitchen and carried breakfast trays into the cells; afterward, they counted the knives on the returning trays. They passed out medications, shaving cream, and razors and watched like hawks to make sure that all the razors came back with blades. Jail inspection followed a flurry of activity with brooms and dustpans, mops and buckets, as inmates cleaned their own cellblocks. And inmates had their hour in the exercise yard as usual, weather permitting.

But tension was creeping in, setting everyone on edge, and it couldn't all be laid on Glenner.

She wasn't the only murder suspect in the Hancock County jail. Philip Willoughby was there, too. He'd been transferred from the jail in Kennebec County the day before Glenner was brought in.

Bishop had good reason for the special directive he issued Monday morning. A corrections officer typed the order into the log in block letters: "MAKE SURE DOOR FROM COURTHOUSE BASEMENT IS CLOSED AND LOCKED WHEN WILOUGHBY IS IN JAIL DAY OR NIGHT. MUST BE CHECKED. BE SURE TO PASS ON TO YOUR RELIEF."

Willoughby was accused of the kidnapping and murder of University of Maine student Paula Roberts over the Christmas holidays when she was working at an ice-cream stand near Augusta.

On Monday, November 5, when jury selection for Willoughby's trial began upstairs in superior court, deputies stood guard in the corridors and at the courtroom doors. Everyone entering the courtroom had to pass through a metal detector, an unheard-of measure in Hancock County. The word was that someone had threatened Donald Alexander, the judge hearing the case. There was concern, as well, about the safety of witnesses and of Willoughby himself.

Willoughby's stepbrother had also been charged with Roberts's murder. When the two Willoughbys started accusing each other, the judge ordered their trials separated. The stepbrother had been cleared, but family members, loyalties divided and passions inflamed, were now pitted against one another.

In mid-afternoon on Monday, Bishop ordered a lockdown in the jail, and Dave Gordon entered another order in the jail log: "INMATES NOT ALLOWED TO GO INTO OTHER CELLBLOCKS FOR ANYTHING." They'd be allowed into the dayroom of their cellblocks for meals only, and outside in the yard for their daily hour of exercise one cellblock at a time.

While Willoughby was in court on Monday afternoon watching the tedious process of jury selection, corrections officers moved his few belongings from Brown cellblock to the adjacent Blue in preparation for Glenner's arrival. The two cells in Brown opened onto a dayroom, and Glenner, designated a special-management inmate, would occupy the entire cellblock alone. State law required the staff to check these special inmates every fifteen minutes around the clock and keep a written record of each check. A seg log, it was called. Glenner was to be segregated in the block usually reserved for juveniles or women.

The lockdown ended sociability in the jail and didn't set well with some inmates, one of whom demanded to talk to his attorney. At 5:09 P.M., while Glenner was being booked in, a corrections officer logged the complaint: "Randall running off at the mouth about being locked up all the time."

Bishop ordered a corrections officer to keep watch all night in the observation room, the glassed-in cubicle in a corner of the large multipurpose room at the center of the jail. From this vantage point, a guard could see the colored doors—brown, blue, tan, green, orange, and gray—to all six cellblocks around the perimeter of the room, which ordinarily served as the inmates' lounge, dining, and TV room. Now, until lockdown was lifted, the lounge would be off-limits.

Tuesday, Election Day, brought some relief to the staff. The courthouse was closed, so no one had to escort inmates back and forth to district or superior court for bail hearings, arraignments, and trials, or stand guard outside the courtroom.

On Wednesday, jury selection resumed in Willoughby's trial and Glenner was arraigned. The judge's denial of bail, not unexpected, called for a decision about where Glenner would stay.

Neither Bishop nor Clark wanted their small jail burdened with the long-term care of a special-management inmate. Glenner's trial would be months away, and the jail was already turning away juveniles from other counties because Glenner occupied the space designated for them.

The Maine State Prison in Thomaston agreed to take Glenner. The sheriff, although he could transfer an inmate to another county facility anytime he wanted, needed a court order for transfer to a state facility.

On Wednesday afternoon, Clark handed his motion for transfer to superior court clerk Rosemary Merchant, and she placed it in the wire basket on her desk. She'd show it to the judge, she said, and let Bill know when a hearing was scheduled.

"By the way, Bill," Rosemary said, a gleam in her eye, "congratulations. We all knew you'd wipe out your opposition." Rosemary was not the first to kid him about his victory in the previous day's election.

"I know. I ran such a top-notch campaign that my opponent was virtually invisible." Bill rolled his eyes at Rosemary and left her office.

The truth was that no one had opposed him in the election. He hadn't needed to campaign at all. He hated standing up in front of people, tooting his own horn. He'd had enough of that in the June primary when Ted Springer ran against him on his own party ticket.

Sometimes Clark wondered why he'd wanted the job as sheriff, anyway. He hadn't expected it to have so little to do with solving crimes and so much with personnel and financial matters, contract negotiations, and problems with their jail. He hadn't had time to be involved with jail matters when he first took office. But when his jail administrator left, he didn't have a choice.

Thinking about that reminded him that he needed to check a jail budget item with the county commission clerk. He headed down the hall to the commission office.

The courts, in the jockeying between individual rights and the rights of the public, had for some time been coming down on the side of the individual, insisting that inmates be treated much the same as citizens at large. The state had responded with sweeping revisions in jail standards. As a result, the Hancock County jail, only five years old, needed radical overhauling to comply with the new standards.

"Congratulations, Bill," said Clerk Jean LaBelle, looking up from her desk.

He steeled himself for a ribbing, then saw she was serious. "Thanks, Jean."

He finished his business quickly and walked back down the hall to the stairs.

Clark was glad he'd found Bishop up in Aroostook County. Although Bishop had spent more time with the Aroostook County Sheriff's Department than the jail division, he'd certainly done a good job with the Hancock County jail. Just last month, when Bishop had been on the job only six months, the evaluation report for county jails had come out, and Hancock County received high marks in everything but the facility itself. They were stuck with a new, out-of-date jail.

While Clark was at dispatch talking with Larson, he saw Bishop drive into the yard. Watching as Bishop and Nate escorted Glenner up the front steps, Clark realized they were returning from the doctor's office in Blue Hill. As they walked past him on their way to the jail, Clark caught Nate's eye and, with a nod of his head, indicated he'd be in his office. In two minutes, Nate joined him there.

"So, what happened?" Bill asked.

"What happened?" Nate repeated. "Samantha lost her femininity, that's what."

"What do you mean?"

"The doctor got rid of her breasts. Cut them off with a razor."

"Shit, Nate. What the hell are you talking about?"

Nate, who'd been standing in the doorway, crossed the room to sit in a chair beside Bill's desk. "What I'm talking about are Glenner's falsies. They weren't stitched on, like Bishop thought. They were glued on, and her chest hair had grown into the nylon and foam rubber. Bishop probably mistook the matted hair for stitches. Anyway, it was a mess. Tyler had to use a razor to get the falsies off. Well, one of them, anyway. The other one was already falling off."

"Yeah, but who told him to get rid of the things in the first place? I'm not so sure that was a good idea."

"Oh, I see," said Nate. "Samantha's attorneys have got you worried. It's okay, Bill. You know that smell Bishop was talking about? It was a skin disease. Impetigo, I think. The doc had to remove the falsies to treat the skin. He prescribed some stuff for the rash."

"Okay. As long as there was a medical reason. I just want to be very careful about Glenner's rights. His lawyers have been trying to educate me about transsexualism. I'm doing my best to understand, but you know I'm just a simple country boy at heart."

"Good luck, Bill. I'm glad it's not my job to understand the psyche of everyone I arrest. To me this is just a murder case."

The phone on Bill's desk rang. While he was talking, Bishop came in and sat next to Nate. "What's going on?" he asked.

"Bill's working on sympathy for transsexuals," Nate said. "Tolerance, sophisticated attitudes, and all that."

Bishop grimaced. "Me, too. I'm developing more sympathy than I know what to do with. This morning I gave Samantha back her cosmetics case."

"Good for you, Bish. I hear you give Willoughby makeup to cover the scars on his face."

"Well, that's different. Can't let a scar prejudice the jury, you know."

Bill, who'd been dividing his attention between their conversation and his phone call, hung up. "I'm more interested in hormones," he said, returning to the conversation. "What did Tyler say about that, Bish?"

"The doctor talked a long time with Glenner," Bishop said. "He decided, on the basis of her history, not to recommend regular use of estrogen for the time being."

"I'll bet we haven't heard the end of hormones," Bill said. "Our next step is getting her transferred out of here."

Bishop stood up. "My next step is to call Mrs. Askeborn and have her come pick up her son's breasts."

Clark raised his eyebrows. "Oh? Where are they now?"

"In my office," Bishop said. "In a paper bag."

On Wednesday night, Al Luck, a corrections officer, came to work well before midnight as usual. He liked working the midnight shift alone with no boss looking over his shoulder. From the booking room he could see the dispatcher and yell to him if he needed backup. Dispatcher Linc Ehrlenbach, especially, always seemed to know immediately when something was wrong and would come back to help. If there was trouble in the jail when Debbie was dispatching, she'd call the Ellsworth Police Department, across the street, for reinforcements.

Larson was on the phone as Luck walked through dispatch to the jail. Dave Gordon, nearing the end of his four-to-midnight shift, was booking a guy on a domestic violence complaint.

Leaving Dave to catch up on the log, Luck went outside for the routine yard and vehicle check. The night air was balmy for early November. He flashed his light along the base of the wood fence around the exercise yard and into the white van parked beside it, then glanced up at the lighted windows in the brick wall of the jail. Behind one of the front windows, he knew, Glenner would be sleeping. She was always asleep before lights out at midnight.

When Luck returned to the booking room, Gordon, still at his typewriter, asked him to put Randall back in his cell. Randall had complained that he hadn't had his full hour in the exercise yard during the day, so Gordon had made an exception to the lockdown and let him use the weight machine in the multipurpose room. Then Luck did his jail check: thirteen inmates inside, one in visiting, waiting for a ride home, and one trusty allowed special privileges—Roode—out cleaning the floors. Luck gave Willoughby a second bedsheet, brought an extra blanket to Reynolds, who had complained that he was cold, and was about to return to booking when Palmer called out from the maximum security cell. He said that something had just hit his cell window.

Luck stayed inside while Gordon and Lenny Ober, who happened to be in the patrol room, went outside with their portables and flashlights to investigate. Gordon climbed onto the first-floor roof of the courthouse while Ober searched the grounds below. They found nothing. Luck reassured Palmer and promised to keep an ear out the rest of the night.

It was nearly twelve-thirty when Luck sat down with Gordon for a briefing on the evening shift. The county always got more than its money's worth at a change of shifts, when the new corrections officer arrived early and the departing one stayed past the end of his shift.

Roode returned from cleaning the floors, Gordon left for home, and the jail finally belonged to Luck.

He'd spend most of the night as he had Monday and Tuesday, in the observation room, a confining but peaceful twilight zone overlooking the dark jail. Ambient light filtered in from the laundry and booking rooms behind him. The jail, an echo chamber, magnified every sound. He could hear inmates whispering, even breathing, in their cells. Very different from five months ago when he started the job.

Then, when the guards dimmed the lights, the inmates took over and turned the jail into a jungle. The result was that they were comatose most of the next day. With Bishop's blessing, he and Joel Guildford, the other night man, had insisted that inmates get up for breakfast, exercise regularly, and stick to a disciplined schedule all day. Instead of simply turning down the lights at midnight, or at 2 A.M. on weekends, they cut the lights completely. A flash from the cellblocks told them that an inmate had lit a cigarette. If the light didn't die out immediately, they knew that someone had a "jail candle" going. They'd go in and confiscate the contraption, usually a bar of soap with a wick of string or thread.

Last July, Luck wouldn't have been able to hear the crinkle of plastic on a mattress as an inmate turned over, or the sound of running water. Now he could tell whether the water was cold or hot.

Tonight he was late turning off the lights and making his first log entry. He drew the log toward him and in the light from his Mini-Mag flashlight wrote, "Checked white van. Okay. Locked and sealed," the same entry he'd made at the beginning and end of every shift since the big drug bust in Corea in mid-July, five days after he started the job. Everyone said it was the department's biggest bust ever.

They'd confiscated the white Dodge van, a brown sedan, two Zodiak boats, other equipment, and eighty-seven bales of marijuana—nearly two tons, which, figured by the ounce, had a street value of about $5 million. The bales were still stashed inside the white van parked beside the exercise yard. Someday, the sheriff joked, they'd pour oil on the marijuana and burn it right there next to the jail while inmates gathered at the windows, inhaling and weeping.

At 1 A.M. the Ellsworth Police Department brought in an arrest, and Luck left his post to call Ray Saunders, one of the bail commissioners. While Saunders did his paperwork, Luck made a jail check. Glenner was asleep, which Luck would note in the seg report. He looked in on the rest of the inmates, and all fourteen were sleeping like babies.

Asleep, one inmate was the same as another to Luck. It made no difference that Glenner and Willoughby were charged with murder, and Walls with the attempted murder of an elderly woman he'd robbed, assaulted, and left for dead. Or that Randall was an escape risk; he'd jumped over the fence in the exercise yard last spring. That's why there was razor wire on top of the fence now. The escape had also convinced the county commissioners that they needed a second guard on duty during the day.

Luck was grateful that when Madore was snoring, he wasn't banging on the shower or breaking things to get attention the minute the guard turned his back. And sacked out, the guy in Tan, who Luck thought was a complete loony (he crawled under his bunk and howled when the lights went out) was as sane as anyone. Luck had noticed that the guy's dilated pupils didn't change in the shine of his flashlight. He suspected that the fellow had some physical problem. Luck would keep an eye on him.

All in all, this was a heavy-duty bunch for the jail to have in its care all at the same time. No wonder Bishop had the jail in lockdown. Although Tuesday, when Luck had pulled a double shift and worked during the day, he'd realized again that the violence of their crimes wasn't any indicator of their behavior in jail.

The murderers and baby rapers could be pussycats, Luck had observed. Take Glenner, for instance. He . . . she was a model of politeness and cooperation. Willoughby, too. It didn't matter to Luck what they were charged with or whether they were guilty or innocent. How they behaved in jail was all that mattered to him.

Leafing through the seg log, Luck had noticed that some of the corrections officers referred to Glenner as "he" and some "she." Personally, he had no problem with Glenner's sex. If the guy wanted to be called a she, why not?

Luck raised his head to locate the sudden sound of splashing water. Someone in Orange was taking a leak. In a minute he heard the crackle of plastic—the guy was back in his bunk. It was probably Mr. Macho, the one Luck had heard bragging on the day shift on Tuesday that doing time was "nothing." He'd said, "I can do it standing on my head." Luck hadn't bothered to point out that might have something to do with the number of tranquilizers he was popping. A lot of the inmates were on meds: tranquilizers, antidepressants, and painkillers. A good 20 percent of the inmates insisted that they "needed something" for some pain somewhere.

Luck knew that the jail had some real problem guys, and it was hard sometimes not to think of them as scumbags. Especially the "golden oldies," the ones who kept coming back. Once, Luck and another corrections officer had looked through the old "jail bibles," the bound volumes listing all arrests, and seen the same names over and over. Crime was a generational thing, a way of life in some families, he thought. It was depressing to look at the birth announcements in the paper and see that one of these families had had another child.

Some of the longtime guards admitted taking pleasure when they wrote "Deceased" across the cover of a golden oldie's thick file. Sometimes, of course, a regular seemed to decide he was sick of spending time in jail, and he'd never be seen again. Or he'd turn thirty, thirty-five and finally grow up. But to consider jail as a "correctional" institution and himself as a "corrections" officer? He didn't think they corrected anybody.

At 4:58 A.M., Luck let the bread man into the kitchen and chatted with him—only for a minute, though, because the inmates were starting to wake up. He'd no longer be watching over inert bodies and would have to deal with personalities, egos, and a pecking order that, no matter what the jail population, seemed inevitable. There was always a boss and a hierarchy of domination by one inmate over another. Of course Luck was the top boss, the big daddy of the whole jail family. When there was screaming and hollering in a cellblock, he'd go in and ask them to please keep it down. When that didn't work, he'd get a little tougher: "Hey, just shut up!" When that failed, he'd threaten to take away first their TVs and then their tobacco, and then to lock them in their cells. The other day he'd had to resort to tougher measures when a guy got out of control; he was setting fires, attacking other inmates, stopping up the johns, and letting the water run. He'd flooded the jail twice. Luck stripped the guy to his undershorts and shackled him to his bunk, and still he was yelling up a storm. He finally told the guy to shut up or he'd strip him bare and call in the other inmates to make fun of his pecker. The threat kept the guy quiet for forty-eight hours.

Threats weren't something that Luck would boast about to the shrinks who came in to counsel inmates, but the shrinks didn't have to live with loonies.

This morning, Luck's jail family was cooperative, making only a few demands, which he took care of easily. He liked it better when being courteous and respectful worked.

Glenner had breakfast at 7:12 A.M. A half hour later, when Luck entered Brown to retrieve Glenner's tray, he brought her tan vinyl cosmetics case so she could primp for her appearance in court. This was special treatment. Not even the women housed overnight in this cell were allowed makeup. Luck had checked the twenty or so bottles inside to make sure they contained only cosmetics. Then, concerned about the broken mirror in the flip-up top of the case, Luck stood near Glenner as she dotted the thick beige paste onto her cheekbones, chin, and forehead. Luck was careful not to stare, but in the few casual glances he allowed himself, it seemed to him that the tall, quiet inmate had done a tasteful job. Perhaps her lawyers had advised her to go easy on the makeup.

Thursday was supposed to be the last day of jury selection for Willoughby's trial, but trouble developed Wednesday. And on Thursday, the trial came to a halt. It would have to wait until the Maine Supreme Judicial Court issued a ruling on the exact nature of privileged communications. Alexander continued the trial and dismissed the jurors. The move was unusual, he explained, but was in this case necessary in the interest of justice.

On Thursday morning, the staff began arranging for Willoughby's transport back to jail in his own county. Glenner was due in court, and the day corrections officer prepared himself for the clamor he knew was about to erupt. As he led Glenner from her cell, inmates, peering through the narrow windows of the cell doors, began banging on the doors and hooting and yelling comments. Glenner, striding through the multipurpose room, paid them no attention.

Upstairs in the courtroom, Sheriff Clark argued to have Samantha Glenner transferred to the state prison in Thomaston. Segregating Glenner in a special cellblock reduced the total capacity of the jail, Clark explained, and prevented them from housing juvenile inmates altogether.

"Why did you decide to segregate this inmate?" Justice Alexander asked.

"Well, even though Dr. Hogben at Maine Coast Memorial Hospital determined Glenner to be a male," Bill answered, "it was obvious to all of us that Glenner identifies somewhat with the female gender. We segregated her to avoid conflict or adverse interaction with the other adult males. We can't hold him—I mean Ms. Glenner—with the general male population."

Clark paused for a response from the judge. Alexander, his mouth pursed and eyebrows knit, said nothing. "And if I acted consistently with her insistence that she's a woman," Clark continued, "I would have her shipped to another facility. We send our females to Penobscot County and take their juveniles for them. I don't know what would happen in Penobscot if I sent Glenner up there as a woman."

It wasn't Glenner's fault that she was a transsexual, attorney Sandra Collier argued, and that the prison system says you have to be either male or female. Glenner's expressed desire was to remain in Hancock County. Collier said she therefore shouldn't be locked up in Thomaston.

"Just because she hasn't had the advantage of an operation, she will be jailed as a male, which will be extremely harmful to her," Collier said. "Samantha Glenner regards herself as a woman. It is critical for her to be treated as a woman. Thrusting her into an all-male institution would jeopardize her psychological makeup.

"Transsexualism is not a matter of cosmetics," Collier continued. "It's a matter of need. Ms. Glenner has a right to remain in the county jail unless the sheriff can show she creates a security problem. She is not violent. She is not a security risk. And she has not posed problems with other inmates."

Alexander, who the day before had cited Glenner's record of violence in denying bail, granted the sheriff's motion for transfer. The defendant's presence in the Hancock County jail, he said, was demanding extraordinary measures and was a potential risk to jail security. "We cannot consider just the person at issue. We have to consider the sheriff's responsibility to house not only this prisoner but all others."

Forty minutes after the hearing ended, Glenner was shipped off to the Maine State Prison. Three hours later, Kennebec County dropped off another prisoner and picked up Willoughby. Hancock County was no longer extending its hospitality to two murder suspects.

On Friday morning, jail administrator Bishop decided that the inmates could be let out of their cellblocks and stay out for the afternoon.

"As long as they don't screw up," he warned.

Chapter Fourteen

IN THE ALL-MALE MAINE STATE PRISON IN THOMASTON, Amy's accused killer was segregated from the other inmates, even having separate time in the prison recreation yard. Askeborn/Glenner had been referred to as Samantha Glenner, a female, in the courtroom and by most of the news media. A confused public said variously "he" and "she" and even "it." But in the state prison Askeborn's "Samantha" disappeared with the symbols of her persona. Like the other inmates, Askeborn wore civilian clothes, which at Thomaston, of course, meant men's attire. Women's clothes, cosmetics, and foam rubber breasts were left in the safekeeping of his parents in Hancock.

Askeborn left more than symbols behind when he went to prison to await trial. Those of us touched by the murder were left to deal with feelings stirred up by the violent crime committed in our midst.

Before the arrest, when I'd come home at dusk, my shadowy woodpile turned menacing and my heart pounded as I walked by. My fingers fumbled with the key at my front door, and I could hardly wait to lock myself inside.

In daylight it seemed silly to think that Amy's killer was waiting to jump out at me. I was relieved, though, to hear that others were afraid, too. My neighbor Hal Church admitted to looking around apprehensively when he stepped outside for a breath of night air.

After Askeborn's arrest, the fear subsided. But Taunton Bay and home still didn't feel as safe as they had before.

Sadness, too, lingered beneath the surface of daily life. I kept thinking of Amy, remembering little incidents now cast in a different light. I thought of the spring afternoon she had dropped by when I was building my house. She reached out to greet me with a hug, stopped abruptly, and drew back. "Some people don't like being hugged," she said accusingly, and she cut me off when I tried to protest. I didn't know then how troubled and suspicious of everyone she'd become. I didn't know when I phoned her for what turned out to be the last time that she was treating others with the same distant coolness.

By the time I understood that Amy, under her facade of coolness, had been in distress and that maybe I, or someone, could have helped, it was too late.

And what were we to do with our anger? Askeborn, the obvious target, was a suspect only and deserved to be treated as innocent until proven otherwise. But feelings weren't an elective, of course, and I for one was often angry at Amy's suspected killer.

Emotions evolved in a process of their own, like the seasons. The tourists, Maine's company for the summer, went home. Long lines at the supermarket and traffic jams on High Street disappeared. Colorful foliage turned brown. Late fall winds scattered dead leaves over the freezing landscape. In the first week of December, blustery winds delivered winter's first snowstorm, which along the coast turned to sleet, icing up the power lines, producing scattered outages and forcing schools to close.

As winter progressed, Askeborn and the murder on Taunton Bay faded from the news, and other matters took their place: the annual downtown merchants' Christmas parade in Ellsworth; a drive-by shooting in Sullivan, for which two men were arrested; the first public speak-out in Ellsworth by incest victims; a report that a new law requiring hunters to wear blaze orange supposedly reduced the number of fatalities during the deer-hunting season just past; and a visit by Senator George Mitchell to discuss a bill setting permanent boundaries in Acadia National Park.

Away from the news spotlight, attorneys for the state were quietly flooding the defense attorneys with discovery, disclosing evidence they might use in an upcoming trial: transcripts of Pinkham's interviews with Glenner, the defendant's statements to police who were

transporting her, and reports of Glen Robert Askeborn's criminal history from the FBI, the Connecticut State Police, and police in Suffolk
County, New York. Defense attorneys responded by filing motions to
suppress nearly everything.

One snowy day during the week before Christmas, attorney Collier and artist Robert Shetterly drove to Thomaston to see Askeborn.
In the prison lobby, they waited with gift-bearing families until at last
they were led through metal detectors and steel doors with bullet-
proof glass to a windowless room in the concrete-walled basement.

Under the watchful eye of a guard, Askeborn sat at a table, his
prison shirt open to the waist, revealing a chest plucked free of hair.
As Askeborn described the man he called Tony, whom he was finger-
ing as a suspect in the murder of Amelia Cave, Shetterly listened and
sketched a portrait of Tony for the defense attorneys. Watching, every
now and then Askeborn reached out a large hand and with his long
fingernails indicated Tony's features by using the artist's face as a
model. If Shetterly minded, he kept it to himself.

Hours later, the snow was still falling as Collier and Shetterly
crossed the prison parking lot to their car. Had they spent the day
serving the cause of justice? Shetterly had his doubts.

On January 4, Justice Donald Alexander listened to Pinkham's
long taped interview with Glenner before the arrest. The judge decided that Samantha had been given a proper Miranda warning and
had made a voluntary statement. It would not be suppressed. Neither
would disclosures made to Pinkham after the recorder had been
turned off. Nor Samantha's repeated plea to police not to disturb the
rock wall built behind the boat, nor evidence seized in four searches
on the Askeborn property. The Askeborns, Samantha included, had
given valid consent to these searches, the judge ruled.

Over defense objection, Alexander granted the state's motion to
obtain samples of the defendant's handwriting. The state had good
cause, he said, based on the report of an expert examiner of questioned documents, the document in this case being Amelia Cave's
$2,700 check.

The defense asked for a change of venue due to the amount of publicity that the case was receiving in Hancock County. The judge, agreeing, tentatively set the trial in Knox County to begin on March 27, 1985, less than three months away.

Justice Alexander was sitting in Waldo county when he considered the motion to suppress, and because Askeborn was still technically a Hancock County prisoner, Nate and Dickson had transported him to and from Belfast for that hearing. They bantered occasionally with their prisoner. "How come you're taking me without a cage?" Askeborn had queried during one transport.

"I've never lost a prisoner yet," Nate told him. "If you want to run, go ahead."

"I'm good," Askeborn said, "but not good enough to do anything at sixty miles an hour." Then Askeborn, solicitous, warned them they were too trusting. He'd been through the system, he said, so he knew people a lot better than they did. Still trying to implicate someone else in the murder, he boasted he'd give them "the other guy," or at least part of him. Nate said he'd prefer the whole guy. Askeborn replied that he had no control over that.

Dickson, reflecting later, decided there'd been a change in Askeborn's manner now that he was no longer Samantha. He seemed masculine and cold, even vicious. As though he'd kill you in a heartbeat, Dickson thought.

But then, Dickson told himself, some of the change might be in the eye of the beholder. He knew that he looked at Askeborn differently than he had Samantha.

In early February, the state filed a motion seeking eighteen hairs, the standard FBI sample, from Askeborn's head to see if they matched hair found in debris vacuumed from the driver's side of Amelia Cave's car. The state said that the hair, about six and a half inches long, light to medium brown, was consistent with gross characteristics of the defendant's hair as observed in open court. Askeborn had denied getting into Amelia Cave's car last October, the prosecution pointed out, so a match would be highly probative evidence of the defendant's guilt. The judge granted the state's request.

In mid-February, prosecutors paid a visit to the state prison in Thomaston. Armed with a court order, they acquired handwriting samples from a reluctant Askeborn to compare with writing on the face and back of the $2,700 check drawn on Amy Cave's account.

Near the end of the month, Sheriff Bill Clark, his attention focused on other matters since Askeborn's arrest, announced that the Hancock County jail would be renamed the Merritt P. Fitch Correctional Facility in honor of the man who had served the county for nearly thirty years, twenty of them as sheriff.

Merritt had died in August. When Clark looked from his office window across the driveway to the hundred-year-old brick jail, now empty, where Merritt had lived as sheriff and raised his six children, he would think of his old friend and the stories he'd loved telling.

Inmates had been part of Merritt's family. They'd played horseshoes in the yard with his kids, whittled with them in the barn behind the jail, and taught Ernie, the youngest, to ride a bike and play cribbage and poker. They helped Dot clean and cook, and they worked in the garden that fed them all until the government decreed that inmates' food must be government inspected. Even wardens were no longer allowed to bring moose and deer meat for the inmates' meals.

Merritt used to wrestle a drunk to the floor, then rub his back until he fell asleep. For a long time it had been legal to arrest someone for just being intoxicated, and you could "slap him around," as Merritt put it, if he didn't do what you told him. Merritt had taken cases to court that a few years later wouldn't get past the district attorney.

During Merritt's twenty years as sheriff, the department acquired the first police radio, first cruiser, first patrolman, first full-time deputies, and first paid cook. Dot had cooked inmates' meals with no pay for fifteen years. Merritt hired a man from the opposition party for the first time, too. "I hired for the man, not his politics," Merritt was fond of saying.

It surprised no one when Ernie Fitch followed in his father's footsteps. He'd always been fascinated with law enforcement. He had stood on a chair before he was five years old to peek through the keyhole into the booking room, and later he taught new employees to use the teletype and went on cases with his dad.

By the end of February, Hancock County began to thaw out. Days were growing noticeably longer and pussy willows were budding when Samantha Glenner, a.k.a. Glen Robert Askeborn, filed a civil suit against the sheriff, the commissioner of the Department of Corrections, and the warden of the state prison. Despite repeated requests, the complaint stated, they had refused to provide Glenner with the medical treatment she needed. Glenner wanted the county, the state, or someone to pay for hormone treatments.

On a Friday morning in early March, I set out in my car along the coast to a hormone hearing at the Knox County Courthouse in Rockland. I would finally get my first prolonged look at the accused killer as he/she took the witness stand—and would respond with a vehemence that took me completely by surprise.

Chapter Fifteen

SHERIFF CLARK LEFT FOR THOMASTON with his jail administrator at seven o'clock Friday morning in an unmarked blue Chevy Malibu. As they drove away, the dispatcher called to alert the Maine State Prison of their estimated arrival time to pick up Glen Askeborn.

The sheriff had eaten breakfast at home. Bishop would skip breakfast altogether; he said he was watching his weight. The cruiser's gas tank was full, so the two men thought this would be a nonstop drive from Ellsworth to Thomaston.

Route 1 along the coast was bare pavement, and a clear sky showed no signs of an impending snowstorm. In a few months the tourist traffic would make it impossible to breeze through Searsport, with its antique shops (most of them closed now), or through the resort towns of Camden and Rockport. To their left, sun glinted off the bays and brightened the crotchety mood in which they had both set out for this nuisance hormone hearing at the Rockland courthouse.

Until they reached Camden, they had avoided any mention of the hearing, which the sheriff, especially, was tired of thinking about. Then Bishop asked casually, "How do you think things will go down today, Bill?"

"Damned if I know," Clark answered sharply. He'd been running around getting ready for today since Monday, when a reporter called to ask for a comment on the civil suit that Glenner had just filed against him and others. How could he comment? It was the first he'd heard about it.

"I don't see providing Glenner with hormones as a medical emergency," Bishop said. He looked over at his boss for a response, but Bill, staring straight ahead, said nothing. "We take a prisoner to the dentist for a toothache," Bishop continued. "Or to the doctor for a bellyache. But hormones? I'd call that elective treatment. What's next? A sex change operation?"

That got a response. "Wouldn't the taxpayers love that!" said Bill. They'd been over this before, but if Bishop wanted to talk, well, why not? "What did Glenner's attorneys say hormone treatments might run, about two hundred dollars a week?"

"Which figures out to ten thousand four hundred dollars a year," Bishop added. "Our medical budget for the whole jail is only about twelve thousand a year, for God's sake."

They'd be finding out shortly what the judge had to say about it. Samantha's attorneys were claiming that hormone treatments were necessary for her health and well-being, and that before her incarceration she'd been taking hormones regularly for what they called gender identity dysphoria.

The sheriff had experienced some dysphoria himself since he'd heard about this suit. He'd hightailed it to the clerk's office in superior court to read the complaint, then called the Maine Sheriff's Association to see if it would represent him. An interesting, unique request, the association said, but no, it wouldn't. He hadn't really expected it to; it wasn't their bailiwick.

The sheriff hadn't really expected Mike Povich to take him on as a client, either, when he went upstairs to the district attorney's office. Povich's job was to represent the county commissioners, not the sheriff. Mike told him that the commissioners would probably authorize him to get a private attorney.

That's just what happened when the sheriff walked downstairs to the first floor and consulted with the clerk and commissioner Walter Bunker. He'd chosen attorney Eugene Coughlin in Bangor and spent the next few days writing a synopsis of the murder case, photocopying reports, and talking on the phone with Coughlin and state corrections officials.

He'd asked for more time to prepare for the hearing, but the judge turned down his request.

When they reached Rockland, the sheriff radioed ahead to Thomaston, the next town, to notify the prison booking office of their imminent arrival.

As the cruiser entered the horseshoe-shaped drive in front of the prison, Bill glanced up at the brick building, a massive, box-shaped structure that had burned early in the 1920s and was now a combination of old and new. A metal plaque on the three-story section in the center told him it was built in 1924. Another plaque on one of the older wings said 1824.

The ten-acre site used to be called Limestone Hill. Prisoners had been put to work quarrying the limestone. A quarry pit in the middle of the complex had been filled in some time ago with dirt and old cars and trucks and now was an exercise yard, complete with baseball diamond.

"Let's leave our guns in the trunk," Bill said, reaching for his holster. "It'll save us having to check and retrieve them inside the prison."

They greeted the guard in the small front office, passed through the metal detector, climbed two flights of stairs, and handed their court order to the control officer. Then they walked down the hall to booking and release to wait for Askeborn.

As a guard approached with the prisoner, Clark and Bishop noticed immediately one vestige of the old Samantha: Askeborn's shirt was gathered in front and tied jauntily at the waist. He met their eyes briefly, nodded, and said hello in a soft, tentative voice. The sheriff, standing aside as Bishop handcuffed Askeborn, saw the rash that covered his pale face—the result, no doubt, of an overzealous bout with a razor.

With their prisoner sitting silent in the rear seat of the car, Bishop headed back to Rockland. He and Bill were silent, too, private conversation squelched by the presence behind them. They'd both heard stories about the sparring that Nate and Dickson had engaged in with Askeborn during the winter as they transported him to court hearings. Neither of them was in the mood for banter today. Askeborn's Samantha was old to all of them by now.

As they turned into the courthouse parking lot in Rockland and pulled up next to another car, Bill looked over and saw Justice Donald Alexander getting out. Bill opened the passenger door and greeted the judge.

Alexander looked surprised to see him. "What are you doing here?" he asked.

"Protecting my interests," Bill said, stepping out of the cruiser.

The judge assured him that Hancock County wouldn't have to bear the cost of hormone treatments for Askeborn, even if the court did order them.

That's not what I've been hearing, Bill thought as Alexander walked off toward the courthouse. Bill followed Bishop and Askeborn to a side door, where a deputy in the Knox County Sheriff's Department met them. The deputy and Bishop escorted Askeborn upstairs to a holding area next to the courtroom. Bill went next door to the Knox County jail to chat with the new sheriff.

I found the courthouse in Rockland easily, parked my car in the lot, then stood outside wondering where to go. There seemed to be two entrances, one in the three-story brick building facing the street and the other in the more modern addition in front of me. I looked up at the white cupola and weathervane on top of the older section.

"What's the matter, you lost?"

I turned to the voice behind me. "Bill!" It was good to see a familiar face. The public, he said, entered through the main courthouse, but I could use the other entrance as long as I was with him.

Inside, Bishop joined us and we stood chatting in the lobby.

"There's going to be hell to pay here," Bill told us. "Last night in the Knox County jail, an inmate swallowed some of that caustic fluid they use to clean the cells."

"No shit. Did it kill him?" Bishop asked.

"He's in the hospital."

Bishop raised an eyebrow. "Well, here goes another lawsuit, no matter how the guy does." He looked at his watch. "We better head upstairs."

As we waited for the elevator, I noticed that Bishop's cheek wasn't puffed out with his usual wad of smokeless tobacco. He explained that this particular judge disapproved of the habit in his court. As we got off the elevator on the top floor and entered the older section of the building, Bill remarked on how awful Askeborn looked. "Worse than I've ever seen him," he said.

"Huh?" Bishop said. "I thought he looked better than she usually does." Bill and I laughed, and Bishop, realizing what he had said, laughed, too.

I didn't know if Askeborn looked better or worse when I saw him sitting at the table with his attorneys. He looked pale, though, and I felt a little sorry for him, exposed as the male he didn't want to be in gray men's slacks and a rumpled cream-colored shirt, his hair pulled back severely by a rubber band into a limp ponytail. Four months in prison were taking their toll.

The door behind the judge's high bench opened suddenly and Justice Donald Alexander, black robed from neck to shoetop, swooped into the courtroom like a giant crow. He addressed the prisoner, calling him Ms. Glenner. He'd been surprised, he said, to receive a letter from Ms. Glenner requesting new counsel. Glenner's attorneys seemed surprised, too. They and their client stood to face the judge. Glenner mumbled something about a change of mind and nodded when Alexander asked if she were now satisfied with counsel, and nodded again when the judge suggested she had written the letter "in the heat of the moment."

Sandra Collier and Anthony Beardsley (who had been appointed by the court to join Collier) asked for a recess to confer with their client. They left the courtroom, and the remaining state's attorneys and clerks chatted among themselves. Sitting alone in the first row of the benches beyond the courtroom arena, I glanced idly around the large room.

Ornate wooden pillars along the walls rose to a high ceiling. In the cornice around the sides of the courtroom were the words *Hope, Honor, Faith, Charity, Liberty, Justice, Equality, Prudence.* Interesting, I thought, that so many were women's names. And *Liberty* and *Justice* are traditionally portrayed as women: Liberty raising her torch high at the entrance to New York Harbor, and Justice in a flowing white dress, holding the balance scales of justice before her.

I was thinking about the number of women judges in Maine and had come up with only one when Glenner and her attorneys returned. Sandra Collier called her first witness.

Brian Rimes, a clinical psychologist in Augusta, admitted right away to limited experience with transsexuals and gender identification dysphoria. But he'd done some homework, reviewing literature at a medical center and through a computer service.

Responding to questions from Collier, the soft-spoken and unassuming Rimes shared his newfound expertise with the court. The first step for people unhappy with their gender, he said, was psychotherapy. Therapy often continued into the next phase of hormone treatments, which affected secondary sex characteristics such as the growth of hair and musculature. During the two phases, endocrinologists and other specialists were called in as consultants. Clients persisting in the desire to change their sex—sexual reassignment, it was called—were advised to make "a real life test."

"Those individuals are requested to insert themselves actively into the culture as the desired sex," said Rimes, sounding as though he were reading from a textbook. That stage might last from one to five years. Surgery, the final phase for those who wanted it, involved a four- or five-step operation for the change from male to female.

The judge, zeroing in on the purpose of the hearing, asked what the physical and psychological consequences would be if, in that one-to five-year period, the person were to stop taking hormones.

Rimes said there would be a reversal of physiological changes. Psychological consequences, he believed, would depend on whether the change was at the candidate's request or not. If hormone treatments were withheld unilaterally, that could be very disturbing to the client, he warned.

Was he acquainted with Samantha Glenner, also known as Glen Robert Askeborn? Collier asked.

Rimes said he was. At Collier's request, he had met with Ms. Glenner at the Maine State Prison for an interview, which lasted four and a half hours. They had discussed Rimes's politics and the rights of patients, and then he had spent ninety minutes collecting a preliminary history. He administered some psychological tests and left more tests for Glenner to complete and return to him. During the interview, he said, Glenner seemed distressed about not looking more feminine and apologized repeatedly for her appearance.

"Did you discuss her past treatment?" Collier inquired.

"Yes. We discussed her history starting in 1977–78 when apparently to her . . . phenomenologically—"

"What?" the judge interrupted him.

"Phenomenologically. In terms of her perception," Rimes explained, "she was not performing as a male but as a female trapped in a male body. That's my own expression," he told the judge. "Ms. Glenner thought and felt like a female."

Thought and felt like a female? I bristled, ready to do battle at any stereotyping by gender. But there was no time for philosophizing. Tape recorders weren't allowed in the courtroom, and I was always scribbling down one piece of testimony while listening to the next.

Now Rimes was talking about Glenner's involvement with a group at Mt. Sinai Clinic, in New Haven, Connecticut, called the Double X Club, named for the female's two sex chromosomes, XX, in contrast to the male's XY chromosomes. The clinic helped people explore the process of changing their sex, Rimes said, but he was uncertain to what extent Glenner had participated in the program. Glenner had told him, though, that she started cross-dressing in public five years ago, and she began taking estrogen that spring and continued on a regular basis through the day she was arrested.

"What is Samantha's attitude toward her anatomical organ?" Collier asked.

"She is not interested in her penis," Rimes said, "except to urinate and keep clean. Otherwise it's excess baggage from which she receives no genital pleasure." He found no evidence of physical or genital abnormality, he said, and no schizophrenia. Only situational dysphoria and anxiety due to being in prison.

The judge asked Rimes his opinion about Glenner's competency to stand trial. Rimes said he hadn't specifically evaluated Glenner for competency and would reserve judgment on that.

But, Collier asked, had he made a diagnosis of transsexualism and gender identification dysphoria?

He had.

And might there be adverse consequences in prolonged deprivation of treatment?

Given Glenner's persistent belief in her femaleness and her apparent attempt to become a woman over a period of four and a half years, Rimes thought the consequences might be quite serious.

Collier asked him to please elaborate.

Well, there was some possibility she might make an attempt to take her own life, said Rimes. And there was risk of psychiatric depression and schizophrenia of a paranoid nature. In fact, Rimes added, it was quite probable.

Collier walked purposefully from the witness stand to the table where Glenner was seated. She turned back to Rimes and, after a calculated pause, asked, "You say one of the potential risks is suicide?"

"Yes."

Collier sat down, leaving her client's possible suicide hovering like a specter over the courtroom. Glenner leaned forward, one elbow on the table, chin propped on the palm of one large hand, fingers cradling her cheek.

The honeymoon for the expert witness was over. Anne Catlin, attorney in the civil division of the attorney general's office, immediately began pressing Rimes to distinguish between sexual identity dysphoria and situational dysphoria induced by stress, such as incarceration in prison. Rimes said he hadn't split hairs to that extent. He did admit, however, that a lack of persistence by Glenner in getting hormone treatment would cause him to reconsider his position.

Eugene Coughlin, the sheriff's attorney, then introduced a doctor's report refuting Glenner's claim of having taken prescription drugs on a regular basis. The report gave a different history. According to Dr. Robert Tyler, who had interviewed and examined Glenner in Hancock

County four months earlier, Glenner had admitted taking estrogen only sporadically since 1982, obtaining it not by prescription but from street sources. On the basis of this history, Tyler had not recommended regular estrogen treatment.

Catlin asked Rimes if this conflicting history made a difference in his assessment of Ms. Glenner.

It did, Rimes said. If Samantha had lied to him, he would have to reconsider his opinion about the possibility of adverse effects from withholding estrogen treatment. He'd need to know more about the periods of time in which she had gone without estrogen and whether they involved forced deprivation or choice.

Coughlin brought up the matter of secondary transsexualism, in which some of the concerns of a transsexual were less deep seated. Rimes agreed that it would take a fairly sophisticated team of specialists to determine the difference.

"This team that you talk about would include a qualified medical physician?" asked Coughlin.

"Yes, as it should for everyone using drugs. As a psychologist, I don't prescribe or recommend the use of drugs."

"So," the judge said, "you're not recommending that treatment today?"

"No. Just strong consideration of a continuing process."

"If Glenner were to dress as a woman," Coughlin asked, "would her condition improve?"

"I imagine so," Rimes said.

"So that would be likely to reduce the chance of an untoward result?"

"It might offer some assistance in reducing psychological distress, I think."

Sandra Collier was relying on the testimony of only one witness to plead the case for hormone treatment for her client. That witness, about to leave the stand, was in trouble. Damage control was clearly called for.

Collier rose from her chair and in a firm, confident voice asked,

"You do recommend the continuation of the process, though, even if it includes hormonal reassignment and therapy?"

"Yes," said Rimes.

The judge had his own parting question for Rimes: "In your understanding of this matter, you are relying on what you were told in your interview on December 31?"

"That's correct," Rimes said. The judge excused the witness and declared a ten-minute recess.

In twenty minutes, Collier reappeared with Rimes and asked that he be recalled to the stand.

"What do you remember regarding prior hormone treatments in the December interview with Samantha Glenner?" Collier asked.

Coughlin objected. "That has been asked and answered before."

"Overruled."

Rimes, subdued, answered. "That she obtained medicine from prescription by a physician for her use. Obtained through a drugstore, or other means—I don't know which."

"I thought you said before that the drugs were not obtained through the underground," the judge said.

Rimes sighed. "There was no doubt in my mind. But I'm not sure how specific my questions were or if I drew the wrong conclusion."

"And if they were obtained illegally or legally, what would be the effect?" asked Alexander.

"Well, if Samantha lied, it would bother me a great deal. But," Rimes said, "maybe it was my mistake in interpreting what I heard."

"Either way," the judge persisted, "she told you she was getting hormones regularly?"

"That's right. But it's possible I made some assumptions and did not ask the right questions."

Attorney Coughlin reminded the doctor that he hadn't equivocated in his written report. The judge reminded him that his statements on the stand had been unequivocal, too.

Rimes became apologetic and said he'd have to reconsider some of his assessments. Collier, in a final rescue attempt, asked if his diagnosis of gender identification dysphoria remained firm. Rimes said that it did.

As Rimes left the courtroom, Collier did, too. She had another appointment. Her colleague, Tony Beardsley, called Samantha Glenner to the stand.

This was the first time I'd heard Samantha Glenner speak, and I was shocked at the small, high-pitched voice coming from such a large person. I strained to hear the whispered responses to Beardsley about Glenner's decision in the late 1970s to change gender, about meeting doctors through the Double X Club, and about not having money for medical treatment.

As Glenner was warming to the story about starting hormone injections, moving to Maine that November, and receiving drugs sporadically from friends who scrimped to share their own supplies, I was distracted by a vague sense of uneasiness.

I continued jotting down the testimony: "In Connecticut, at first I dressed in women's clothes only on my boat that I was living on. I didn't go cold turkey. I had courage, but not that much. I did it gradually."

Glenner sighed. "Eventually, dressing as a woman destroyed the boat-designing business I was trying to start." Her large hands fluttered before her and dropped to her lap.

"But you dressed as a woman full-time living in the State of Maine?" Beardsley continued.

"Oh, yes," Glenner breathed. "No other way exists. For me to put on male clothes, why I'd feel as conspicuous as anyone in this room if you were to change your gender."

I stopped writing and stared at the witness, the thought I'd been shoving aside suddenly clear: Had those hands closed around Amy's throat and strangled her to death? Everyone was listening politely to the story. This is crazy, I thought. This person is accused of murdering Amy, and we're all listening to a chat about hormones.

I told myself that I had no choice but to put on a polite mask and listen too. We heard about migraine headaches lasting five to six hours. Taking Tylenol. Feeling antagonistic. Coming close to losing her temper with other inmates. Feeling depressed. Drawing boats as a safety valve.

A thrust of the chin accompanied one defiant announcement: "But I'm most definitely going to have final surgery sooner or later."

Really? I thought. While Askeborn was sitting in prison for murder, that's what he'd been thinking about? Final surgery?

Anne Catlin began interrogation for the state. "Ms. Glenner, you were associated with Mt. Sinai hospital or clinic in New Haven?"

"Well, sort of. Not the hospital directly, although I had contact with some of the counselors and medical doctors. There was a gynecologist and a speech therapist."

"What was the role of the speech therapist?"

"Well, for a lot of us, if you're asked to speak like a woman, you can't do it. Take any one of you gentlemen here." Glenner said with a knowing look around the courtroom.

I was aware of a sudden tension in the room, of the men squirming in their seats. I caught the judge's eye and rolled mine—unprofessional, I knew, but I couldn't help it.

Samantha grew increasingly irritated as Catlin tried to pin down her medical history. Only five visits in eight months to one doctor, the attorney pointed out.

Maybe so, was the response, but there'd been other doctors, too. She couldn't recall their names or addresses. So what if she hadn't mentioned any history of hormone treatments to Dr. Coopersmith at the Maine State Prison. She'd become increasingly disenchanted with Maine doctors. They had tunnel vision.

"Have you made any complaints since you've been at Maine State Prison?" Catlin asked.

Samantha sighed. "It would be futile. I mentioned some when I was first there."

"Have you had any medical symptoms requiring attention?"

Glenner sighed again and mumbled something about headaches, seeing a nurse, and not being able to get the needed medicine. No one there had any experience with gender identity dysphoria. If there was anyone in prison who could handle depression well, she didn't care to meet that person. She'd been handling it adequately on her own, certainly, but not "well."

Glenner held out a hand, beseechingly. "I'm not normally antagonistic. I don't frequently lose my cool."

"But you did come close to losing your temper, didn't you?" asked Catlin.

"Yes," Glenner admitted in a near whisper.

"Why?" Catlin asked.

Glenner turned to the judge. "Do I have to answer that?"

"I don't see the relevance of the question," Alexander said.

Coughlin took over and riled Glenner into snapping responses, such as, "I just told you that" and "That has nothing to do with the matter before this court."

Coughlin asked for the names of friends who had provided the hormones. Beardsley objected. The judge overruled the objection.

"I'm not going to answer," Glenner declared with another jut of the chin. "It was a very important favor, and I think you're out of line."

Beardsley stood quickly and extended his hand, palm out like a traffic cop, warning his client to stop.

"If I have to," said Glenner reluctantly, "I'll give up one source."

"Shall I consider this a refusal to answer in a civil procedure?" Justice Alexander asked.

"I believe I've already done that," Glenner snapped back, then looked at Beardsley, who was still standing, stern faced, and added, "It wouldn't do any good. The person has already had reassignment surgery. Revealing her name wouldn't serve any purpose."

She did remember a Dr. Anderson and a Dr. Knight, but couldn't recall Dr. Knight's first name or his street address. Perhaps she'd never known them, she suggested, but then added that she recalled Dr. Knight being very personable.

"He was about fifty-five, a Negro, very nice, a gentleman. He would talk to any of you gentlemen." Glenner turned to the judge. "He'd talk to you, even." Alexander smiled.

"All right," said Coughlin. "Dr. Knight and Dr. Anderson—how many times did you see them?"

Glenner was irritated. "I don't know how many times. I didn't keep track."

"Then give us the name of a pharmacy where you bought the drugs."

"Well, one was in East Haven. On Main Street. Call the East Haven Police Department. They'd know. Metcalf's Pharmacy—that was it. And I got drugs by mail."

"How did you pay?"

"In currency and other ways. I suppose you'll ask me to tell you what other ways."

Coughlin obliged. "What ways?" he asked.

"Forget it," Glenner shot back.

"Mr. Coughlin," the judge intervened, "get to the issue."

Coughlin asked again about the incident in prison when Glenner had come close to losing her temper.

What had happened in prison, I wondered, that the state's attorneys were so interested in getting on the record? They weren't succeeding, though, for Glenner just rambled on about feeling testy, having headaches, taking Tylenol, and sleeping a lot. And about being refused cosmetics. "But," she declared, "the medicine is infinitely more important."

It was one o'clock and Glenner had been on the stand for thirty-five minutes. I'd never seen a witness allowed such leeway to ramble and bicker with attorneys and aim caustic comments at the judge.

But then, I'd never been in the courtroom when a man was asking the state to provide female hormones to ensure his competency to stand trial for murder.

The state called Morton G. Coopersmith, physician at the Maine State Prison, to the stand. I looked over at Glenner, who was glaring at Coopersmith.

The prison doctor, licensed for twenty-seven years in osteopathic medicine and medical surgery, exuded confidence on the stand, especially compared to Rimes, who by the end of his testimony had appeared shaken.

Coopersmith had examined the prisoner in the infirmary a week after arrival, he told Catlin, and found a physically normal individual with generally male characteristics. Glenner's skin still needed treatment, and they were continuing the erythromycin prescribed at the Hancock County jail, as well as pHisoHex surgical soap. The prisoner hadn't made any complaints about the treatment.

"In your opinion," Catlin asked, "is there any medical necessity for the administering of hormonal drugs?"

Coopersmith answered quickly. "The use of hormones was never brought up by Mr. Askeborn."

Beardsley rose from his chair. "Objection!"

"Overruled."

"By Ms. Glenner," Coopersmith, conciliatory, corrected himself.

"So," the judge interceded, "do you see any necessity for the use of drugs?"

"No," said Coopersmith. "Glenner did not request them and personally, as the prison physician, I see no reason for them in this particular case."

He said he was aware of a number of possible side effects of the class of drugs mentioned: The drugs might be carcinogenic or cause gastrointestinal upset involving the urinary tract and kidneys.

Coughlin had no questions for the doctor. Tony Beardsley had a few. Addressing him deferentially as "sir," he asked Dr. Coopersmith if he had ever diagnosed anyone as having gender identification dysphoria.

Never, said Coopersmith.

Had he ever had any experience with anyone having this condition? Coopersmith said he hadn't.

Was he aware that these drugs had been successfully prescribed for a variety of treatments?

He was.

Was he aware that the drugs had been successfully prescribed for people with gender identity dysphoria?

Yes, under controlled conditions.

In Coopersmith's opinion, Beardsley asked, might Glenner have the condition known as gender identity dysphoria, or GID?

No, the doctor said, not on the basis of his physical exam.

When the judge asked what his physical exam had shown, Coopersmith started to speak about Glenner's genitalia, but the judge, apparently concerned about the doctor's lack of sympathy about the psychological aspects of GID, cut him off. "Doctor," he said, "you basically have no idea about any of this."

Coopersmith's testimony ended. He had been on the stand for less than ten minutes.

It was after one o'clock and there'd been no recess for lunch. Alexander announced he would hear closing arguments the following Wednesday and asked the attorneys to address the competency issue and his authority to intervene on the grounds of competency. It was unlikely, he said, that Hancock County would be required to foot the bill for any medical treatments even if he did order them, and he had serious doubts about the justification for such an order.

Beardsley stood to address the judge. "Your Honor, my client won't attend the hearing next Wednesday."

"Why not?" Alexander asked, looking at Glenner.

Samantha, head down, mumbled, "I don't see any point in it." Sounding even more dejected, she added, "To sit here all day?"

I wasn't happy about sitting in court for four hours either, especially while Askeborn was on the stand, painting his strange picture of women in his simpering, Marilyn Monroe voice. It was a relief to finally move around outdoors in the fresh air. When I closed my car door and started to pull out of the parking lot, I let off steam with a loud hoot. It felt good.

At a crosswalk in the center of Rockland, I slowed the car to a stop to let a pedestrian cross. A stocky, middle-aged woman in a bright purple and pink parka smiled her thanks. I nodded back and began mimicking Askeborn's breathy voice: "It's not easy to talk like a woman. Any of you gentlemen here—you couldn't do it." I laughed and stepped on the gas.

Driving along a winding uphill road out of Camden, I realized I hadn't looked down the side streets for a glimpse of the picturesque harbor. There were ocean vistas ahead to enjoy if I'd just focus on them instead of the drama of the morning.

But along a dull stretch of road with no view, I drifted back to the scene in the Rockland courtroom: the black-robed judge, symbol of authority, sitting above the other players. Below him are the lawyers, adversaries in a game of who's right and who's wrong, fencing with one another, thrusting and parrying to discredit and disparage their opponent. Into this arena of blacks and whites enters Dr. Rimes, a psychologist dealing with human emotions in infinite shades of gray. A sympathetic observer, not a judge of the human condition, he's out of his element in the legal framework.

And how much would anyone reveal of himself, anyway, to a doctor who he knew would be critiquing him in court?

But most out of kilter in my eyes was that all of the players were addressing a six-foot man with his hair pulled back in a ponytail as "Ms. Glenner" and talking about Ms. Glenner's penis. "Ms. Glenner receives no pleasure from her penis. . . . Her penis is that of a normal male."

And gender identity dysphoria? Such a serious-sounding label by experts wrapped in the cloak of medical authority.

So Askeborn was not happy with himself as a man. Would calling himself a woman, gluing on foam rubber breasts, ingesting hormones, and even surgically altering his penis make everything all right? I doubted that changing the packaging would change what's inside.

Between Lincolnville and Belfast, I began wondering why anyone would change gender these days when gender roles were themselves changing, allowing men and women their feminine and masculine sides. Today, if people saw a presidential candidate cry in public as Ed Muskie had, they might not dismiss him so readily as unstable. They might even see him as compassionate. Why didn't Askeborn just get in touch with his feminine side?

As I looked down on Ellsworth from Bridge Hill to the white church spire and the brick courthouse across the Union River, I thought how awful it would be to mutilate your body to become someone else and then find you didn't like the person you'd become. Or that you were the same person you'd always been.

The following Wednesday, Justice Alexander heard the attorneys' closing arguments in the hormone hearing and decided that Glenner might be at risk if no treatment were provided. "Some relief is necessary," he said. "I'm not ordering drugs, but I am ordering an independent examination by a person with expertise who will then recommend a treatment program. The prison doctor demonstrated substantial insensibility to Glenner's condition. I recognize that this is a sensitive, difficult issue. But we take our prisoners as we find them."

When the state's attorney suggested it might be difficult to find a qualified expert within the state of Maine, Alexander told him perhaps they'd have to consider releasing the prisoner pending trial. Glenner must be presumed innocent until proven guilty.

The judge directed attorneys for both parties to come up with a list of three licensed Maine physicians expert in psychiatry and endocrinology before March 26. If drugs were ordered, so be it, he said. His court order would extend only until the end of the trial. And he certainly was not talking about forcing anyone to pay for a sex change operation.

In response to a motion by the state, Alexander also ordered Glenner to be examined for competency to stand trial by an expert recommended by the commissioner of the Department of Mental Health.

With the matter of competency and hormone treatments still to be dealt with, the judge set a tentative date and location for the murder trial. Askeborn/Glenner, if found competent, and with or without hormones, would stand trial for murder in Rockland during the last week of April.

Part Three

Chapter Sixteen

THE EARLY MORNING SUN REFLECTED OFF TAUNTON BAY and shimmered in a lively dance over the ledges and tree-lined shore. I could hear seals barking on Burying Island Ledge and loons calling to each other from somewhere near the Sullivan shore.

The ice in the shadow of the boathouse behind me had disappeared only two weeks ago, and pesky blackflies would arrive any day now. But today—Monday, May 20, 1985—was a perfect spring day. The trial of Amy's accused murderer would begin in one hour in an Ellsworth courtroom.

Sitting by the water enjoying the bay she had loved, I could feel Amy's presence. The trial seemed to have nothing to do with her. It was for the rest of us she left behind.

At 8:30 there were already more people than I'd ever seen in the courtroom, and by 9:00 all five long rows of wood benches were filled. I sat in the front row, which had been reserved for the media—another first in that courtroom. Bangor TV reporters and all the local newspaper and radio reporters were there. And new faces, too.

Word passed along the media row that the young blonde woman sitting at the other end was with *People* magazine. Two artists with sketch pads sat in the jury box. There would be no jury in this trial.

Less than two weeks earlier, Askeborn's attorneys had asked for a jury-waived trial, which meant that a change of venue was no longer needed. The trial had been returned to Hancock County.

People sat erect in churchlike reverence, speaking with one another only occasionally and in hushed tones. But at 9:15 when security guards led Askeborn into the courtroom, even the whispers stopped.

All eyes devoured the large, subdued man and followed him to the defense table as he sat down. He wore black slacks and a black blouse with multicolored stripes. His frizzy hair was pulled back with a rubber band into a long ponytail. Sandra Collier leaned over Askeborn and in a deliberate gesture placed her hand on his shoulder and kept it there. If this were a jury trial, I'd suspect it to be a calculated move designed to elicit sympathy from the jurors. As it was, I thought Collier might be offering comfort to her client and making a statement to the rest of us who were staring at him as though he were an exotic fish in a glass bowl.

At 9:30, the judge had still not entered the courtroom. Attorneys for both sides were milling about: Foster, Beardsley, and Collier for the defense and two men from the attorney general's office—Jeff Albanese and Nick Gess—for the state. Dave Giroux, because he'd been in charge of the murder investigation for the state police, was seated at the prosecutors' table.

I looked around the familiar courtroom at the dusty pink walls and off-white rococo woodwork and was checking out the narrow vertical stripes in Askeborn's bat-wing–sleeved shirt—alternating shocking pink, bright blue, plum, and aqua—when the door behind the bench opened.

"All rise," boomed the voice of court officer Earland Linscott.

A gray head and then a black robe bobbed into sight as the judge climbed the steps to the bench platform.

In a monotone and on a single breath, Linscott rattled off: "All persons having anything to do before the superior court held here this day in and for the County of Hancock come forth and declare it, and it shall be heard." He paused for a breath. "The Honorable Justice Eugene F. Beaulieu presiding. You may be seated."

Beaulieu busied himself with papers at the bench as courtroom visitors looked him over. A round head and full cheeks and jowls gave him the appearance of a cherub. That impression vanished when he raised his head and flicked sharp, spectacled eyes around the courtroom. With no sign of surprise at the unusual crowd and without ceremony, he jumped to court business.

For the record, he said, Philip Foster, who had previously repre-sented the interests of Askeborn's parents, had now entered the case on behalf of the defendant. And the court had received a defense re-quest, which he would grant, that a "viewing party" look at scenes outside the courtroom. Witnesses were to be sequestered and not dis-cuss trial matters with anyone but attorneys.

Sandra Collier rose from the defense table to state that Mr. Giroux was a key witness in this case and therefore should not be seated in the courtroom.

Beaulieu said that Giroux could stay until it became evident that the officer's presence would be prejudicial in a particular instance.

Jeff Albanese complained that the defense had violated discovery by not making available a doctor's report for the state to study before questioning the doctor on the stand. Beaulieu ordered the defense to give the report to the state by the end of the day.

At 9:40 the trial began. As at the previous hearing, in the court-room the defendant would be addressed as Samantha Glenner, fe-male, not as Glen Askeborn, male.

Albanese announced that he would present no opening state-ment. I was surprised. If there were a jury, I suspected, he'd have plenty to say.

Collier was left to paint the picture of the upcoming trial, and I began finding fault with her every brush stroke. Glenner lived in Han-cock, not Franklin; Amy hadn't moved to Maine seeking seclusion, as had Glenner. I bristled at Collier's picture of Amy and Samantha as bosom buddies who shopped and dined together, and of Glenner as the poor victim of prejudice and Amy as a depressed, paranoid creature whose life had been filled with loneliness, rumors, and bur-glar alarms.

Collier hadn't even known Amy. It wasn't a fair picture. But being fair, I knew, was not Collier's job. She was a defense attorney.

"No doubt Amelia Cave was a victim, and her murderer should be brought to justice," Collier said, winding up her ten-minute state-ment. "But Samantha Glenner is not guilty and should not become another victim."

The state called its first witness, Patrick Toman, assistant to the chief medical examiner.

As Toman described digging up the body that Saturday morning in October on Taunton Bay, the state introduced exhibit number 11, a photograph of the grave site and Glenner's boat. Then Toman, who'd attended the autopsy Saturday afternoon, held up his hand to show the court exhibit number 54.

It was, he said, a test tube of Amelia Cave's blood.

How had it seemed just this morning that this trial had nothing to do with Amy?

The second witness, a medical technologist in the Kennebec Valley Medical Center lab, had a soft voice and had to be reminded repeatedly to speak louder. But that was the least of Sandra Hanley's problems.

When Hanley was asked to present the lab test results, Collier moved swiftly into attack mode. What were Hanley's qualifications? The state hadn't established a proper chain of continuity. Exactly how were the samples handled?

Nick Gess protested that Hanley had more than twenty years' experience, and lab personnel knew that lives depended on their handling of samples. What were the chances, anyway, Gess asked, of there being another Amelia Cave whose vitreous fluid was analyzed the same day in the same lab?

What conditions were maintained in the lab? Collier persisted. Why did Hanley put blood in the refrigerator at the end of the day?

Flustered and growing meeker with each response, Hanley said she didn't know if refrigeration was necessary or if temperature affected the potassium level of vitreous fluids.

Finally, irritation overcoming meekness, Hanley announced in a strong voice, "My job is to analyze the samples, that's all."

People stirred in their seats, agitated, and I began to feel anxious, like a hostess at a dinner party whose guests were getting bored. I willed them silently to hang in there. Real trials, unlike *Perry Mason*, were not good theater. They moved slowly in fits and starts, seemingly in no sensible order, and bogged down in details that appeared to have little to do with justice.

"Point well made," Justice Beaulieu told Collier. He struck most of Hanley's testimony but allowed the test results.

Thomas J. Dewyer, a chemist at the Department of Human Services public health lab, was better equipped to deal with Collier and explain the lab's handling of fluid samples, the dissipation of alcohol in the body, and human metabolism. Over Collier's rapid-fire objections, the judge allowed Dewyer's testimony. His conclusion: There had been no alcohol in Amelia Cave's blood.

After a twenty-minute recess to arrange a time for the outdoor viewing, Iva Patten took the stand. I could tell she was nervous.

Iva, who was naturally chatty, found it hard to stick to the artificial courtroom dialogue of simple yes and no responses. Asked if Amy's drapes were closed when she and Mrs. Askeborn had entered Amy's living room, Iva said yes, they were, and went on to explain pleasantly that some folks protect the inside of their homes from the sun by pulling their drapes. She herself didn't do that, however.

Iva smiled out over the courtroom. Her audience, who for the first time seemed included in the proceedings, smiled back at her.

At 11:50, the judge ordered a lunch recess until 1:00, when the viewing party would meet at the courthouse before leaving for the Cave property. I wondered if "viewing party" included reporters. No one I asked was sure. I was told that it was up to the judge.

I returned to the courthouse before one o'clock and, walking past a black limousine parked in the yard, noticed Justice Beaulieu seated alone inside. I stood beside the car, and when he rolled down his window I asked if reporters could attend the viewing.

Beaulieu seemed annoyed and didn't give a direct response. But he hadn't said no, so I drove to Amy's house. Only one other local reporter, who also knew where Amy had lived, showed up. We both brought cameras, which weren't allowed in the courtroom but might be outdoors. Staying discreetly in the background, we snapped an occasional photo, expecting that at any minute we'd be told to stop. I overheard a whispered comment to the judge about confiscating our film. The ax didn't fall until after we'd left Amy's house.

On the way through North Sullivan, the caravan of vehicles I was following came to a stop in the middle of the road. I pulled onto the shoulder and stopped, too. Dave Giroux shuttled among the cars, the go-between for officials riding in them, then walked back to my car. They were going to the Askeborns, he explained, and because it was private property, reporters wouldn't be allowed.

That made sense. And it was a relief to have someone deal openly with the matter. I didn't mind the role of adversary when it was necessary. But being a reporter shouldn't mean I had to wear boxing gloves all the time.

"Let the record reflect that at the Amelia Cave residence, we pointed out the windows of her house, the proximity of her home to the bay, and the location of Burying Island," Sandra Collier said when the court reconvened at 3:34 P.M.

She explained that at the Askeborn property, the viewing party had entered Glenner's trailer, noted paths between the residences and the network of dirt roads to the shore, and had seen the boat, the pilings, the two rock walls, and the relative proximity to Amy Cave's house across the water. And the location of Burying Island.

Why the emphasis on Burying Island? Was Collier implying that the real murderer had hidden out on my family's island, as though the name itself—Burying—should conjure up images of skullduggery?

The first day of the trial ended with brief testimony by Merrill Taylor, the caretaker for Amy's property, and Crawford Hollidge, her friend and neighbor.

Working in the darkroom was a welcome respite after a full day at a murder trial. And now with photos spread across my desk, I chose one—not typical fare in our newspaper: A female referee in a striped bathing suit was leaning over two women in tights wrestling on the mud-covered floor, arms and legs so entangled that it wasn't clear which limb belonged to which body.

Female mud wrestling wasn't typical fare in Ellsworth, either. The previous Thursday night, however, it had been the Lion's Club choice as a fund-raiser at the Round Up, a Country-Western nightspot, and had brought in $1,600 for service activities.

As I typed a caption for the photo, I imagined someone browsing through our paper in another hundred years and coming upon this picture. Did female mud wrestling, like the Roman circuses, deserve to be recorded for posterity? Probably, I decided, as much as some of the city council meetings I'd covered.

Tuesday morning, the prosecution continued carefully laying a foundation for the introduction of each exhibit and building a framework for the testimony of each witness. The proceedings moved forward like molasses.

Pete Hartford's testimony boiled down to one essential fact: On patrol the evening of October 4, he had seen Amy's car parked outside her garage.

Nate Anderson detailed breaking into Amy's house, searching for her, and learning about the check that led to Samantha Glenner.

Asked to identify Glenner, Nate, looking toward the defense table, began a verbal description for the record. Samantha, suddenly the focus of attention, smiled across the room at Nate and wiggled her fingers in a coy greeting. Nate looked away without responding.

Just who was Glenner using for a female role model, anyway? I wondered. No woman I knew would act like that in the courtroom. Coyness was inappropriate.

After the noon recess, the state called Wendy Spearin, Amy's insurance agent, then Gusti Duschek, who had visited Amy the day before she disappeared. Gusti's spine stiffened noticeably at Collier's questions.

"You knew that Amy was friends with Samantha?"

"Not really. She was friends with Mr. and Mrs. Askeborn."

"But you also knew that she knew Samantha?"

"No, I didn't."

"Amy never mentioned Samantha to you?"

"No."

Collier had failed to elicit a picture of Amy and Samantha as buddies, as she had claimed. Leaving the stand, Gusti seemed stern, but satisfied.

John Keenan's testimony, I assumed, was designed to forestall the defense pointing the finger of suspicion at an unidentified person at Amy's house just before she disappeared. Keenan, who'd stopped at Amy's after finding his car blocked in while he was clamming with his brother and uncle, said they'd moved the barricade, hot-wired the car, and later found the key behind the seat. Keenan had recognized Amy on the TV news and called the sheriff's department to tell them about the dark-haired woman he'd seen with her. The woman turned out to be not the abductor whom Keenan suspected but Amy's friend Gusti.

Taking the stand next were Felix Duschek; Robert Cochrane, president of Security Central, which had installed Amy's burglar alarm system; and two men who had dug clams on the Askeborn shore in the fall, Raymond Piper and his brother-in-law, Peter Carney.

Piper said that on October 7, three days after Amy was last seen, he'd noticed that several rocks had been moved from the beach to build a wall behind the old boat sitting there.

Carney, the next witness, was with Piper that day and had seen the rock wall, too. He said he'd clammed in the same spot the year before; the boat had been there but not the rock wall.

Carney returned to the shore two days later and started up the path through the woods after he'd finished clamming. Samantha appeared behind him carrying a bow and arrow. She reminded Carney that he was on private property, then followed him along the trail. Carney stopped finally and set down his bucket of clams, explaining that it was heavy.

"Don't tell me about heavy," Samantha had retorted. "I built that big rock wall down on the shore."

Collier chastised Carney for trespassing on the Askeborn property, then asked about the elusive Tony. Carney said that the only Tony he knew was Tony Chick, and he laughed at the idea of Tony Chick owning a thirty-eight-foot boat. He didn't believe that a boat that size could get close to the Askeborn shore because the water was too shallow.

State police Detective Sergeant Ralph Pinkham had barely taken the stand when Samantha sent him one of her flirtatious finger waves. Maybe this was grandstanding, I thought, Glenner wanting the audience to see how cozy she was with the cops.

Pinkham, like Nate, ignored the greeting.

Albanese, introducing the transcripts and tapes of Pinkham's interview with Samantha, asked to play the tapes in court. Collier moved to suppress the entire interview and asked if the state intended to use the interview for the purpose of impeaching Glenner.

The tapes would have to be heard, the judge pointed out, before they could be characterized. He added that the defense should have brought forward its motion to suppress before today.

At 3 P.M. the state began playing the taped interview. The audience, straining to listen, heard Samantha's soft, breathy voice for the first time. When the first tape ended, the judge said he'd listen to the others in chambers. He adjourned court for the day.

The next morning when Pinkham returned to the witness stand, attorneys, using transcripts of the interview, argued the relevance of one section after another. Albanese claimed that virtually the entire interview addressed the matter of the defendant's veracity. He cited Glenner's statement that her only previous trouble with the law had been a few parking tickets and that she was familiar with the Miranda warning only because she'd seen it on TV.

The judge excluded these statements and much of the rest of the interview as irrelevant. Pinkham resumed answering questions.

"You directed considerable attention toward a person named Tony, didn't you?" Collier asked.

"Yes, after Glenner brought up Tony."

"Why were you interested?"

"Because Glenner was so evasive about Tony," Pinkham said. "She didn't even know Tony's last name."

"Do you consider it important to locate Tony?"

"We'd like to."

Collier, her tone accusatory, asked, "You're still investigating this case, aren't you, officer?"

"I guess you'd say that. Yes."

The state called Alice McInnis of Bangor Savings Bank and introduced Amy's banking records for the previous two years. The last check written on Amelia Cave's account, McInnis said, was for $2,700 and was made out to Samantha Glenner. Bangor Savings had not honored that check.

The judge allowed Pinkham, sequestered as the other witnesses were, into the courtroom for the testimony of the next witness.

John Hargett, of Bowie, Maryland, examiner of questioned documents, had impressive credentials: more than twenty years' experience identifying handwriting and hand printing, twelve of these with the Secret Service dealing with letters threatening the president of the United States. He had lectured for the Secret Service, published papers and articles, represented the government in foreign countries, and testified more than a hundred times in this country.

"None of us writes exactly like anyone else," Hargett said. "We all develop speed and individuality, until at about twenty-five years of age we reach graphic maturity."

Hargett had examined a letter written by Amelia Cave as well as ten of her checks and her bank signature card.

"Handwriting holds more clues to the identity of the author than most of us realize," he said, "the size of one letter in relation to another, for example. Amy's capital 'A' in Amelia," he pointed out, "is much taller than her 'C' in Cave."

Another clue was the stroke at the beginning and end of words. A tapered stroke at the beginning showed that the pen was already moving as it hit the paper. Amy's pen created a slight tapering at the beginning of her signature and in the release stroke at the end, indicating that her pen was moving rapidly as she lifted it from the paper.

Shading within the signature was also an indication of speed, Hargett said. Consistent pen pressure was generally the result of slower writing.

He looked for idiosyncrasies, too: the placement of the dot over an *i* or the placement of words in relation to the line, for example.

He checked connecting strokes to see if they were made with underhand, overhand, or straight-line movements. And he noticed the slant of letters. Amy's small *a* at the end of Amelia pointed toward twelve o'clock and her small *e* in Cave toward two o'clock.

The format of the entire check was important, too, Hargett said. For instance, after the amount, Amelia Cave wrote a slanted *and,* then two small zeros or the number of cents with a line underneath and nothing under the line.

"However," Hargett said, "in exhibit eighteen, the questioned document—"

"Objection! The specimens haven't been properly authenticated."

"But we indicated earlier that this witness would be called out of order," Albanese protested. "My understanding was that we concurred on that."

The judge, agreeing, allowed the testimony with the understanding that the underlying documents would be introduced later. Collier should continue objecting for the record, though, Beaulieu suggested.

On the questioned document, the $2,700 check, Hargett continued, the format was different. He pointed to the numerical amount, which was followed by a period and a line with nothing above the line. Amelia Cave always indicated the number of cents. And instead of her slanted *and,* the author of the questioned document had used an ampersand.

Albanese held up a packet of Amy's checks. "In all of these checks, did you ever find any different format?"

"No, never," Hargett said.

The signature on the questioned check was different, too, both in the size of the letters and the speed with which the words were written. Blunt terminal strokes and consistent pressure within the signature indicated that it had been written slowly.

"Through my examination," Hargett said, "I have concluded that the Amelia Cave signature on state's evidence number eighteen is not a genuine signature of Amelia Cave but is a simulation or drawing of her signature."

He added that there may have been an attempt to copy some of the conspicuous features of Amelia Cave's signature, but he'd found nothing to suggest that she had written the face of the check. He believed that the endorsement on the back of the questioned check was written by Samantha Glenner, whose specimen writings he'd witnessed himself. But because the check signature was a simulation, there was no way he could identify the author.

Hargett had to catch a 2:30 flight, so the judge postponed the noon recess for Collier's cross-examination. Collier began by pointing out variations in the signatures on Amy's checks and suggested that intoxication might have affected Amy's signature.

But Hargett stood firm. He said he'd found none of the classic characteristics of writing under the influence—uneven pressure or spacing, illegibility, missing letters, and writing over or under the line—on the $2,700 check. And no evidence of tracing, no indentations around the letters, no traces of carbon. He'd concluded that it was a freehand simulation.

Hargett left for the airport, and court recessed for one hour. I hurried out of the courthouse to buy some snacks, hoping a light lunch would make it easier to stay awake in court, then rushed back to the office. As I was eating and reading my messages, Mel Stone laid a newspaper clipping on my desk.

"Kessler's piece? I didn't think it was going to come out 'til after the trial."

"It was in *Newsday* over the weekend," Mel said. "We've got their okay to run an excerpt in tomorrow's paper."

Newsday, on Long Island, where both Amy and the Askeborns had lived, had sent Bob Kessler to Maine after Glenner was arrested in the fall. I'd steered Kessler to people to interview and driven him to Amy's house and the Askeborns'. Kessler invited me to come in while he interviewed Glenn, but I said that it was his show and he'd probably do better one-on-one.

I scanned the article. Kessler had done a good job. *Newsday* had used the picture of Samantha I'd taken at the time of the arrest. And a head shot of Askeborn as a man—the first I'd seen. Nice-looking man. A strong face with dark-rimmed glasses. Thin mustache. Short cropped hair. The eyes, narrow and slanted, were all that reminded me of Samantha. Askeborn, I decided, was a better looking man than woman.

Hmm . . . here was something I hadn't heard. Kessler said that in the early 1970s, according to law enforcement sources, an acquaintance associated with organized crime had suggested that Askeborn could solve his financial problems by committing crimes for the Colombo organized-crime family and that his two robberies on Long Island were part of that effort. His cut for the first robbery was $200 and for the second, $10.

"But more important than the money," Kessler wrote, "was that he was proving his worth to the organization."

The canon of the Hartford church where Askeborn attended sex change counseling sessions had described him to Kessler as "a spinner of a lot of tales" involving secret projects with the submarines he was building, important people in Washington, and lucrative government projects.

An artist whose studio was near Askeborn's business had told Kessler that Askeborn said bizarre things were happening to his body as a result of swimming through radioactive water when he was a SEAL frogman in Vietnam. According to navy records, Kessler wrote, Askeborn had never been a SEAL and had never been exposed to radioactivity.

Chapter Seventeen

CHEMIST ALLEN ROGERS, A BROWN UNIVERSITY GRADUATE, had worked for Union Carbide for nearly twenty-eight years, he said, and was now the company's quality assurance manager in the manufacture of Glad Bags.

My light lunch had been a smart idea. Two and a half hours of testimony about trash bags threatened to put everyone to sleep. Two things indicated that the testimony might be important, though: Albanese's persistence and the defense's frequent and vehement objections.

During the manufacturing process, Rogers explained, as polymers and resins are pulled into film and wound into rolls, they gradually degrade and produce lines, which at first are only an aesthetic concern. But after about eight hours, the lines become so pronounced that the machines have to be shut down and cleaned.

Knowing the rate at which the die turns and the lines move across the film makes it possible to determine the sequence in which bags were manufactured within a batch.

"Do you recognize this?" Albanese asked, handing Rogers an envelope marked state's exhibit 44.

"Yes," Rogers said. "It's the green plastic trash bag I examined in the latter part of March. I took a sample and initialed the bag."

"And do you recognize this?" Albanese asked, indicating another bag.

"Yes, exhibit forty-seven is a similar bag that I also examined and tested in March."

No one explained that one bag had covered Amy's body and the other had been taken from Samantha's trailer, so the audience in the courtroom didn't understand the implications of Rogers's testimony. I didn't think that Perry Mason would have left his viewers in the dark listening to lengthy testimony about resin content, thermal transitions, differential scanning, and double inflection in curves. He would have made certain that everyone understood the importance of the witness's conclusions when he finally made them. In fact, the two bags were manufactured by Union Carbide—no other company manufactured trash bags in that color that year—and the two bags were so consistent with each other in terms of their lines that they must have been manufactured within six or seven bags of each other. Or even closer. They may well have come from the same box.

Perry Mason, I decided, would have made it clear that the trash bag found on Amy's body had almost certainly come from Samantha Glenner's trailer.

It occurred to me as Rogers left the stand that if TV cameras were ever allowed in Maine courtrooms, the courts would find a way to combine good legal practice and good theater.

Beth Sargent, teller and office supervisor at the High Street branch of Key Bank, took the stand next. She identified Samantha Glenner as the person who'd presented a $2,700 check to her on October 9. Glenner waved across the room to Sargent, a more circumspect wave, though, than the previous ones to Nate and Pinkham. No flirtatious wiggling of her fingers.

Albanese asked Sargent if she'd had any conversation with Glenner.

Sargent said Glenner had volunteered that she owned a boat, which had been damaged, and that a person she said was her silent partner was putting up the money to fix the boat. But Amelia Cave's name had never been mentioned in either of Glenner's two visits.

Curtis Ramsey, of The Bangor Window Shade Company, identified the cups that Albanese showed him as similar to the ones in which Amy had served him and Richard Roberts hot chocolate when they delivered a divan to her home on October 4. Amy told them she'd spoken with her insurance agent that morning. She was dressed in bright-colored clothing, Ramsey said, and had a towel around her head because, she explained, she'd just taken a shower.

On that intimate note, the third day of the trial ended.

At my desk late that afternoon, I scanned my trial notes for a lead for the next day's paper. Weeding out the objections, attorneys' conferences, introduction of exhibits, and testimony that hadn't yet been explained, there was only one thing to say. I wrote: "Amelia Cave's signature on a $2,700 check cashed by the person accused of killing her was a forgery, an expert witness for the state testified in superior court in Ellsworth yesterday."

I was late to court Thursday morning. When I arrived at 8:50, Ronald Roy, the deputy chief medical examiner, was talking about the day he and his helpers exhumed Amy's body on the shore of Taunton Bay. A first tentative exam of the body, he said, had revealed marks on the front of the neck, hemorrhaging on the eyelids, and lacerations of the mouth.

The eyelids. The mouth. Amy had become "the body."

At the autopsy that afternoon, they'd cleansed the body and found evidence of a head injury: a laceration of the scalp above the left ear; swelling, bruises, and abrasions around the nose; and lacerations of the cheek and tip of the tongue. One hand was swollen and broken, perhaps from a defensive effort at warding off blows, Roy said. Internal examination showed hemorrhaging of the temple area, postmortem hemorrhaging of the larynx, and fracture of the thyroid horns, indicating trauma directly to the larynx, possibly the result of manual strangulation.

I looked at Askeborn's huge hands resting on the table in front of him.

Earlier, I'd felt sorry for the man hunched over the table in his tan silk blouse, crossed arms hiding a chest deprived of breasts by prison officials, and beneath the table, men's black prison shoes. I felt no sympathy for him now.

As part of the autopsy, blood samples had been taken for routine serology and blood alcohol testing, and fluid from the eyeballs to analyze for potassium, Roy said. The body generally starts metabolizing blood alcohol in a few minutes, he explained, but once cell death occurs, metabolism stops. Potassium, however, accumulates after death.

The longer a person has been dead, the higher the level of potassium. But in this case the body essentially had been refrigerated in a cold, damp atmosphere, so it was harder to determine the time of death. Roy's rough estimate was that Amelia Cave had been dead somewhere between seven and ten days, probably closer to a week.

What about the hands? Beardsley asked. Were they tied before or after death?

Roy said that the ligature marks on the hands and ankles were probably postmortem.

And the broken hand and scratches—couldn't they have occurred if the body had been dragged? asked Beardsley.

During life, possibly, but not after death.

I was relieved when Roy left the stand. Clinical language and a professional manner had not been enough to ward off images of Amy fighting for her life.

The next witness, smartly dressed in a gray three-piece suit, looked familiar. I'd seen Detective Charles Downing testify in another murder trial.

Nothing seemed to throw Downing off balance, not even the defense when it pounced on him.

Downing said he'd been present when exhibit 44, a green plastic bag, and exhibit 43, a birdseed bag, were seized from Glenner's trailer. He'd locked them in his car, taken them to Augusta on October 15, and turned them over to Ron Kaufman, a forensic chemist with the state police.

Downing fielded questions about several more searches, including one at the Cave residence. Among the items seized there were a bag of birdseed and a plastic bag from the garage, which he had also turned over to Ron Kaufman on October 15.

This statement would come back to haunt him.

Then suddenly Beardsley asked, "Do you recall making a statement under oath that you recovered no green garbage bags from Samantha Glenner's trailer?"

"No, I don't recall that."

Beardsley handed Downing a document, an application for the

affidavit supporting a search of Glenner's trailer. "Please read the first sentence of paragraph twelve on the last page, your statement written after the search."

Downing obliged: "The search of the trailer did not reveal any garbage bags or string of the kind used to bind Amelia Cave."

"Your Honor," said Beardsley, "I'm introducing a copy of the statement into evidence for the purpose of impeaching this witness."

Albanese jumped to his feet and began bombarding the witness with questions. Answering them calmly, Downing testified that he had seized the bag, exhibit 44, in Glenner's trailer on October 13. Present then were Corporal David Giroux, Sergeant Len Ober, and Chief Deputy Dickson. Downing said it was his writing on the bag, which he turned over on October 15. Two days later he'd written his statement, and all of his statements were absolutely true.

Still relaxed in the face of an accusation that he had lied, Downing offered an explanation: Maybe the problem was his use of the terms "garbage" and "trash." He took garbage bag to mean a small white bag and trash bag to mean to a large green bag.

But, Beardsley pointed out, in Downing's own photos taken inside the trailer, there was no large green plastic bag, was there?

That was correct, Downing admitted.

This would not be the end of exhibit 44.

The next witness, Joseph Roy Gallant, state police firearms examiner and crime scene processor, said he had been at the scene when the body was exhumed and had taken possession of a birdseed bag found in the victim's mouth, a white bag over her head, and a large green plastic bag covering her upper body. He'd also lifted finger- and palm prints from Amelia Cave's car and at the autopsy had collected hair, blood, and fingerprint samples and the victim's clothing.

Albanese held up a plastic bag containing state's exhibit number 49. "Do you recognize this?" he asked.

"I recognize exhibit 49 as the slacks the victim had on. I collected them at the autopsy and brought them to Augusta and gave them to Ron Kaufman, on October 18, I believe."

Then Gallant identified Amy's blouse and her red parka. I was glad that Richard and Susan Cave weren't in the courtroom. Amy's tan print blouse, so familiar, was more personal, more disturbing to see than the vial of her blood.

As Gallant left the stand at 11:13 A.M., I looked around the room and counted sixty people, a surprising number to survive the hours of tedious testimony. Most hadn't known Amy. Some no doubt had been merely curious to see a transsexual, at least at first. Once there, they had evidently been hooked. In addition, Amy's disappearance, played up by the media, had evoked widespread concern even before a suspect had been identified. Maine people rallied when their neighbors were in trouble.

The state called Stanley Wong, Amy's financial planner at Prudential Bache in New York.

Amy had been his client for ten years, Wong said, and they'd become friends. He'd visited her in Maine and had planned to do so again last October but hadn't been able to reach her by phone. One of the reasons for his wanting to visit had been to discuss how they could bring her cash reserve account back to the usual $10,000 he recommended she keep for emergencies. The account, depleted by Amy's purchase of land, was less than $2,000 at the beginning of October.

"What were Amelia Cave's total assets?" Collier asked.

"Do you mean the assets I control?" Wong inquired coolly, as though asking what that private information had to do with Amy's death.

"Yes," said Collier.

Wong hesitated, then sounding openly hostile, replied, "About two hundred thousand dollars."

Wong had traveled from New York to testify. He was on the stand for only twelve minutes.

The next witness was already in the courtroom and had only to move from the prosecution table to the witness stand. The fact that Dave Giroux had not been sequestered still bothered Collier, and she moved to strike all his testimony concerning the search of Samantha Glenner's trailer.

The motion hanging, Albanese brought up the subject of the green plastic bag again. Giroux said he'd seen it in the southeast corner of Glenner's living room and had directed Sergeant Ober to empty it of the clothing inside.

Again Collier said it wasn't fair that Giroux had been in the courtroom to hear the defense make an issue of the green bag.

The judge denied the motion to strike, and Giroux's testimony stood.

Albanese asked a final question: "How many rock walls were there behind the boat on the Askeborn shore?"

"Behind the boat, sir?" said Giroux. "There was only one rock wall."

I remembered Collier had made a point of seeing two rock walls at the viewing. Apparently the significance of there being one or two walls was to be revealed later, for Giroux left the stand.

During the noon recess, I checked with the court clerk to see what I'd missed earlier. Amy's attorney, Frank Walker, had testified, the clerk said. So had Gerald Upton. An officer at Key Bank, Upton had said he'd talked with Glenner about the $900 owed the bank as a result of drawing against uncollected funds. Glenner told him she didn't have the $900 then but expected to shortly and would repay the bank.

Glenner had also offered Upton an explanation for the apparent forgery of the $2,700 check: There'd been problems with the pen that Amy used, so Glenner had traced over everything on the check.

When court resumed, Ronald Richards—evidence technician and processor of major crime scenes—testified that the front seat of Amy's car had been set as far back as it could go, in the position to accommodate a tall person. Amy was only five feet five inches tall.

Richards also examined latent fingerprints (those scarcely visible but which can be developed for study). He had processed latent prints on eggshells, a coffee can, a saucepan, and cups and saucers from Amy's kitchen. None of them were Glenner's. Neither were the palm prints and fingerprints on Amy's car.

Richards said that he had vacuumed the floor and seats of Amy's car and turned the debris over to forensic chemist Ron Kaufman of the state police. Kaufman had examined the debris and found human and animal hairs. None of the human hairs matched the defendant's.

And none of the string, twine, and rope seized from several locations on the Askeborn property, including the boat, were similar to the cords found on the body, Richards testified.

The state called Ron Kaufman, forensic chemist, to the stand. Kaufman said that all the bags and clothing evidence had been in his possession until the trial began. He'd taken green bags, state's exhibits 44 and 47, to Connecticut and had been there when Allen Rogers of Union Carbide examined them.

When the state tried to enter the bags into evidence, Collier objected. There was serious question, she said again, about the chain of custody and the origin of the bags. Even as the bags were being admitted, Collier insisted that the matter of what happened to the bag taken from the Cave residence had not been resolved.

Then, slowing her tempo and smiling slightly, Collier asked Kaufman, "So you were never given, by any police officer, any cord or twine with any similarity to that found on the body?"

"That is correct," Kaufman said.

As Kaufman stepped from the stand, Albanese announced, "The state would call Glenn Askeborn."

The courtroom rustled with an expectant stir as the tall blonde woman in a black pantsuit and white blouse moved, erect and dignified, past the defense and prosecution tables to the stand. She listened with an intent frown as the clerk read the oath, and swore to tell the truth.

Samantha wiggled her fingers at her mother, who seemed not to notice.

Albanese, leading Mrs. Askeborn through introductory questions, directed her to please speak up. On the Thursday she'd come home from the hairdresser and seen Amy's car in her yard, where had Samantha told her Amy was?

Glenn said she couldn't remember. She didn't think that Sam had told her where Amy was.

Glenn could remember so little in response to Albanese's questioning that he finally asked, "If you listened to the tape recording of your interview last October, would that refresh your memory?"

Glenn sighed. "I suppose so."

Albanese pushed Glenn to admit she had misled and lied to police last October. Frustrated, he finally said, "Your Honor, request permission to treat as a hostile witness."

"The court will not rule her a hostile witness," Beaulieu said.

Albanese reminded Glenn that she was under oath, then continued his questioning. "Mrs. Askeborn, when you took Samantha to the bank, where did she tell you she got the money from?"

"Objection. Leading the witness," Collier said.

"Overruled. You may answer."

"Well, ah, she'd helped a fellow on his boat."

"Objection. Nonresponsive reply."

"She helped a fellow on his boat and had several small checks from him."

"And that's why you went to the bank?"

"Yes."

"Did Samantha have a check from Amelia Cave?"

"No," said Glenn in a small voice.

"Please speak up, Mrs. Askeborn."

"You know, sir, I'm having trouble hearing you, too."

"Anytime you're having trouble hearing," said Beaulieu, "you may ask Mr. Albanese to repeat the question."

"Mrs. Askeborn, were you ever aware of Samantha borrowing money from Amy?"

"I knew Amy had loaned Samantha some money."

"And when was that?"

"Well, this, ah, the winter of '83."

"And when did you find out?"

"Amy told me. I don't remember when."

"Did you ask Amy to loan Samantha money?"

"No."

"But in the October 12 interview taped at the sheriff's department, you said Samantha never asked to borrow money from Amy."

"But that's just it," Glenn said triumphantly. "She never asked. Sam never asked to borrow money."

Glenn was obviously pleased with her answer. Albanese was not. He paused, then renewed his attempt to get Glenn Askeborn to admit she had lied to the police last fall.

"On October 13, Mrs. Askeborn, were you not asked if you and Samantha had any conversation on your ride to and from the store about where Amy was?"

"Ahh," Glenn sighed, "I don't remember."

"You don't remember Sergeant Pinkham asking you on tape where Amy was?"

Another sigh. "No, I don't remember, but—"

"You don't recall—"

"Objection," said Collier.

"What are you objecting to?" asked the judge.

"Mrs. Askeborn is not being allowed to complete her sentences."

"I don't remember," Glenn said again, adding, "Maybe I said Amy was on the boat. That's what I assumed, anyway."

"Mrs. Askeborn," Albanese said sternly, "on October 13, 1984, your memory seemed to have been a lot better about what happened."

"I don't have a very good memory lately," Glenn said. "My memory is obsolete. But I'm answering to the best of my ability."

Albanese gave up. He asked that Glenn be directed to listen to her taped interview to refresh her memory.

The judge adjourned court for the day. Mrs. Askeborn would listen to the tapes, he said, and court would resume at 8:30 the next morning.

"Glenn is doing a good job of not remembering," I told Iva on the phone that evening.

"She did it very well last fall, too," Iva said.

"You know, Iva, as I sat there watching Glenn, I couldn't help wondering what I'd do in her shoes. What would you do if you suspected that one of your kids committed a crime. Would you tell?"

"Oh, dear God. I'd have to do a lot of thinking, wouldn't I?"

"Not fun to think about, is it?"

"No, not fun at all. It's hard to know what I'd do." Iva was silent a moment. "Of course two wrongs don't make a right, do they? I suppose waiting would just be putting off the inevitable."

We began sharing memories of how we'd handled transgressions that our children had committed when they were young. Standing by as they returned stolen pencils and apologized to a shopkeeper. Helping them tell the truth and face the consequences. Helping them grow up to be responsible adults. Patting ourselves on the back.

"Iva," I finally said, "this isn't even in the same ballpark with what Glenn's going through, is it?" It had become uncomfortable playing the game of "what if?" with our offspring as pawns. "Sorry I brought this up."

"So, how much longer do you think the trial will last?" Iva asked.

"Probably through most of next week."

"If you have time," Iva said, "call me tomorrow, will you?"

"I will. I promise."

On Friday morning Glenn Askeborn returned to the witness stand in the same black pantsuit but a different blouse, similar to the one Samantha was wearing, with a flouncy bow at the neck. Both were in black and white.

"Mrs. Askeborn," Albanese began, "now that you've had an opportunity to listen to the October 13 tape, has that refreshed your memory?"

She said it had, although she still didn't recall what time she left home on October 4, and she didn't remember asking Samantha where Amy was when she drove Samantha to the store to buy a bottle of wine. And she didn't know where Sam went when they returned from the store. In fact, she couldn't remember seeing Sam again that day or seeing Amy at all.

"Had Amy been to your house before October 4?"

"We visited back and forth constantly," Glenn replied.

"When she came to your house, was it to see you?"

"Yes. She always came to see us. But I had told her I wouldn't be at home."

"When?"

"When she called to say she'd be over."

So Glenn had known that Amy was coming to her house that day.

Glenn Askeborn was not breaking down on the stand, admitting knowing anything about Amy's murder or who drove Amy's car back to her house. Maybe she knew nothing. Or maybe she was a mother tiger protecting her cub.

"No more questions," Gess said. Collier had no questions at all for the witness. Glenn rose from the chair and walked through the court-room, her dignity still intact.

"I strenuously object," Collier said when the state recalled Charles Downing. "The witness has had a chance since his testimony to con-fer with attorneys from the AG's office and other officers."

So what? Nick Gess in effect said. He stated that the purpose of the rules of evidence was to ascertain the truth. After Downing testi-fied, he had made it known he was confused and of course he (Gess) had talked with him. It was Gess's job to talk with the state police. Downing's testimony would be no less reliable because of it. Anything affecting the ends of truth and justice was relevant, he said.

Those were the very reasons why Downing shouldn't be recalled, countered Collier, because that would mean that any witness from whom one wanted a different answer could be recalled on the grounds that he or she was confused.

Beaulieu pointed out that the state hadn't rested its case and most of the witnesses hadn't been dismissed when they left the stand. He allowed Downing to take the stand again.

"Now," Gess said, "I direct your attention to yesterday and your testimony on cross-examination by Mr. Beardsley that you seized a green plastic bag at Amelia Cave's residence in Sullivan."

"Yes, I said I did."

"Objection," said Collier.

"Noted," said Beaulieu.

The bag had covered snow tires in Amelia Cave's garage, Downing said, and he'd removed it from the tires but had never packaged or marked it as evidence because it didn't match the description of the bag on the body. He'd been present when the body was exhumed and had also called the lab to double-check the color of that bag. The color and size of the bag in the garage were both wrong.

"Are you absolutely certain you did not seize that bag?" Gess asked.

"Objection," said Collier. "Leading the witness."

"Sustained."

Collier continued to object as Albanese led Downing through the details of both searches and the chain of possession of evidence seized. Downing produced an evidence receipt for items turned over to the lab from both the trailer and the Cave residence.

But at the conclusion of all of Downing's self-assured testimony, Collier posed a question that cast doubt in the matter of a mix-up of trash bags. "What did you do with the green trash bag that you seized from Amelia Cave's garage?"

"I can't recall if I threw it away or took it back to the Cave residence," he admitted.

The next witness was nervous, and with good reason. Susan Cave had been sequestered in a small room with her husband since the trial began five days earlier. Albanese urged her gently to speak louder, but all Susan had the chance to say was that Amy was her husband's aunt whom she'd known for fifteen years.

Collier objected to Susan identifying Amy's handwriting in the letter and checks examined by the expert. Susan seemed close to tears for the twenty-five minutes that the attorneys argued back and forth.

The judge excused the witness and retired to his chambers to read cases provided by Collier about the extent to which a layperson could give testimony authenticating handwriting and to decide which exhibits were to be admitted as evidence.

When court resumed in the afternoon, Collier continued her argument. In Maine law there had been no clear ruling concerning authentication of handwriting. But because of the extreme seriousness of this case, which, Collier pointed out, was based on extremely circumstantial evidence, she would ask the judge to apply a more stringent test than usual.

In the end, Beaulieu said he was satisfied that Amy's handwriting had been properly authenticated.

Collier made a last-ditch effort to have the plastic bags excluded. She detailed how Downing, a critical witness, had testified today that he didn't know what he'd done with a green plastic bag seized from the Cave residence. Yesterday he'd said he turned the bag over to Ron Kaufman on October 15, and Kaufman had testified that he'd received the bag marked exhibit 44.

"We submit," Collier continued, "that the state police should not be believed. Downing claims he called the lab to corroborate the color and size of the bag found on the body before conducting the search of Amelia Cave's residence. That is impossible. Roy Gallant said he collected that bag on October 13 and turned it over on October 18. Downing was vague about the information he received on the phone. We submit that the phone call did not occur."

Gess remained calm. Downing had answered too rapidly the day before, he said, and had made a mistake. But it was simply a matter of semantics. The inference that Downing couldn't have learned about the bag found on the body by calling the lab was incorrect. Joseph Roy Gallant worked at the lab, had been at the grave site, and had seen that bag.

The match-up of the bags was novel evidence, Gess continued, presented only two or three times previously in the history of the country's courts. What possible motive could the state have in fabricating evidence about this matter? It had so much more probative evidence.

Beaulieu finally admitted the bag numbered 47, found on the body, and bag number 44, in an envelope labeled, "seized in the southeast corner of Glenner's trailer." There had been other witnesses who testified about the latter bag, and the evidence and chain of possession had been well documented, he said.

At 1:53 P.M. on Friday, the state rested its case.

Collier moved for acquittal. For the next forty-five minutes, Collier and Albanese argued back and forth. At 2:39, Justice Beaulieu denied the motion and declared a recess for the long holiday weekend. Court would reconvene on Tuesday at 8:30 A.M.

Chapter Eighteen

IT WAS A RAINY MEMORIAL DAY MORNING. A new Ellsworth police cruiser, a Volvo, led the parade down Main Street, followed by the Ellsworth High School band, scout troops, veterans, and a few representatives from city businesses.

Onlookers took cover under shop awnings or stayed in their cars. Memorial Day weekend was for many area residents the start of the summer season. They planted their gardens, opened summer camps, and gathered for family barbecues.

At the bottom of the State Street hill, the small parade stopped at the Union River bridge. Marchers watched in silence as VFW and American Legion veterans scattered flowers from the bridge in memory of the men and women lost at sea. Blossoms floated downriver with the outgoing tide.

The parade continued up State Street to the monument on the city hall lawn for speeches and a memorial service for veterans.

While I was covering the Ellsworth festivities, other *Ellsworth American* reporters were covering similar ceremonies in other Hancock County towns. I left for home after the parade and in a few hours returned to Ellsworth for a dedication ceremony at the jail.

The family and friends of former sheriff Merritt Fitch were gathered on the steps of the jail being named in his memory. At first I didn't recognize the uniformed man standing at attention with a wide-brimmed hat hiding his face and his head tucked down so fiercely that it gave him a double chin. Then, looking through my camera lens, I saw that it was Sheriff Clark. I'd never seen him in military posture before.

"So, Bill," I said after the ceremony, "it's almost over now." He knew what I meant.

"What do you think?" he asked. "Will they put Samantha on the stand?"

"Wouldn't the prosecution love that. Think of all the questions they could ask."

Bill went inside where refreshments were being served. I left for the office to develop my film. It would be a short work week, and I'd probably spend most of it in court.

The newspaper office was closed for the holiday and nobody else seemed to be there, at least not in the front office. I snapped on the light to the basement and at the top of the stairs called out, "Hello. Anyone there?"

No one answered. Alone in the windowless basement, I locked myself in one of the darkrooms and concentrated on developing the film as quickly as possible. When I finished, I hung the film in a drying cabinet.

Upstairs, large windows looked out onto Main Street, and I breathed easier. I could see out and the world could see in. I didn't remember being afraid when I'd been alone in the newspaper office before Amy's murder.

Passing my desk, I saw that someone had left the uniform crime report there. A quick glance told me that crime in Maine was down 3.5 percent from last year and was considerably lower than in the other New England states and the country as a whole. The statistic offered little comfort at the moment.

I wanted to salvage a little of the holiday for myself, but I'd take a minute to check the statistics for murder. Twenty murders last year in the whole state, four fewer than in the previous year. Ten of the victims had been killed with firearms. In Hancock County, there had been just one murder last year. Amy Cave had been the only homicide victim.

The courtroom was packed on Tuesday morning, May 28, when security officers escorted Samantha Glenner up from the jail. Curious eyes scanned Glenner's attire for the day: dark slacks and a pastel plaid blouse tied at the waist.

At 9:03, bailiff Russ Cook peered into the superior court and nodded across the room to Earland Linscott. "All rise," Linscott called out as the judge appeared, then settled at the bench. "You may be seated," Linscott said.

Beaulieu nodded toward the defense table. "Miss Collier?"

Deliberate and assured, Collier pushed back her chair and stood to face the judge. "The defense rests, Your Honor."

This was it? I wondered. The defense would call no witnesses? No wonder Collier and Beardsley had been so aggressive, had objected so fiercely and often to almost everything. Discrediting witnesses, poking holes in the state's case while it was being presented *was* the defense case. I'd never seen this happen before.

Collier renewed her motion for a judgment of acquittal, and Beaulieu again denied the motion. The trial was over except for closing arguments.

Jeff Albanese, who must have suspected or known that the defense would rest, launched into a straightforward summary of the state's case, punctuated with an occasional observation: "By 9:37 on October 4 (when Pete Hartford, on patrol, saw Amy's car parked outside her home), I submit to the court, Amelia Cave was dead. She didn't sleep in her bed that night because she was dead. She had been killed."

Based on the facts—that the check was forged; that Amelia Cave's body was found under the rock wall that Glenner built and twice asked police not to disturb; that the bags on the body and in Glenner's trailer were manufactured from the same lot within seven of one another; that no one saw Amelia Cave after October 4; and that her car was parked in front of her house within two hours after the defendant, according to her own statement, had been with Amy—based on all these facts, Albanese asked the court to find Samantha Glenner guilty beyond a reasonable doubt of the murder of Amelia Cave.

Attorney Beardsley, with no trace of his usual ready smile, began closing for the defense as Collier and Foster looked on. Listening to him suggesting several unsubstantiated hypotheses, I reminded myself that it was not the job of the defense to prove anything, only to raise doubt about the state's case. In addition, I realized, by making a tactical decision to present no formal case, the defense was making it harder for prosecutors to disprove their hypotheses.

Samantha Glenner and Amelia Cave were good friends, both socially and in business, Beardsley was saying. Cave's check number 324 to Harbor Divers was an indication of what good friends the two were. They spent Thanksgivings together and had other meals together. Amy Cave liked to help people start in business and to that end she'd wanted to help Samantha Glenner repair her boat.

The state's case, Beardsley said, was based on questionable theories and depended on the drawing of too many inferences. In the first place, why was Amelia Cave's grave so conspicuous? With a small rock wall built over only part of the body? Why wouldn't the defendant have built a wall over the whole body? When Glenner asked police not to disturb the rock wall, she'd been talking about another wall to the side and some distance from the boat.

The state's expert witness had said that the trash bags might have come from the same carton. But the condition of the bag found on the body would have made it difficult to identify. And obviously there could be serious questions raised about which bag had been delivered to the lab for analysis. Downing had testified that he seized one bag from the Cave residence, only for the state to later retract that testimony. The second bag could have come from the Cave garage or been taken off Glenner's boat.

The handwriting expert, Beardsley said, had been given a limited number of the defendant's signatures and asked to compare them to one on a questioned document. The inference had been made to him from the start that the check was questionable, and that wasn't fair. And Miss Cave did have the financial capability to lend Samantha Glenner the $2,700.

Beardsley said that the state had not shown any indication of violence or any motive for Glenner to murder her friend. There were just too many unanswered questions. Why would someone of Samantha Glenner's intelligence have put the body of her friend right next to her boat? Why wouldn't she have hidden it in the woods? Why wouldn't she have used string and rope from her boat to tie the body? None of the string or rope on the body matched any on the boat. And considering the location of Amy Cave's home, there was every likelihood that she had been brought to the grave site by boat.

Beardsley further stated that the alarm system in Amy's house wasn't working. Her home could have been entered before the deputies broke in. In addition, her car was seen at her home on October 4, but Crawford Hollidge had seen it drive past his house on October 8. Someone else could have been driving her car. And what about the hairs found in her vehicle? The long brown hair found on the driver's seat was not Amy's or Samantha's. Amy's hair had been found in the backseat, yet there was testimony that she always drove the car herself. Someone else had driven her car and she had been in the back seat.

Animal hairs were found all through the vehicle, yet Samantha Glenner had no animal. Neither did Amy. Whose animal was it? The evidence suggested that someone else was involved.

After a clear review of all the evidence—the plastic bags, the signature, the hair samples—it was obvious, concluded Beardsley, that the state had not met its burden of proof beyond a reasonable doubt.

Before Beardsley had even taken his seat at the defense table, Albanese jumped to his feet. "The defense asks what motive there could have been. That's obvious: the twenty-seven-hundred-dollar check."

And of course other fingerprints had been found on the car, he continued. It had been at the victim's home for several days and numerous people had been there. Iva Patten, for one, had said that she opened the car door. And there was no question about the rock wall: The defendant had referred in her statement to the rock wall behind the boat.

At 9:50 A.M., Justice Beaulieu asked the clerk to bring all the case material to his chambers. "I will come to a decision during the course of this day," he announced.

At two o'clock, the sheriff and Pinkham, arms folded, stood next to the bench at the front of the room. Ernie Fitch joined them, then

Bishop and Dickson. They waited in silence, shifting from one foot to the other. Near them, Alan Calor, head of probation and parole, sat alone on the single bench along the side of the room.

Samantha Glenner, flanked by two security guards, walked stiffly past them to the defense table and sat down. She faced her moment of judgment with no outward sign of emotion.

Susan and Richard Cave, faces solemn, stole to the rear of the courtroom as though hoping not to be noticed and found seats in the next to the last row. The court reporter arrived—always a sign that the judge was about to appear.

"All rise," Linscott ordered at 2:15 as Justice Beaulieu entered through his private door. At the bench he poured himself a glass of water and drank two sips.

"For the record," Beaulieu said, "I thank the attorneys for the state and for the defense for the professional and competent manner of their presentation to the court. It would be appropriate for the court to give the reasons for its findings."

He did so in the impersonal, formal language of the law.

The first question was whether the state had met its burden, the defense having none whatsoever, in proving that on or about October 4, Samantha Glenner, also known as Glen Robert Askeborn, had intentionally and knowingly caused the death of Amelia Cave.

The court found that the body removed from the location at the rear of the boat on Taunton Bay was that of Amelia Cave, but it must also find that the death of the victim was intentionally and knowingly caused. The court was satisfied, Beaulieu said, that Amelia Cave did not die of natural causes. Her death was the result of an act of murder. Considering testimony during the trial that the victim's death was due to asphyxiation, that there were lacerations and trauma to the head, and considering even the manner of burial with a birdseed bag in the victim's mouth and the victim's hands tied, there was no possible explanation other than that the person responsible had committed the act intentionally and knowingly.

Next, the court had considered the issue of whether there was proof beyond a reasonable doubt that the defendant had intentionally and knowingly caused the death. Attorneys for the defense and the state correctly indicated in their arguments that the evidence was circumstantial. It must be proved that the circumstantial evidence supported beyond a reasonable doubt that there existed no reasonable alternative explanation.

Much of the testimony concerned the disappearance of the victim, Beaulieu noted. Several witnesses said their last contact with the victim occurred on October 3 and 4. The court was satisfied, based on the testimony of the mother of the defendant and the defendant, that the defendant was with Amelia Cave on October 4. Other evidence showed that the victim was not seen after that point in time.

The court had drawn no specific conclusion from the substantial testimony regarding the victim's home and the manner in which her car was parked other than that Amelia Cave had not occupied her house since the morning of October 4. It might well be that someone else parked the vehicle there.

The court was excluding evidence, Beaulieu said, regarding the green garbage bags. But it had concluded from the evidence that Amelia Cave did not write the face of check number eighteen. Based on contradictory statements made by the defendant, the court was satisfied that it was not Amelia Cave's handwriting on the check and that the defendant knew this.

Regarding the location of the body, as the viewing and exhibits had shown, the burial site was within the very shadow of the boat that was the personal property of the defendant. It was also within the area of the so-called rock wall and was, as officers testified, freshly dug. Red slacks had been found on the body, and the defendant had told Pinkham that Amelia Cave was wearing red slacks on October 4.

The birdseed bag found in Amelia's mouth was similar to one found in Samantha Glenner's mobile home. And although the court had excluded evidence concerning the green bags, it was satisfied that they were the same type of bag.

The most incriminating evidence, Beaulieu said, was the location of the body. In considering the lifestyle of the defendant, there was no other conclusion than that her boat was the focus of her activities. The defendant had told police officers, and others had testified, that she had no car and no other means of transportation. Even the loan was in reference to the boat. Considering the location of the grave, there could be no other conclusion than that Samantha Glenner knew that Amelia Cave was buried there.

Common sense dictated that with all the miles of coastline, no other person selected that site. The court was satisfied that the wall that covered Amelia Cave was placed there by the person who caused her death.

"The court's finding," Beaulieu concluded, "is that Samantha Glenner caused the death of Amelia Cave and that the state has met its burden."

Glenner's attention, which had been fixed on the judge, now shifted to the three defense attorneys, who clustered around her, whispering. Collier turned to the judge. "We have nothing further at this time, Your Honor."

"The court is not in a position to sentence at this time," Beaulieu said. "It will allow a reasonable time for the filing of motions and will order a presentence investigation. Court is adjourned, the matter before it continued until sentencing."

When Beaulieu left the bench, others rose and quietly left, too. There had been no outcry in the courtroom, no visible reaction to the final judgment. Stony-faced, the now-convicted killer was led away by the officers.

Samantha Glenner stayed overnight in the Hancock County jail and at 6:56 A.M. the next day was returned to the Maine State Prison, to be again identified only as Glen Robert Askeborn and classified as a male.

A little later that same morning, before work, I sat by the boathouse watching the gentle lap of water against the ledge at my feet. It would be a long time before Glen Askeborn would see Taunton Bay again.

And then I looked across the bay to Amy's empty house.

Chapter Nineteen

Now I had no excuse not to make the telephone call I had been putting off until after the trial was over and Askeborn had been found guilty.

Early Sunday afternoon when I sat down on my living room couch next to the phone, my heart was pounding. But what was the worst that could happen? She could yell at me and hang up.

No, even worse, she could hear what I had to say in contemptuous silence and then hang up.

I dialed the number and listened to the phone ring and ring before I started counting. Three more rings and I'd hang up. Maybe she'd moved and the number I had was outdated. I'd probably never find her. I hung up finally, relieved but disappointed. I knew I had to try again.

All afternoon I dialed the Connecticut number. No answer. Between calls I set out annuals in my garden; a stiff breeze kept away the blackflies and mosquitoes. Sometimes I became so engrossed in planting that I forgot the call hanging over me.

At 6:30 I dialed again. The ringing stopped and I heard a click.

"Hello?" The voice was soft and pleasant.

"Hello. My name is Pat Flagg. I'm a reporter with a newspaper in Ellsworth, Maine. Is this Martha?"

The "yes" was cautious and ended with a question mark.

"Are you the Martha who was married to Glen Askeborn?"

I heard the sharp, indrawn breath before an even more cautious "yes."

Apologizing for intruding on her privacy, I asked if she was aware of the trial that had been going on in Maine.

I thought she wasn't going to answer. Then she said yes, that a reporter from a newspaper on Long Island had told her about it sometime during the winter.

I said that would be Bob Kessler; I'd met him and had read his article about Glen Askeborn in *Newsday*. She hadn't read it. I told her that I'd covered the trial and it was over, but I wasn't calling her for a newspaper interview. I was writing a book about the murder.

"Writing a book?" she asked in disbelief.

I explained that I'd known Amy Cave, the murdered woman, and I lived on Taunton Bay, where the murder took place. So my interest was more than that of a reporter.

"You're writing a book?" she said again. "Why on earth would anyone want to capitalize on someone else's misfortune?"

When I didn't answer, she asked about the trial. I told her that it had ended last Monday and Glen had been found guilty of murder.

Martha said she wasn't surprised. But she sounded sad. Quietly, as though talking to herself, she said that Glen had serious emotional problems during the last couple years of their marriage and she'd been very angry that she couldn't get help for him when he needed it.

Glen had been emotionally affected by his tour in Vietnam, Martha continued, although the problems hadn't surfaced until later. He wasn't coping well as a male and was vulnerable to anyone with a sympathetic ear, such as transsexual counselors looking for a feather in their caps. She wanted Glen to find a good therapist, not people with an agenda of their own who said, Okay, if this is what you feel like doing, go with the feeling. She said that wasn't what he needed.

Martha said that Glen was a very loving, kind person, and if she'd been able to get him the help he needed, he certainly wouldn't have hurt Amy Cave.

Was she blaming herself? I wondered. I pointed out that he had hurt his stepchild much earlier, probably before she even knew him.

"What do you mean, 'hurt his child'?" She sounded furious. "He never hurt a child!"

Oh, my God, I thought. She doesn't know about that. What could I say? I explained that Glen had been taken to court in California because of it.

"That's not what the case was about!" she snapped. "Who told you that?"

"I was just quoting from the *Newsday* article," I said.

She was silent for a moment, then asked what else it said.

How had I gotten into this? "Well, apparently," I explained, "he forced the child's head into a tub of scalding water. That's why he was discharged from the service."

"Putting someone's head in scalding water? That's not sane. Sane people do not molest their children." She said she'd learned a lot—although nothing about the scalding—from Glen's parole officer, a man she respected.

So she must know about the armed robberies and his time in prison, I thought, but I wasn't about to bring that up. Anyway, we hadn't really established that she wanted to be quoted by someone writing a book.

"Look," I said, "why don't I call you back when you've had time to think about this."

She welcomed the idea. "It's just too bad that people will hang this whole thing on transsexualism. I don't know if Glen was a transsexual or not. It might have just seemed the easy way to go. I feel badly that you people up there see Glenn only as a transsexual and a murderer."

"Martha, it's hard not to right now. I was hoping you'd help me know him better. I'd like to hear some of the good things."

"Okay, I'll talk with you," she said, warming for the first time.

We agreed I'd call her back in a week. I knew she might change her mind, but I liked what I knew so far about Martha and hoped she would decide to talk with me.

If I were in her position, however, I doubted I'd confide in a stranger over the phone.

The following Tuesday, Samantha Glenner's attorneys filed a motion for a new trial.

They claimed that the judge had reached his decision on a finding that the birdseed bag in the victim's mouth was similar to the birdseed bag found in the defendant's trailer, when in fact both the brand and the size were different.

Furthermore, testimony concerning two plastic trash bags had sufficiently tainted the entire proceedings that the defendant was denied a fair trial. Finally, the testimony of John Hargett, examiner of questioned documents, shouldn't have been admitted. The specimen signatures provided to Hargett were never properly authenticated, and Hargett had insufficient foundation and an insufficient number of checks on which to base his opinion.

Justice Beaulieu would rule on the motion for a new trial on August 12, when sentencing might also take place, if the presentence report had been received by then. Difficulty in getting out-of-state information on Askeborn's background was delaying the report.

Sunlight was still streaming into my living room at five o'clock Sunday afternoon when Martha and I finished our second conversation a week after I'd first called her. We had talked for forty-five minutes. I sat by the phone thinking about what she'd said, then grabbed a sweater and left the house. The bay was calm and the tide high enough to float a boat at the bottom of the boathouse ramp. June 9 was late in the season to put my boat in the water for the first time, but somehow my usual sense of urgency was missing. I didn't feel the same about Taunton Bay this year.

I headed down the bay away from Burying Island and away from the dilapidated old boat near Egypt Stream. Moving at full throttle stirred up a breeze, which which felt good on my face. A gull on a boulder near the Carrying Place inlet cocked its head at me, ready to fly away. I slowed the motor and gave the boulder wide berth, and the gull settled back on its perch.

Martha said she had loved Glen. They'd lived together four years, married only the last two. How had she put it? "I am very straight sexually." When Glen started dressing as a woman and wearing lots of makeup, she couldn't take it. He loved her, too, he said, but this was just something he had to do. Martha moved out, and he holed up in the apartment and wouldn't go out or see anyone. He'd talk on the phone to a few people—the minister, for one. Martha acknowledged that maybe Glen did have some kind of hormonal imbalance. She didn't know.

Did I have to think about this now? On such a beautiful day? I looked deliberately across the river to the Sullivan shore and the remains of the old stone wharves and made myself think about the schooners that had docked there, loaded with supplies from far away. Sugar from Haiti. Codfish from the Grand Banks to be dried in people's yards and shipped out again. The schooners left with lumber and granite from the local quarries. Two-, three-, four-masters had been sailing in this bay only fifty years ago.

I imagined a four-master approaching in the distance, sails filled, prow piercing clouds of sea mist as it drew closer and closer.

My mind drifted back to Martha. She said she'd been feeling guilty for doing nothing about the case. After our first talk she had read newspaper accounts of the murder and had phoned Glen's mother. Mrs. Askeborn had always been good to her, she said. Martha agreed to give Glen's lawyers the names of friends who knew about Glen's problems.

It was probably too late now, Martha had said to me. If he'd killed someone, she wouldn't want him walking around anyway. But it was a shame to think of him in prison. He'd probably kill himself or someone else. He ought to be in a hospital where he could get help. If only she'd been able to find help for him back then. Everyone had told her that there was nothing she could do until he did something, or hurt someone.

What was it Martha had said almost in passing about Glen's father? "I think Glen may have spent his whole life trying to get his father's attention." He had certainly accomplished that, I thought, by becoming a woman, a carbon copy of his mother.

The Singing Bridge loomed ahead. I didn't intend to get too close to the granite piers, where swirling eddies could push around a boat much larger than mine. I slowed the motor to an idle and listened to the song of tires whirring across the open metal grille overhead. The pitch rose and fell as traffic passed over the long span from one shore to the other. I'd learned only recently why the tune changed from one section to the next: Metal traction studs embedded at different times on the grille had worn down to different heights and, like frets on a guitar, produced different sounds.

A strong current was pulling me downriver. I turned up the throttle and veered the bow around to face west. The setting sun lined the clouds with gold and streaked the sky with shafts of light that spread out like a fan. Amy would have seen the same view from her picture windows and could have watched the yellow-red globe sink to the evergreen horizon—the horizon directly behind Askeborn's boat. Would I ever look toward that shore and not think of Amy's grave?

Martha wanted to forget, too, she'd said. She'd go just so far, she said: talk to the lawyer and that was it, for she had a new life now. She and her husband-to-be had agreed to seek counseling as a safeguard against repeating destructive patterns in their own lives.

I wasn't sure that Martha and I had decided whether I might quote her in my book. I wouldn't use her full name, of course. But soon the matter became academic: Sandra Collier filed a court document using Martha's name, as well as information about Askeborn that Martha hadn't shared with me.

I discovered the document in the superior court office on a Wednesday afternoon in late July during a last-minute check for the next morning's paper. Askeborn's "Motion for a New Trial II" included an affidavit by Collier and a supporting memo by Beardsley.

Collier's sworn statement stemmed from a phone conversation in June with the defendant's former wife, Martha Evarts. During their marriage, Collier wrote, "the defendant repeatedly suffered from episodes of violent behavior during which his personality and behavior differed greatly from that of his usual gentle self. On at least one occasion the defendant lost control and attacked Martha with a knife, but afterwards had no awareness or recollection of the incident, this conduct despite the fact that the defendant and Martha Evarts had a close, loving relationship. Martha Evarts and other friends tried to get the defendant to seek psychological or other counseling but the defendant refused. . . . Knowing the defendant as she did, Martha Evarts is of the opinion that if the defendant did in fact commit the acts charged, he must not have been in his right mind."

What had I started by calling Askeborn's former wife? Could he plead insanity at this late date? And claim amnesia? How convenient.

"The defendant only recently admitted to me," Collier continued, "that there were in fact several incidents such as described by Martha Evarts which the defendant acknowledges she did not realize even happened until afterwards when others related her conduct to her."

In his memo, Beardsley acknowledged that an earlier exam had shown no evidence of the defendant's incompetence to stand trial. However, Beardsley wrote, a closer look at the psychological report showed that Glenner had failed or refused to complete tests and had refused to provide pertinent details of her past. The examiner had based his conclusions on the defendant's own statements denying any past history of mental illness.

The defense attorneys wanted their client tested again and asked for money for psychological testing. And they moved to change Samantha Glenner's plea to not guilty by reason of insanity.

Chapter Twenty

OUR CHAT HAD STARTED CASUALLY AND BEEN FRIENDLY ENOUGH, but in the end I almost ran to get away from the man in the small lobby outside the Ellsworth courtroom.

He'd been sitting in a chair having a smoke when I came out of the courtroom. I walked to the window and stood looking down on State Street two floors below.

"What's going on inside now?" the young fellow asked.

"The judge is sentencing someone for OUI," I said.

"I'm getting sentenced this afternoon, too," he volunteered. "What are you here for?"

"For a hearing in the Samantha Glenner case," I said. "It was supposed to have started a half hour ago."

"Samantha Glenner? Isn't she . . . he . . . the one who killed that woman?" I nodded. "How much time did he get?"

"He hasn't been sentenced yet," I said. "Probably in another week or so."

"Well, if he ever gets out, he damned well better not hang around here." His face grew crimson and the veins in his neck stood out. "If he does, I guarantee there'll be another homo chucked off the Sullivan bridge." I retreated from an ugliness I didn't quite understand, but once inside the courtroom it hit me: the Charlie Howard incident. There'd been a lot of publicity recently about the beating death of Howard, a homosexual, whom teenage boys had thrown off a bridge, although it was in Bangor, not Sullivan.

I wished I'd responded to the guy in the lobby. Not for his sake but for mine. I was always taken aback by threats of violence—to burn down someone's house, put sugar in someone's gas tank, cut loose someone's lobster traps—all classic threats in down east Maine.

I glanced at my watch—it was 1:40—and looked up to see Samantha Glenner entering the courtroom escorted by Richard Bishop, who sported a new mustache. He'd grown it on his vacation, he told me this morning. Glenner wore a striped pastel blouse gathered on a band at the hips. Why did I always notice Glenner's clothes? I didn't pay attention to what Sandy Collier was wearing, or anyone else for that matter.

The judge's private door opened suddenly, and in a moment he was seated, listening to the attorneys debate about a new trial. Beardsley argued that this was the last chance for the defense to address the judge as fact finder and determine whether he, the judge, was "free from taint." Albanese responded that the judge was trained to exclude and accept evidence but that he needed to hear the evidence first before he could make a decision.

In the end, Beaulieu denied the first motion for a new trial and reserved decision on the motion to reopen the evidence and permit a change of plea. A fishing expedition, Albanese called it. A fundamental question of justice, argued Collier.

There was no need, the judge said, to act on the motion before imposing a sentence, which he planned to do within the next two weeks.

The minimum sentence in Maine for murder was twenty-five years. The maximum, since Maine had done away with the death penalty, was life in prison.

The Channel 5 camera caught Glenner fiddling with her bangs as two deputies escorted her up the sheriff's department steps. In the lobby they walked swiftly past Mrs. Askeborn, who was seated and shaking visibly, and disappeared into the jail. I nodded at Mrs. Askeborn and took the elevator upstairs to the courtroom. No one else was there for the sentencing. Where were all the people so fascinated with the trial two and a half months earlier?

Would Askeborn speak on his own behalf, I wondered. Would

anyone else speak for him? I'd recently heard a minister extol the
virtues of a convicted sex offender who'd begun attending his church
while awaiting sentencing. Wasn't the minister the least bit skeptical
about the timing of this man's finding the Lord?

At a sound in the rear of the courtroom, I turned to see Mrs.
Askeborn slip into a seat nearest the door. Then the defendant entered from the front of the room. Then the judge.

Beaulieu noted for the record that counsel on both sides had been
sent copies of Glenner's presentence report. He himself had received
a written statement from the defendant.

The state was asking for a life sentence, announced prosecutor
Albanese. Mr. Robbins, the probation and parole officer who prepared
Glenner's report, had also recommended life. It was, Albanese said, an
appropriate sentence because of the brutal and vicious nature of the
crime, the killing of a middle-aged woman for pecuniary purposes.

Then, too, this was the defendant's fourth conviction for a violent
crime since 1967. Askeborn had been twenty-four years old when he
inflicted second-degree burns on a three-and-a-half-year-old child by
immersing his head in 167-degree Fahrenheit water. For that he'd received a suspended sentence with probation. When he was twenty-
eight, the defendant had taken part in two armed robberies, for which
he received a ten-year sentence. After that he'd been convicted of
forgery and failure to pay wages to employees and had received a two-
year suspended sentence. And, Albanese said, according to the presentence report, the defendant was now talking about retaliation
against an unidentified person.

"The fact that he has shown no remorse, that there is no chance
of rehabilitation, warrants the full, maximum sentence allowed under
the law," said Albanese.

The facts warranted no such conclusion, argued Collier. There
had been no eye witness and no confession, and the defendant maintained her innocence and was in fact doing so before the court today.
The evidence was not there to support premeditation. Ms. Glenner
had no recollection of that afternoon, and the matter of criminal re-

sponsibility had not yet been resolved. The defendant's last thorough mental evaluation had been in the late sixties in California, and she had been found to be suffering only from "unsocialized adult reaction."

In Glenner's letter to the court, she wrote about what she did and didn't recollect and what she'd begun to realize about her problems, Collier pointed out. She expressed remorse if she indeed did perpetrate this crime. Her lack of memory would be consistent with other blackouts she had suffered since 1977.

Furthermore, the defendant had cooperated fully with authorities before her arrest. Her lack of cooperation after that was the result of anger and frustration, largely because of mistreatment at the hands of the state, as she had described in her civil suit.

Collier said that in the stores and around town, people regarded Samantha Glenner as a normal, nice person. Martha Evarts said she was a good person. If Samantha Glenner did commit this crime, she was not in her right mind. A life sentence would be like locking the door and throwing away the key and should be reserved for defendants shown to lack any possibility of redemption. This defendant had already started counseling in Maine State Prison and was recognizing that she might have problems beyond her control. Her sentence, said Collier, should satisfy the public but permit her to have a life after prison.

Collier sat down next to her client, and they both looked up at the judge. The judge peered back at them over the top of his glasses.

"The court has been advised that there's been no request for the defendant to speak," Beaulieu said. He paused, and hearing nothing to the contrary, proceeded to address the defendant's pattern of violence and record of prior convictions. He concluded that there was nothing in the presentence report to indicate that the defendant's previous experience with the system, including services received, had resulted in any change in the pattern of violence. The possibility of rehabilitation seemed negligible. He found little that was encouraging, except for the defendant's own statement.

However, because of the length of time since the last conviction, he had decided to stop just short of the recommended life sentence.

Beaulieu stopped speaking and waited for Collier and Glenner to stand. Then he announced that Samantha Glenner, also known as Glen Robert Askeborn, would be remanded to the care of the Maine Department of Corrections for a period of forty years.

I squelched the impulse to turn around and look at Mrs. Askeborn; it would be too obvious in the nearly empty courtroom. I did look back, though, as Askeborn was being led from the room. His mother had already left.

I stared at the chair where Askeborn no longer sat. Forty years. A huge chunk out of anyone's life. Askeborn would never serve all that time, though, even if his appeal failed. The jails were too crowded. There'd be reductions for good behavior and all sorts of things.

The courtroom was nearly empty. I approached the prosecution table, where Jeff Albanese was gathering up papers, and asked the standard question.

"Yes," Albanese responded. "I'm basically satisfied with the sentence. Considering that his last violent crimes were committed in the late sixties and early seventies, I think it's appropriate. There'll be an appeal, I'm sure, and the judge still has to rule on the second defense motion for a new trial and change of plea."

"What was that reference to retaliation?" I asked.

"Oh, it was in the presentence report," Albanese said. "The parole officer claims Askeborn told him that only three people knew about Amelia Cave's death—himself, Cave, and a third unidentified party. And Askeborn said the day he was found guilty, the third person had signed his own death warrant. Askeborn said he was having someone track down the person."

Downstairs, Bishop told me that Askeborn was already on his way back to the state prison. He hadn't been allowed visiting privileges at the jail. Bishop and I did some fast figuring on the time that Askeborn might actually spend in prison if his conviction or sentence weren't overturned. Then I stopped at the dispatch desk to check with Dave Brady and make sure nothing major had happened that should be in the next morning's paper.

"You mean like finding a dead body?" Dave asked without looking up.

"Yep, anything like that." Then he did look up, challenging me with a poker-faced stare. "Dave? You're kidding. Aren't you?"

"Dad's down in Sullivan now investigating the report of a body found in the woods about a mile off Route 1." Dave wasn't kidding. "The state police and the sheriff are already at the scene."

Couldn't they find a body at a more convenient time than 3:15 on a Wednesday afternoon, the day before the paper came out? I still had Askeborn's sentence to write up. Brady gave me directions to the scene, then I checked in at the newspaper, grabbed my camera, and headed for Sullivan. On the way it occurred to me that it would be hard traipsing through the woods in the flimsy sandals I had on. I made a flying stop at Trader Don's in Sullivan and in record time found a pair of ugly but practical black shoes. As I neared the nursing home on Route 1, I spotted police cars at the side of the road and pulled off behind one of them.

Pete Brady, Bill Clark, Ralph Pinkham, and two other state troopers were standing by the cruisers talking with one another. They turned in unison as I walked toward them.

I wouldn't be needing a change of shoes. They told me that there was no point in my hiking into the woods. The body, discovered in a swampy area by a couple surveying their property, had been there for some time. All that remained was a skeleton. They knew of just one person in the area reported missing and never found: Harold Jacobson.

"The name sounds familiar," I said.

"You remember," Bill said, "the guy that owned a little yellow submarine. Didn't you write a story about him?"

"Oh, yeah. Yes, I did. I remember his telling me that everyone assumed there was something sinister about a little yellow submarine."

The medical examiner's office would do an autopsy the next day, so the results would be too late to include in this week's paper. I'd take a picture of the officers and go with a cutline about their discovery.

"Pat," Bill called after me as I started to walk away. "What happened in court?"

"Oh, you don't know, do you? He got forty years."

Pinkham, Brady, and the sheriff, who ten months ago had been caught up in the investigation of Amy Cave's murder, now had little to say. They'd gone on to other things, possibly even another murder in the same town.

I'd sparked their interest with Askeborn's comments about a third party, though, I thought on the drive back to Ellsworth. Not that they believed it. But threatening retaliation did seem a strange thing to share with your probation officer, especially if you were claiming you had no memory of the day of the murder.

I hadn't had much time to think about the sentencing that I'd be writing up in another few minutes. Askeborn's attorneys had certainly covered the waterfront, hadn't they? They had said that their client was "maintaining his innocence even before you today." But if he did commit the crime, he was sorry. And if he did, he hadn't been in his right mind. He couldn't remember the events of that afternoon last October. Yet he said that he was one of three people who did know what happened and had already taken steps to go after the third person.

At my desk I called upon my "just the facts, ma'am" voice and began writing: "Forty-two-year-old Glen Robert Askeborn, also known as Samantha Glenner, was sentenced yesterday to 40 years in prison for the murder last October of Amelia Cave of North Sullivan."

As I was finishing, a typesetter stopped by my desk to see if she should wait for my copy or come in early the next morning.

"Just a minute," I said and began typing the last paragraph: "With the maximum possible time of 13 days a month allowed for 'good time,' Askeborn's 40-year sentence might effectively be reduced to slightly more than 23 years.

"He would then be 65 years old."

Judges do not regard insanity pleas lightly, I knew. Two months ago a judge had accepted an insanity plea from an Auburn couple charged with murder in the oven-burning death of the woman's four-year-old daughter. How could anyone think that a sane person would burn a child in an oven?

There was a case to be made, I supposed, that taking the life of any human being was insane. But sanity in the eyes of the law was measured on a sliding scale, with criminal responsibility the determining factor.

Of course in Askeborn's case, there was an added factor: His insanity plea came after he'd already been tried and found guilty.

As Albanese wrote in opposition to the motion for a new trial, "The defendant's trial strategy—that others besides him committed the murder of Amelia Cave—failed, and now, the verdict in hand, he seeks to rearrange the deck chairs on the Titanic and attempt a different strategy."

Less colorful but more to the heart of the legal matter, Albanese's argument included the five-part burden that Askeborn must meet in seeking a new trial on newly discovered evidence: that the evidence would probably change the result if a new trial were granted; that the evidence had been discovered since the trial; that the evidence could not have been discovered before the trial by the exercise of due diligence; that the evidence was material to the issue; and that the evidence was not merely cumulative or impeaching, unless it was clear that such impeachment would have resulted in a different verdict.

Eugene Beaulieu had considered the matter and come to a decision. It seemed fitting that his decision would be in the October 10 issue of the paper, exactly one year after Iva had called the sheriff's department to report Amy missing. One year after Nate, Pete, Iva, and Glenn had entered Amy's home expecting to find her inside.

I was in the clerk's office reading the judicial order, with its arcane language and citing of precedents, when I came across a sentence that struck me as so nonlegal and full of ordinary common sense that I laughed aloud.

"There's something funny in a judge's order?" Rosemary was clearly skeptical.

"Maybe it's just me, Rosemary, but there's all this staid language and legal stuff supporting Glenner's insanity plea. And Beaulieu disposes of the whole matter in one sentence. Listen. 'It is difficult to conclude from the fact that the defendant's former wife was battered that the defendant suffered from a mental disease or defect.'"

Rosemary just looked at me. "I guess you had to have been there," I said and continued reading to myself.

There was no evidence, Beaulieu concluded, that the defendant suffered from a mental disease or defect at the time the crime was committed. Citing a precedent ruling, he said he wasn't persuaded that the evidence before the court would change the verdict if a new trial were granted. The defense motion failed on a second ground, too: Facts known to the defendant at the time of the trial did not constitute newly discovered evidence for purposes of a new trial motion, even when the defendant saw those facts in a new light. He cited another precedent.

Beaulieu denied the defense motion for a new trial and concluded that therefore the other motions—to change the plea and to receive more money for psychological testing—were not in order. He denied all motions.

The Maine Supreme Judicial Court agreed with Justice Beaulieu in its decision the following August. "A defendant cannot preempt the discretion of the court by withholding an insanity plea for tactical reasons until after a finding of guilt," wrote Justice David Roberts.

The high court concluded that the superior court had committed no error. It affirmed the judgment of the superior court and upheld Samantha Glenner's conviction for the murder of Amelia Cave.

Epilogue

Early Spring, 1994

Agreat blue heron, its long, skinny neck and legs stretched out in streamlined flight, glided over my boat as I landed on the beach. I watched the bird disappear among the treetops in the island rookery.

The herons had come back to their old nests in early April, about a month ago. I was returning to Burying Island after a long winter, too.

Sometime since last fall, storm tides had cleared the gravel beach of decaying seaweed, and had washed up new debris—a large green soft-drink bottle, two lobster buoys, a broken piece of barnacle-covered piling, and a child's red plaid sneaker.

I walked the length of the beach and back before climbing the bank to my log cabin. At the top, I stopped and craned my neck back to search for the huge nest a pair of bald eagles had built three years ago in the pine tree that towered over the shuttered cabin. For the last two years they had nested there and raised chicks, but today the nest looked ragged and seemed abandoned.

Moving to the front of the cabin, I turned to face the bay and the Bar Harbor mountains on the horizon beyond, and was reminded of Shawn O'Brien. This was the spot where he and I had been standing fifteen years ago when an eagle floated down and nearly landed on his head.

Disturbed by the memory, I moved quickly to the corner of the cabin and stared unseeing up at the nest again. Shawn had died in February 1995 of a heart attack when he was only forty-five years old.

∞

Leaving the empty nest and memories of Shawn behind, I turned and headed along the shore trail to the north point. Bob and Liz, both artists, would arrive next month for their island summer on the point. Near their cabin I spotted the green casing of a spent shotgun cartridge, telling me that last fall hunters had lain in wait here for unsuspecting ducks and Canada geese on their way south. Prompted by the unwelcome image, I scanned the far shore where Askeborn's old boat used to sit. That ugly reminder of Amy's murder was gone, the engine removed and the hull burned on the shore sometime after the accidental deaths of Glenn and Wesley Askeborn.

Glenn had died in July 1996, after an episode in which she choked on a bagel. Her obituary made no mention of her son or of Samantha. Wesley was killed a few months later, in October. He was putting heat tape on outside pipes for the winter when he apparently slipped and fell. Neighbors discovered him several days later in a pool of water. Wes's obituary stated that he had no children.

As I resumed my tour of the island, I wondered whether Wes and Glenn had known that in 1994 their son had been questioned in connection with an unsolved murder case in Connecticut where he used to live. Maine investigators learned of that murder in 1995 when they contacted East Haven police to research Askeborn's background. A young woman, never identified, had been killed in 1975 and her body found in a drainage ditch two streets away from where Askeborn lived at the time.

Police in both states were impressed by the number of similarities between the two crimes. Both victims had been strangled to death. Both had their hands and feet tied behind their backs and gags placed in their mouths. Their heads were covered with a towel in one case and a small plastic bag in the other, and trash bags were drawn on over these.

Glen Askeborn had not been questioned at the time. When East Haven detectives requested an interview in 1985, he refused, but eventually agreed to talk to them in 1994. At that meeting, which took place at the Maine State Prison, Askeborn denied any role in the Connecticut killing. The East Haven police still did not rule him out as a suspect, but although they said they probably would talk to him again, they have never done so.

The 1994 interview received more press coverage in Connecticut than in Maine, so maybe Askeborn's parents had not been aware of it. There'd been no proof of their son's involvement—only a suspicion—still, I hoped they hadn't known.

Where will Glen Askeborn go when he gets out of prison? I thought. What will he do with the rest of his life? With his boat gone and the property now sold, he is not likely to return to Taunton Bay. He is scheduled for release on November 12, 2010, after serving twenty-six years of his forty-year sentence, and will then be sixty-seven years old.

I entered a grove of cedars, where a spicy fragrance filled the air. Breathing deeply, I determined to enjoy the present—a resolve that lasted only moments before I began thinking of the people I miss seeing regularly now that I am no longer a reporter. Bill Clark is one. He is still sheriff, although I've heard him speak wistfully about going on to new challenges.

Richard Dickson has done that already by becoming a banker. I still smile when I remember how Dickson created a Stephen King movie out of that Friday night on the Askeborn shore.

Nate Anderson, too, always seemed to thrive on adventure, something he probably doesn't find much of in the electrical supply house where he now works. More important to him, though, is spending a lot more time with his family.

Dick Bishop has moved from jail administrator to chief deputy, Dickson's old job. He was glad to return to law enforcement, facing new ventures each day. Bishop still hasn't given up smokeless tobacco —just changed his brand.

I stopped at the spring for a dipper full of cold, sweet water, then made my way to Shipyard Point, where I climbed a huge boulder to

look around. An osprey dive-bombed into the water, and before I
even heard the splash, it rose straight up with a fish struggling in
its talons.

Watching the osprey climb higher and higher, I thought of Pete
Brady, who still pilots a plane. He works as a garage mechanic these
days, and flies simply for pleasure, no longer searching for marijuana,
stolen vehicles, or dead bodies.

His son Dave is still dispatching. But not Skip Bouchard, whom
I'll never see again. He died so young, probably only in his early forties, if that. Skip had artistic talent, too. I recalled a large seascape he'd
painted and hung on a wall in the sheriff's department.

I thought also of Ernie Fitch who had been injured on the job.
When his sick leave ran out, others gave him their holiday and vacation time. In the end, ill health forced him to leave law enforcement
anyway. He took with him a phenomenal memory for people and
events, which served him well in police work. Maybe it still does, in
the variety store he now owns in Castine.

Beyond Shipyard Point, I crawled around trees uprooted by winter storms. Some were already dead when the wind threw them over;
others evidently had been in the prime of life. In some places the trail
tilts precariously over eroding banks. Burying Island shrinks a little
each year.

I passed Steve's cabin in the field that was once a raspberry patch,
then rounded the southern tip of the island and looked over toward
Schoodic Mountain and Iva's house in the foreground. Her grand-
daughter Beth lives there now. Iva just celebrated her ninetieth birthday in a nursing home, where she entertains everyone with her dry
wit and gets them to tell her their life stories.

And then, finally, I shifted my gaze to Amy's house. I still call it
that even though it has been sold three times.

I remembered visiting there after the first buyers, the Knowltons,
moved in. It had been strange to sit chatting in Amy's living room. Her
thick carpeting was gone, along with the crystal chandelier she'd been

so proud of, and of course all her furniture. Another woman's furniture, knickknacks, throw pillows, and pictures had taken over Amy's home. Ginny Knowlton sat quietly, letting me look around. Sunlight streamed through the long wall of windows and sliding glass doors that Amy had designed.

"Amy is still very much here," Ginny said softly. "I think of her nearly every day."

"You do?" I felt sudden warmth for the stranger in Amy's house.

"I didn't know her, of course, but I've heard about her." I knew she meant the murder. "I feel her presence here. And when I want to make some change in the house, I consider whether she'd approve or not. Usually, I decide she would."

It had been good to find Ginny so respectful of Amy, I thought as I picked my way farther along the rocky shore, Amy's house behind me now. The house on Evergreen Point would always be a reminder of the woman who'd built it. A day such as this, which Amy would have loved, would be another reminder.

The little cove seemed bare without my cousin Bill's blue and white boat tied on the shore. He'd be arriving soon to spend a summer away from phones, plumbing, electricity, and all the other conveniences of the mainland. Most visitors like leaving those things behind, like the change of pace as their lives slow down.

Summer vacations on the coast, when the weather is on its best behavior, are seductive. At one time or another, most Burying Islanders have toyed with the idea of moving to Maine to live year-round, a fantasy I carried out years ago. I thought back to the first winter, when I had a romance with the Maine coast, and mused about how quickly the winters after that became just something to endure. I could understand why Amy, living alone, far from home for the first time, had become depressed.

I could understand, too, why Susan and Richard Cave have never returned to Maine. At home on Long Island, where Amy had also lived, it is easier to focus on the good times they'd shared with her.

∾

Back at the beach where I'd landed, I noticed that while I had been circling the island in my familiar spring ritual, the tide had turned and was ebbing now toward the mouth of the bay. I could hear the whine of traffic on the Singing Bridge and the sounds of construction on the new concrete span being built to replace it. Soon the Singing Bridge would be only a memory.

Seals splashed and barked, playing near the ledge. I picked a spot and wiggled a nest in the warm sandy gravel. With the fragrance of evergreens in the air and the promise of summer in the warm sunshine, I lay back and looked up into the vast sky to watch for an eagle.

LIFE IS DIFFERENT ON A MAINE ISLAND AND SOMETIMES, SO IS DEATH . . .

Look for these exciting mystery novels filled with the character of the Maine coast.

✧ *A Show of Hands: A Maine Island Mystery*
By David A. Crossman

Retired NSA code breaker Winston Crisp looks forward to a quiet new life on Penobscot Island, but with the discovery of a woman's body frozen in the ice of an abandoned quarry, he just can't help asking some questions. Just for starters, why is her beautiful face coated with 40-year-old theatrical make-up? Crisp quickly finds himself embroiled in a murder investigation, haunted by a red-headed ghost, and targeted by a killer with a strangely twisted mind. PAPERBACK $14.95

✧ *The Dead of Winter: A Winston Crisp Mystery*
By David A. Crossman

Another murder has rocked the Penobscot Island community, and once again it looks like retired NSA agent Winston Crisp is the man to unravel a mystery—this one surrounding a corpse with tears in his eyes, bruises on his knees, and a missing shoe. Surprises are in store as Crisp traces the crime's connection to incidents of espionage and murder from the island's dark past. HARDCOVER $22.95

More Maine mysteries on next page . . .

✂ Murder on Mount Desert
By David Rawson

In the peaceful town of Eagle Harbor on the "quiet side" of Mount Desert Island, Sheriff's Department patrolman Jimmy Hoitt follows the investigation of a high profile hit-and-run death. High-speed chases, sniper attacks, and cliff-hanging suspense propel this rousing mystery to its surprising conclusion.

PAPERBACK $15.95

For a Younger Audience—

✂ The Secret of the Missing Grave
By David A. Crossman

Teens Bean and Ab are expecting to spend a normal, fun summer together on the Maine island where Bean's family lives, but things quickly become exciting when they discover that Ab's house appears to be haunted. The intrepid friends have a series of dangerous and frightening adventures while looking for secret tunnels, buried treasure, and valuable stolen paintings.

HARDCOVER $16.95

All titles available in bookstores or by calling Down East Books at 1-800-685-7962

— PRICES SUBJECT TO CHANGE —